Contents

Foreword

Congratulations! As a trainee chef you have embarked on one of the most rewarding and challenging careers there is. Going to college and working for a City & Guilds qualification is the best start you can get. But don't think the learning ends when you get your certificate.

My career with food started when I was 16, when I went to college. More than 20 years later I am just as passionate about food and still learning and adding to my basic training from all those years ago.

Food has always been part of my life – my father ran a fruit and vegetable business supplying schools and local restaurants and my brother trained as a chef, inspiring me to follow. On day one at Southport Technical College I just knew I had made the right choice, everything just dropped into place and I had found something I truly loved.

I continue to be inspired but now it's more about the individual ingredients, what is available today and how can I bring out the best flavour, what I should pair it with. At the restaurant we never stand still, we are constantly trying new dishes, testing and tweaking until we reach perfection.

Since I started cooking, the world of catering has changed. Chefs are better known, there are more cooking shows on TV and diners have greater knowledge about food than ever before. It can only get better – what a fabulous time to be joining the world of cooking and hospitality, with so many opportunities throughout the industry.

Food alone is no longer enough. Successful restauranteurs need the whole package, which means understanding the consumer, learning to manage a team, handling finances, but most of all it's about hospitality and the whole experience from the moment the guest books a table.

Hospitality is a great industry to work in. It doesn't matter where you start from, if you have determination and ability, if you are prepared to work hard and grab every opportunity to learn, the future will be bright for you.

This City & Guilds course is the foundation to your future – my advice, listen to your mentors, keep your head down and work hard, the sky is the limit!

Marcus Wareing
Marcus Wareing Restaurants Ltd
Marcus Wareing at The Berkeley
London

Introduction

This book has been written to support the practical skills and knowledge required for the City & Guilds Level 1 Diploma in Introduction to Professional Cookery. The aims of the Diploma are:

○ To provide a broad understanding of the hospitality and catering sector and the vocational skills required.

○ To ensure that all achievement is recognised.

○ To encourage progression by enabling learners to develop good basic skills as a foundation for a career in the Hospitality industry.

○ To provide a highly-valued qualification.

The Diploma consists of 12 units that are assessed in different ways (see pages v–vi and Figure 1). It is possible to take individual units (see page viii) but in order to achieve the full Diploma you have to:

○ complete all of the units

○ take a number of practical tests

○ complete synoptic tests.

Methods of assessment

The Diploma is assessed in several different ways.

Unit number	Unit title	GLH	Credit value	Assessment
101	Introduction to the catering and hospitality industry	20	3	Assignment
202	Food safety in catering	9	1	Online multiple-choice test
103	Health and safety awareness for catering and hospitality	10	2	Assignment
104	Introduction to healthier foods and special diets	10	5	Assignment
105	Introduction to kitchen equipment	21	5	Assignment
106	Introduction to personal workplace skills	30	3	Assignment
107	Prepare and cook food by boiling, poaching and steaming	100	10	Practical test and underpinning knowledge test
108	Prepare and cook food by stewing and braising	60	7	Practical test and underpinning knowledge test
109	Prepare and cook food by baking, roasting and grilling	120	12	Practical test and underpinning knowledge test

110	Prepare and cook food by deep frying and shallow frying	30	5	Practical test and underpinning knowledge test
111	Regeneration of pre-prepared food	20	4	Practical test and underpinning knowledge test
112	Cold food preparation	20	5	Practical test and underpinning knowledge test
	Total	**450**		

Figure 1: Assessment methods and Guided Learning Hours (GLH) for each unit. GLH are a guide to the likely delivery time of each unit.

Synoptic tests: These will last for up to three hours and there are two of these tests. You should be told what you will be expected to cook three weeks before the test. You should prepare – and keep – a time plan, your recipes and an equipment list. Your tutor should also give you the grading criteria so you are clear about what you need to do to achieve a pass, merit or distinction. These tests are called synoptic tests because they cover different parts of the qualification at the same time. They do not aim to cover all of the unit requirements. The synoptic tests are important because they demonstrate that you can plan and cook meals in an organised way.

Practical tasks: These are individual practical cookery tests. They can be taken individually or your tutor can combine up to three of these together.

Theory assignments: These are paper-based research and report type activities. You will be given the assignment and should read this against the grading criteria so that you are clear about what you need to produce to get the highest grade possible. Always read the assignment carefully.

The assignments are divided into tasks. You need to complete them all successfully. The tasks may cover the key skills requirements so you may be asked to produce a variety of types of evidence, e.g. to write and deliver a presentation and then answer questions, or to produce a report.

Your centre will give you a time period within which you must complete each assignment. They may be completed away from the centre, in your own time and at your own pace.

You can ask your tutor for some feedback about how your grade could be improved before the final submission of your work. Once the assignment has been formally submitted the grade awarded will stand.

Short-answer questions: These are used in the practical units to check your underpinning knowledge. They will be taken under supervised conditions and are closed-book tests.

On-line multiple choice test (Unit 202 only): Each question will normally have one correct answer and three incorrect answers. The test will be taken under supervised conditions.

Grades

The Diploma is graded at:

○ pass

○ merit

○ distinction.

Grades for practical tests: Once the practical test has been marked your tutor should provide you with written and oral feedback. This will allow you to see if there are areas of your performance that require improvement so you can work towards improving your grades. If you do not fulfil the Pass criteria for the practical test you can re-sit it but you will only be able to gain a Pass or Fail.

Grades for theory assignments: To achieve a particular grade in your theory assignments you must achieve all the points for that grade. For example, if a candidate met all the Pass criteria but only one of the Merit criteria, they would receive a Pass grade. To gain a Distinction all the criteria must be met for every grade.

Task	Pass	Credit	Distinction
	The candidate needs to have	**The candidate needs to achieve everything at pass grade and**	**The candidate needs to achieve everything at pass and credit grade and**
A	demonstrated understanding of the requirements and produced the minimum evidence required provided evidence which demonstrates knowledge relevant to the task	demonstrated sound understanding of the tasks and provided clear and relevant evidence shown the use of a range of relevant sources/resources presented the task well and in an organised and logical sequence demonstrated evidence of analysing research information	demonstrated excellent understanding of the tasks with evidence of analysis and evaluation critically evaluated a wide range of sources/resources which are clearly referenced provided evidence which demonstrates a good breadth and depth of knowledge that has been used to good effect in the task presented the task to a high level provided evidence of creative and original thoughts completed the task with minimal assistance

Figure 2: Example of grading descriptors for a theory assignment

Unit route overview

In order to develop your skills in specific areas the qualification is split into units which can be taught and assessed separately. The unit route is a particularly good way of building skills and allows flexibility in how the content of the unit is delivered. So, it is possible to cover a 20-hour unit over two and half days or over five weeks.

Once the content has been taught your tutor will arrange a 'Practical observation' to assess your skills. Your tutor will tell you what dishes you need to prepare. You need to successfully complete all the dishes. The observation will not cover everything you have learnt in that unit. Each Practical observation has a time limit although in some observations a specified amount of extra time can be added.

Once all the dishes have been completed a marking sheet will be filled in. However, you will still be expected to work in a safe, hygienic and organised manner throughout the practical observation.

Once you have achieved all of the units, if you want to achieve the full qualification, you will need to take practical tests, called **synoptic tests**, to prove that you can organise your workflow to produce a number of dishes in a set time while working in a safe, hygienic, efficient and organised way. These tests are more demanding than the practical observations because you have to produce a number of dishes in a set time period. In order to be successful you will need to plan your time well and practise the dishes before the test. You will be graded at Pass, Credit or Distinction. Your tutor will explain how you can achieve the grades before the tests.

Definition

Synoptic tests – these tests cover different parts of the qualification at the same time. They are important because they demonstrate that you can manage your time and resources as well as cook.

Did you know?

A quality assurance person, someone working within your centre, will check some aspects of your work. This is to make sure that the allocation of grades is fair. A City & Guilds representative, called an external verifier, will then check that the quality assurance meets national standards.

Key features

Look out for the following special features as you work through the book.

All important technical words are defined to help you develop your underpinning knowledge.

Interesting and useful culinary facts.

 Practical ideas and tips from top chef Marcus Wareing.

 Useful practical ideas and good advice – nearly as good as having a real chef to help you!

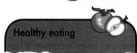 Ideas for healthy alternative ingredients and methods.

 Case study   These short real-life case studies tell you about the experiences of other people working in the catering industry.

 Important points to promote good practice in the kitchen and reminders about safe working practices.

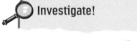 These independent research activities help you explore new areas and extend your knowledge.

 When you see this feature you will know that there is a related video clip for you to watch. The ProActive Catering e-learning site can be accessed at http://www.proactive-online.co.uk

 This feature helps you understand what you need to do to get the higher grades.

Try this!   Short practical activities for you to try in the classroom. Sometimes they may provide evidence for your portfolio.

Test yourself!   Within each chapter there is a set of questions to check your knowledge. These are a useful way of revising the underpinning knowledge for a unit ready for assessment.

Practice assignment tasks   At the end of each chapter (except chapter 2), there are assignment tasks where you can practise applying your knowledge.

This feature tells you the skill level for each process in the recipe.

Preparation	2
Cooking skills	1
Finishing	2

E-learning

The ProActive Catering e-learning site can be accessed at http://www.proactive-online.co.uk. If your centre has a licence then you will be given a login and password.

There are various types of electronic resources available on the site for independent learning:

- Video clips clearly demonstrate skills, e.g. how to cut a chicken for sauté.
- Interactive tutorials teach you about a specific topic, e.g. food safety. At the end of the tutorial there is a short multiple-choice test which checks your understanding.
- You can print off recipes, menus and worksheets as directed by your assessor.

Introduction to the catering and hospitality industry

1

This chapter covers the following outcomes from Diploma unit 101: Introduction to the catering and hospitality industry

- Outcome 101.1 Know the different sectors of the catering and hospitality industry
- Outcome 101.2 Be able to identify relevant qualifications, training and experience for employment within the industry

Working through this chapter could also provide the opportunity to practise the following Functional Skills at Level 1:

Functional English: Reading – identifying main points and ideas and how they are presented in a variety of texts.

In this chapter you will learn how to:

- Describe the structure and sectors of different types of catering and hospitality operations
- Explain the main features of establishments within the commercial and service sector
- Identify the staffing structures and main job roles for different types of catering establishments
- Identify the types of qualifications, training and experience available in the catering and hospitality sector
- Recognise and list employment rights and responsibilities
- Identify the associations related to professional cookery

The catering and hospitality industry

The **catering** and **hospitality** industry is one of the UK's fastest-growing sectors. By learning about and understanding the industry you will give yourself an insight into the widest possible choice of careers and lifestyle. If you are willing to seek opportunities and work hard you will be rewarded at an early age with responsibility, a good income and job satisfaction. The industry is set to benefit from increased investment and a higher profile as London prepares to host the 2012 Olympics, creating an estimated 850,000 jobs.

Structure of the UK catering and hospitality industry

The structure of the hospitality and catering industry reflects the different organisations that make up the industry. The industry is divided into two main sectors:
○ the commercial sector
○ the service sector.

Commercial sector

The commercial sector includes businesses whose main source of income is providing food, drink and accommodation services – e.g. hotels, restaurants, cafés and public houses (pubs).

Service sector

The service sector covers hospitality and catering operations in organisations where this is not the main business – e.g. providing meals in hospitals, schools and workplaces.

In the service sector, hospitality and catering services can be:
○ owned or managed in-house – this means that there is a department within the organisation which provides the service
○ contracted out – this means that the catering provision is provided by an outside company, often called a contract caterer.

Definitions
Catering – the business of providing food, drink and entertainment.
Hospitality – the business of providing services such as catering, accommodation and entertainment.

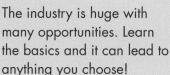

Marcus says:
The industry is huge with many opportunities. Learn the basics and it can lead to anything you choose!

Did you know?
The commercial sector is sometimes known as the profit sector because the businesses are run to make a profit. The service sector is sometimes called the cost sector because the hospitality services are often a cost to the businesses which need them, such as hospitals and schools.

Did you know?
There are over 180,000 people working in the contract food service industry in the UK.

Top marks!
Find out about the organisation that provides the food service in your college.

Operations

The three main operations in the catering and hospitality industry are:

○ catering
○ accommodation
○ hospitality.

Catering

Catering operations involve all aspects of preparing and serving food and drink. Some catering establishments are very small independent organisations run by one or two individuals. Others are multinational companies with many outlets that employ many people.

Accommodation

Accommodation operations provide somewhere for people to stay, usually overnight. Accommodation can be either serviced, e.g. in a hotel or guest house, or self-catering, e.g. in caravans or chalets.

Hospitality

Hospitality operations combine the catering, accommodation and service provision such as cleaning and laundry within one establishment, e.g. a hotel.

Commercial sector

Examples of establishments in the commercial sector are shown in Figure 1.1.

Figure 1.1 Examples of establishments in the commercial sector

Service sector

Examples of establishments in the service sector are shown in Figure 1.2.

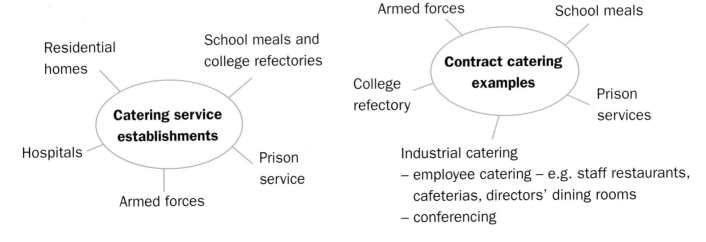

Figure 1.2 Examples of catering service and contract catering

Establishment features in the commercial sector

Hotels

Hotels can be either independent or part of a chain such as Hilton, De Vere, etc. Hotel features vary from low-cost options with limited facilities to expensive five-star hotels, offering a full range of services. These services will consist of food, quality furnishings, accommodation and other hospitality services which might include concierge services, valet and butler service, a spa, leisure and conference facilities and 24-hour room service.

Definition

Catering service – a catering operation run by the company or organisation itself.

Contract catering – where an outside company provides the catering service.

Case study — De Vere Hotel Group www.devere.co.uk

The De Vere Group is one of the most respected hotel and leisure chains in the UK. It has 19 hotels with over 150 timeshare lodges, 16 village hotels incorporating leisure facilities and 15 health and fitness clubs with over 66,000 members.

The upmarket four and five-star hotels operate in cities, as well as coastal and rural locations. They also offer facilities for conferences, banqueting and events. Several hotels have their own golf courses.

The De Vere Village Hotels and Leisure clubs offer extensive food, beverage and leisure facilities within easy reach of major towns and cities. These are complemented by Greens — the company's own chain of standalone health and fitness clubs

Figure 1.3 Slaley Hall is an example of a five-star hotel in the De Vere chain

Did you know?
Hotel ratings
Since 2007, hotels are now graded according to a set of nationally recognised common quality standards which have been adopted by the AA (Automobile Association) and UK tourist authorities. Hotels are placed within one of three categories – hotel, guest accommodation and budget hotel – and are given a rating from one to five stars. These ratings appear in guidebooks and are also displayed on the premises. Owners with star ratings benefit from increased publicity and business.

Lodges

Lodges provide popular, standard accommodation at low cost. They are suited to the business or leisure traveller and are often close to motorways or major towns and cities. They offer limited services – for example, they may not have a restaurant or if they do it may offer a limited choice. Many lodges are sited next to restaurants for convenience. Sometimes the restaurants are run by the same company.

Examples of lodges include Travelodge and Premier Inn.

Did you know?
Food ratings
Every year in the UK, the AA awards up to five rosettes to restaurants and hotels for the quality of their food. If an AA-rated hotel does not have a rosette the quality of food is still usually enjoyable and of a reasonable standard.

Case study

Travelodge is one of the UK's largest operators in the budget hotel sector. It manages a chain of over 300 properties offering over 20,000 beds. The hotels are mainly located in city centres, airports and near major roads and motorways. City centre locations have adjoining Bar Cafés and roadside hotels have the Little Chef facilities.

Budget rooms can be booked online, with offers of time-sensitive discounts – early bookings get discounted rates. Travelodge also offers rooms at its service station locations for drivers to rest for an hour and avoid driving fatigue.

The company continues to expand and is currently refurbishing its existing facilities and aims to open new sites in the future.

Figure 1.4 Travelodge hotels are often situated next to motorway services

Guest houses

Guest houses are usually privately owned and family run, offering bed and breakfast. They tend to be low-cost operations with a limited range of facilities and furnishings. Opening hours and food service depend on the rating. Increased competition has led to improved quality and service in recent years.

Restaurants

Restaurants provide food and drink and not accommodation. There is a huge variety of restaurants in the UK. Menus can be traditional, themed or international – e.g. Chinese, Mexican, Indian or Italian. Facilities vary widely according to location, popularity, quality and type of menu offered.

Many restaurants are owned and run independently. They offer a unique and often high-quality dining experience. Restaurants can be awarded up to three Michelin stars. The prices charged will reflect the quality of the food and the reputation of the chef.

There are over 18,000 Chinese, Indian and other ethnic restaurants in the UK, offering a wide variety of regional cuisine. They are generally small, independently-owned family businesses. The sector is dominated by Indian and Chinese restaurants, which also have a large share of the takeaway market. Other Asian cuisines such as Thai, Vietnamese and Japanese are becoming increasingly popular.

Did you know?

Michelin Guides

These are a series of guidebooks for restaurants and hotels published every year in several European countries. Restaurants of a very high standard are rated with one, two or three Michelin stars. These are the most recognised, influential and highly sought after culinary ratings in western Europe.

Michelin also highlight restaurants which offer "good food at moderate prices" with their "Bib Gourmand" feature.

Other restaurants are owned by chains such as Beefeater or Brewers Fayre. These are designed to appeal to the mass market and have reasonably priced menus.

Case study – Brewers Fayre

Brewers Fayre is a chain of over 440 pub restaurants. It is a subsidiary company of Whitbread plc, which is a large brewery company. Many Brewers Fayre restaurants are located next to Premier Lodge budget hotels (formerly called lodges) that are also owned by Whitbread. Each restaurant has its own unique identity and offers a range of affordable meals and meal deals, including traditional dishes such as a carvery to dishes from around the world.

Figure 1.5 Brewers Fayre is an example of a restaurant chain with outlets in many locations

Traditional cafés

Traditional cafés are usually independent businesses that provide basic food and non-alcoholic drinks.

Cafés are often self-service or offer a combination of self-service and table service, in which food ordered at the counter is freshly prepared in the kitchen and taken to the table. Traditional cafés provide simple, good-quality and good-value meals, snacks and hot and cold beverages. In order to attract more customers some café owners add additional facilities such as TV, free newspapers and wi-fi internet access.

Chain coffee outlets

Chain coffee outlets such as Costa Coffee and Starbucks have an international style. They offer a wide range of specialist Barista style coffees and are often located in busy locations such as airports and town centres.

Fast food outlets

Fast food restaurants serve a limited range of food. Service is quick and usually over the counter. The food offered is quick to make and serve and, depending on the outlet, might include burgers, fish and chips, baked potatoes or sandwiches, rolls and panninis.

Many fast food restaurants are part of very large national or international chains such as McDonald's and KFC. These outlets are sometimes run by managers, and sometimes run as **franchises**. The brands are instantly recognisable and the food and the restaurant decoration is standardised so that customers always know what they are going to get.

There are also many independent fast food outlets, such as sandwich bars and fish and chip shops

Facilities, staffing and opening hours usually are dependent on location and demand. Staffing is mainly low skilled with prices dependent on national rates, quality and reputation.

Definitions

Franchise – an agreement to sell a company's goods or services in a particular place.
Subsidiary company – a company is a subsidiary if another company holds more than 50% of the shares.

Case study — McDonald's

McDonald's is the largest fast food operator in the world. The restaurants are either owned by the company, by franchises or **subsidiary companies**. In the UK more than 2.5 million customers are served each day in over 1250 independent restaurants, including 735 drive-through restaurants and 500 in-house restaurants — these are outlets competing with other fast food operators, e.g. in a service station or shopping centre.

In the UK McDonald's employs approximately 67,000 people, many of whom are young and work part time. McDonald's has an extensive training programme and it will be offering higher-level qualifications in the future. The chain is going through a massive menu change and is introducing healthy options in response to critics and customer demand.

Figure 1.6 The McDonald's golden arches are known throughout the world

 Investigate!
Visit the McDonald's website and find out about the McDonald's quality values to staff and customers.

Public houses

There are approximately 55,000 public houses in the UK. Public houses are licensed to sell alcoholic drinks. Most also sell food. Some pubs market themselves as "gastro pubs", offering a particular style of modern decor and a wide range of traditional and international dishes.

Many pubs are owned by breweries. Some are "free houses". This means they are independent. These pubs often make a speciality of offering a range of guest beers from different breweries.

Service sector
Hospitals and hospices

Hospitals and hospices, both NHS and private, have to cater for large numbers of patients each day. There is usually a standard menu on offer but the establishment must also be able to cater for a wide range of special dietary needs.

In addition, catering has to be provided for staff and visitors in a number of outlets including canteens, coffee shops and vending areas. Private hospitals offer greater flexibility and generally have better-quality food and service standards.

Case study – Cornwall's NHS Food Project

Catering in the NHS is all about producing quality, nutritious meals to patients, visitors and staff every day of the year. Caterers must comply with the NHS plan and the "Better hospital foods" initiative. The five NHS trusts in Cornwall spend around £1.5 million per year on food products. The Cornwall Food Programme started in 2002 and is committed to providing and purchasing as much locally produced food as possible to its hospitals in Cornwall and the South West.

Before the project started, most of the food eaten in the county's hospitals was imported from a national supplier based in South Wales. The Royal Cornwall Hospital Trust has now placed business with local suppliers to provide sandwiches, fruit and vegetables, cheese and ice-cream.

The project has built a food production unit that produces the 5000 fresh meals required each day. The unit **blast chills** and **blast freezes** meals before delivering to each of the county's 20 hospitals. The aim is to increase the percentage of purchasing within the county. The project works with local producers, suppliers and distributors and promotes sustainable methods to protect the environment. It will also provide many skilled jobs in an area of need that traditionally relies on seasonal work.

Figure 1.7 Food service in a hospital must cater for a wide range of special dietary needs

Definitions

Blast chilling – reducing food temperature from +70°C to +3°C or below within 90 minutes.
Blast freezing – reducing food temperature from +70°C to –18°C in no more than 240 minutes.

Top marks!

Investigate the "Better hospital foods" initiative and write a summary of its findings.

Residential homes

Residential homes include private or council-run care homes for the elderly and children's homes.

Catering in residential homes can either be provided privately by in-house caterers, or subsidised through the local authority either directly or contracted out. There are usually set times for meals and refreshments. The facilities and furnishings are often basic and homely.

Schools and colleges

Most state schools and colleges cater only for lunchtimes. They offer a low-cost service with high volume and quick service. Some refreshments may also be available for evening and weekend courses, usually from vending machines or cafés. Some schools and colleges also offer breakfast and/or snacks at after-school clubs. Boarding schools need to provide breakfast and evening meals as well as lunch.

School catering is controlled either by individual schools (especially in the private sector) or through local authorities. School meals are usually subsidised so the prices paid by students are kept down. The emphasis is now on healthy eating and nutrition within government guidelines. In March 2005 the government introduced the initiative "Healthy Food in Schools – Transforming School Meals". It provided additional funding to ensure minimum standards of ingredients and introduced a new qualification for school caterers.

Prison service

Catering in prisons is now provided by staff who are not prison officers or it is contracted out. Prison catering needs to provide high-volume, low-budget food at set meal times. This must be balanced by the need to offer a varied and healthy menu that takes into account the cultural and dietary preferences of the prisoners. Separate facilities and a higher-quality provision are also available for prison staff.

Armed forces

Catering services are provided worldwide in a wide variety of locations such as on ships, in the field and on permanent bases for all three services (Army, Navy, Royal Air Force). The catering services are staffed by both service and contract caterers. They offer a wide variety of high-quality accommodation and food services at subsidised cost.

A new initiative is the "pay as you dine" (PAYD) service. This service is operated by commercial contract caterers in an increasing number of units across all three of the armed services. The contractor is required to provide breakfast, lunch and dinner each day and can only charge up to a maximum price set by the Ministry of Defence. However, the contractors can also offer additional options at competitive commercial rates, such as takeaway snacks, confectionery and sandwiches.

Contract catering

Contract caterers offer a wide range of tailored contract catering services to business and industry. This can include staff restaurants, cafés and deli bars, as well as private and fine dining for directors. Staffing, menus and pricing depend on the type of contract service being offered. Contract caterers sometimes also offer other facility services such as cleaning.

Case study — BaxterStorey

BaxterStorey runs one of the UK's largest independent contract catering operations. It provides the business and industry sector with staff restaurants, private dining facilities for executive managers, cafés, deli bars and other hospitality services.

It provides excellent in-house staff training for chefs. An example of this is the training scheme run by Michelin-starred chef John Campbell at Stockcross Hotel in Berkshire.

Figure 1.8 A typical BaxterStorey staff restaurant facility

11

Investigate!

Choose one of the case studies that interests you. Use the internet to find, select and identify some of the main features of the organisation. Try to cover: menus, pricing, staffing, layout, furnishings, nearest location to you, facilities and opening times. Present the information in a format that suits your purpose — such as a fact sheet or as a presentation and discussion with your group.

Test yourself!

1 Approximately how many hospitality, leisure, travel and tourism establishments were there in Great Britain in 2006?

2 Name the two main sectors of the catering and hospitality industry.

3 Name and describe three kinds of accommodation.

4 Hospitality is the business of providing food, drink and entertainment. True or False?

Identify relevant qualifications, training and experience for employment within the catering and hospitality industry

In order for you to get your career off to a good start, it is important to understand that the catering and hospitality industry has a wide and varied number of career choices available. You may have become interested in a career in catering by watching and learning how to cook or having a part-time job as a waiter or waitress or in a kitchen or fast food outlet.

Whatever got you interested in the industry, you will probably want to develop your career and perhaps run your own restaurant one day. This section will help you identify the qualification routes, skills, knowledge and experience you will need to fulfil your ambitions.

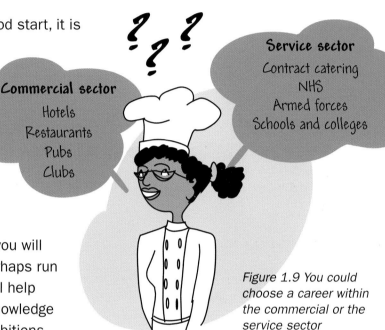

Figure 1.9 You could choose a career within the commercial or the service sector

Figure 1.10 There is a wide choice of different establishments you could work in

Figure 1.11 You might have a dream of opening your own restaurant one day

13

Staffing structures in different types of catering establishment

The commercial and service sectors of the industry that operate the hospitality, accommodation and catering operations all have staffing structures as shown in Figure 1.12.

Figure 1.12 Staffing structure in the hospitality and catering industry

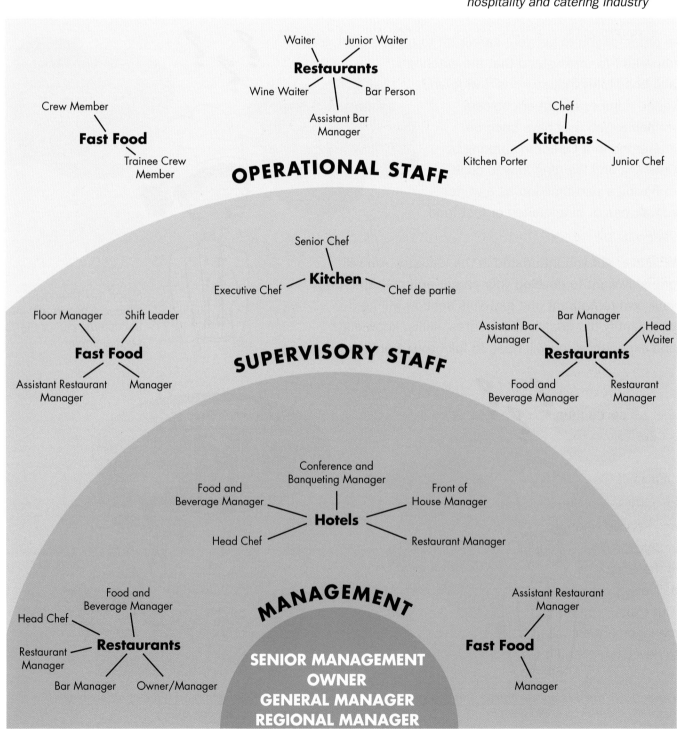

Main job roles
Operational staff

Commis chef

This is the junior position within a kitchen and is an ideal starting point for someone with qualifications but little experience. As a commis chef, your work should be supervised and you should be given opportunities to learn the various sections of the kitchen.

You will be required to carry out basic preparation (mise en place) and cooking and you will be expected to maintain high standards of hygiene. As well as using the skills you have already learnt to produce and present well-cooked and attractive meals, you will quickly need to develop speed and consistency, particularly if the kitchen is busy.

Chef de partie

Once you have gained experience as a commis chef and perhaps been in charge of a particular section of the kitchen, e.g. grill, sauce, starters, you will be ready for more responsibility.

As chef de partie you will report to the head chef. You will prepare, cook and present a range of dishes from your section or sections of the menu in a timely manner during service. In a large kitchen you may be assisted by a full-time or part-time commis chef, a trainee or someone on work experience. Working as part of a team the chef de partie must ensure that the dishes they are responsible for are ready when required for service.

Sous chef

As a sous chef you will be responsible for the day-to-day operation and service when the head chef is absent. You will have a clear understanding of all the sections in the kitchen and play a key role in the management of the kitchen such as ordering food, checking deliveries, food safety and the staff roster. These skills come with experience working in various establishments, level 3 and 4 management and skills training and the opportunities you have taken to develop professionally.

Management

General manager

As a manager you will be responsible for every aspect of the business including:

○ ensuring the customers receive the best possible service
○ monitoring the staff and ensuring that they work together to provide the best possible service
○ making sure that the business is profitable and is managed following the standards set by the owners
○ making sure that the business complies with the law – particularly health and safety, food safety, licensing, consumer protection and employment laws.

Head chef

As the head chef you will be responsible for all aspects of the kitchen, including:

○ planning the menu with an attractive variety and choice of dishes
○ liaising with food suppliers, ordering, organising deliveries and safe storage of food
○ managing the food budget and staff costs
○ supervising, recruiting and training staff to the highest standard
○ co-ordinating the food service
○ liaising with other managers, in particular the restaurant and general managers
○ checking standards and maintaining the food safety management system.

Restaurant manager

As the restaurant manager you will be responsible for all aspects of the restaurant, including:

○ making sure that the restaurant is prepared for service
○ making sure that customer service is of the highest standard
○ liaising with the head chef and kitchen staff
○ supervising, recruiting and training staff to the highest standard
○ dealing with customers by advising them on food and drink choices and solving any complaints
○ managing the budget for staff and restaurant equipment or services, e.g. laundry.

Conference and banqueting manager

As the conference and banqueting manager you will be responsible for:

○ attracting revenue to the business through functions and special events, e.g. conferences, weddings, meetings and exhibitions
○ developing relationships with clients
○ promoting the facilities of other departments within the establishment, e.g. overnight stays and leisure services
○ organising the events, including staff, food and beverage requirements
○ controlling the costs and budget for each event
○ training, managing and supervising staff.

Food and beverage manager

As the food and beverage manager you will be responsible for all aspects of the control of food and drink, including:

○ ensuring tight controls over food and drink to prevent waste, theft or losses
○ managing the head chef, restaurant manager, and other department heads, who will report to you
○ acting as a deputy or duty manager when needed, ensuring the hotel is operated in accordance with the law and the standards set by the owners
○ developing ideas for new menus, promotions and publicity to increase the profitability of the establishment
○ dealing with enquiries from suppliers, members of the public and the general manager
○ training, managing and supervising staff.

Investigate!
Find out the sort of salary you could expect to receive as a commis chef.

Figure 1.13 Whatever your role in the establishment, you will need to work as a team

Hospitality and catering qualifications

All qualifications are designed around the National Occupational Standards which are developed by the Sector Skills Council (SSC). For Hospitality, the SSC is People 1st. Qualifications are developed by awarding organisations and must be accredited by the Qualifications and Curriculum Development Authority (QCDA). This means that your certificate will have the QCDA logo on it, so it will be recognised by employers as a valid and worthy qualification that you have achieved by reaching the required standard.

Definition

NVQ – a qualification gained while working. NVQ stands for National Vocational Qualification.

NVQs

There is a range of NVQs in Hospitality at Levels 1–3, as shown in Figure 1.14.

Level 1	Level 2	Level 3
Food Preparation and Cooking	Professional Cookery	Professional Cookery
Food and Beverage Service	Food and Beverage Service	Hospitality Supervision
Multi Skilled	Multi Skilled	
Quick Service	Food Processing and Cooking	
Front Office	Front Office	
Housekeeping	Housekeeping	

Figure 1.14 NVQ qualifications available in Hospitality

NVQs are suitable for every learner and are available in a number of different pathways. To gain an NVQ you must demonstrate that you are competent in a number of mandatory units plus a selection of optional units which you choose.

Candidates demonstrate their competence in the workplace or sometimes in realistic working environments. NVQs can be assessed by employers or by colleges and training providers. Level 2 and 3 NVQs are compulsory components of the Apprenticeship and Advanced Apprenticeship awards.

Young Apprenticeships (YA)

These are new nationally designed programmes for young people aged 14–16. They provide a combination of on-the-job and off-the-job training. It is an educational route which allows motivated and able 14–16 year olds to study vocational qualifications as part of their options at Key Stage 4.

14–19 Diplomas

14–19 Diplomas offer an exciting new alternative to GCSEs and A levels, focusing on applied learning and including real work experience. The Hospitality Diploma became available from September 2009.

You can do a 14–19 Diploma at Foundation, Higher or Advanced level. To complete your Diploma you will need to achieve success in all the following areas:

- principal learning (about the skills and job roles in the Hospitality industry)
- functional skills (Mathematics, English)
- personal learning and thinking skills (e.g. creative thinking and team working)
- a project which you complete independently
- additional and specialist learning (e.g. a GCSE in a foreign language, or some units from an NVQ).

Entry Level Certificates

These are taught entry level qualifications aimed at learners with learning and physical difficulties. They can provide a progression route to NVQs. There are two entry levels in Food Studies that cover core subjects such as health, safety and hygiene, using kitchen equipment, food preparation and cooking, identification of food and an awareness of balanced diets. The Entry 3 certificate also covers communication and working relationships at work. It offers food and drink service, housekeeping, counter service, food preparation and cooking as optional units.

VRQs

VRQs have been developed to meet the specialist needs of the industry. A VRQ is similar to a GCSE but is directly workplace-related. The qualification involves both classroom-based learning of theory and, more importantly, a demonstration of craft skills. VRQs can be delivered in the workplace by centres, such as colleges and training organisations, that are approved by the awarding body. VRQs are aimed at anyone working in the industry as an addition to their existing qualifications and will benefit the catering operation.

The following are examples of VRQs.

Definition
VRQ – stands for Vocationally Related Qualification.

Diplomas in Professional Cookery

Specialist Diplomas in Professional Cookery are available at levels 1, 2 and 3. Unlike NVQs where you select from a range of optional units, in a VRQ you must achieve at least a Pass mark in all units in order to gain a certificate.

Short courses

There are also many Hospitality-related short courses (typically about 20 hours long) available. These cover specific areas of knowledge and skill. Examples include Food Safety and Health and Safety courses, as well as more specialist courses such as the **Barista** course or the Butlers course.

> **Definition**
>
> **Barista** – a term used for a trained individual who is capable of producing, presenting and serving a full range of non-alcoholic hot and cold beverages.

Advanced/Higher Diplomas in Hospitality and Catering

These are higher-level qualifications aimed at supervisory or senior managers in a variety of hospitality and catering positions and types of establishments. They are set at levels 3 and 4 and require completion of a number of mandatory and optional units. Individuals can tailor these qualifications to their needs by choosing the optional units which relate most closely to their work.

City & Guilds higher level qualifications

As well as being the leading provider of NVQs in hospitality and catering, City & Guilds also offer a range of higher-level vocational qualifications. These include the Advanced Professional Certificate in Hospitality and Catering level 3, the Higher Professional Diploma in Hospitality and Catering level 4, and the Master Professional Diploma in Strategy and Development (Hospitality and Catering) level 7.

Degrees

There is an increasing need for highly-qualified managers and chefs with skills and technical expertise to manage catering operations. Foundation Degrees (FdA) in Culinary Arts or Hospitality and Food Management are intended to fill this need. A person who had achieved a foundation degree could enter employment as a junior manager or progress to the final year of a full honours degree.

Functional Skills

Functional Skills are practical skills in English, Mathematics and ICT that allow individuals to work confidently, effectively and independently in life. They are a compulsory requirement for apprenticeships and for the 14–19 Diplomas. The functional skills qualifications are a qualification in their own right.

Investigate!

What key and functional skills does a head chef need in order to be able to do his or her job? Once you have finished your list, give as many examples for each skill as you can.

Training and experience in the hospitality and catering sector

There are many training opportunities within the hospitality and catering sector. This is one of the fastest-growing sectors in the UK and you will be giving yourself a fantastic opportunity to learn and get promoted across the wide range of career choices available. At the start of your career you should apply and volunteer to gain experience in as many different work placements as you can. This will give you an insight into the reality of what could be a very rewarding career.

You will need to be aware of your career opportunities as you gain experience and qualifications. The UK Skills Passport has an excellent career map showing progression routes from kitchen porter to senior management in over 25 areas in the industry.

Investigate!

Go to the Skills Passport website and find out the progression route you want to aim for. Find out the job descriptions and what salary you could earn.

You can find out about many popular job descriptions and industry roles by doing research on company websites or job advertisements. A full list of industry websites can be found in the *Caterer and Hotelkeeper* magazine advice guide.

Go to www.heinemann.co.uk/hotlinks and enter the express code 3729P.

Throughout your career it will be important to keep your skills up to date and to develop new ones. Any new skills you learn could give you the edge over other candidates at a job interview. Some companies will provide their own training and development schemes through practical or e-learning. Other companies will ask training providers to come in to train, assess and reward your skills with nationally recognised qualifications such as NVQs.

Employment rights and responsibilities

When you start work or you employ someone in your business you must be aware of the range of statutory regulations you need to comply with. It is important to understand the difference between a right and a responsibility. Your rights are what you can expect to receive from your employer. Your responsibilities are what you must do yourself.

Your employment responsibilities

Your responsibilities as an employee are to:

○ take reasonable care of yourself and others and co-operate with your employer in accordance with health and safety legislation – see Chapter 3
○ support the rules of the business
○ stick to the terms of your contract.

Your employment rights

Your employment rights as an employee are:

- the benefits from UK legislation
- maternity and paternity rights
- equality of opportunity
- to receive the minimum wage
- paid holidays
- the right to join a trade union
- protection from discrimination.

The benefits from UK legislation include your legal responsibilities and rights, and those of your employers. They include:

- contracts of employment
- anti-discrimination provisions
- employment equality (religion and beliefs)
- equal pay
- disability discrimination
- working hours and holiday entitlements
- sickness absence and sick pay
- minimum wage entitlement
- data protection
- health and safety
- human rights
- your role in the organisation you work for and the industry as a whole
- the variety of career opportunities and progression routes available to you.

Contracts of employment

A contract of employment is an agreement between an employer and an employee. The contract is made as soon as you accept a job offer, and both sides are then bound by its terms until it has properly ended (usually by giving notice) or until the terms are changed (usually by mutual agreement).

Your rights and duties, and those of your employer, are called the "terms" of the contract.

At first, the contract doesn't have to be in writing and can be a verbal agreement, e.g. shortly after attending a job interview.

But you are entitled to a written statement of the main terms within two months of starting work. The contract should include details of:

- pay
- hours of work
- holiday entitlement
- sick pay arrangements
- notice periods
- information about disciplinary and grievance procedures.

If an employee or employer wishes to end the employment contract they should also follow a set procedures that is designed to protect both parties from unfair treatment.

Employees who believe they have been dismissed or otherwise treated unfairly have the right to take their case to an independent Employment Tribunal, providing certain rules are met about how long they have been employed and the procedures that have been followed by their employer.

Anti-discrimination provisions

There are several laws in place to prevent discrimination against different groups of people in the workplace. Anti-discrimination laws include the following:

- Employment Equality (Religion and Beliefs) Regulations 2003
- Equal Pay Act 1970 (Amendment) Regulations 2003
- Race Relations Act 1976 (Amendment) Regulations 2003 and Sex Discrimination Act 1975 (Amendment) Regulations 2003
- **Disability** Discrimination Act 2005 (DDA 2005)
- Human Rights Act 1998.

Definition

Disability – a physical or mental impairment which affects a person's ability to carry out normal day-to-day activities.

Working hours and holiday entitlements

The Working Time Regulations 2003 apply to all employers in the UK, regardless of sector or size of the company. They are a set of rules about the amount of time that employees can work and the amount of rest time they are entitled to. There are special provisions regarding the number of hours young people and seasonal workers can work but the basic rights and provisions are:

- a limit of an average of 48 hours work per week (though workers can choose to work more if they want to)
- a limit of an average of 8 hours work in 24 for night workers
- a right for night workers to have a free health assessment

- a right to 11 hours rest a day
- a right to an in-work rest break if the working day is longer than 6 hours
- a right to one day off each week
- a right to four weeks paid leave per year.

Sickness absence and sick pay

The amount of pay you are entitled to when you are off sick varies from job to job, and there are also different sick pay schemes in operation – but there is advice available if you have problems. There are two types of sick pay:

- contractual (company, or occupational) sick pay
- Statutory Sick Pay (SSP).

If you take time off from work due to illness, any payment you receive will depend on your contract of employment. This can be either in writing, verbally agreed or implied by "custom or practice" or a mixture of all three.

If your employer runs a company scheme, you are entitled to the benefits of the scheme. Otherwise your employer should still pay you Statutory Sick Pay (SSP). However, SSP doesn't start until your fourth day off work.

What to do if you have problems

If you are unsure about anything relating to sick pay, talk to your employer first. However, if your employer is refusing to pay you sick pay that you are due; this is classed as an "unlawful deduction from wages" and you should seek further independent advice.

Minimum wage entitlement

Almost all UK workers, whether they are full or part-time workers, have a legal right to a minimum level of pay, called the National Minimum Wage. The level is set by the government each year based on the recommendations of the independent Low Pay Commission (LPC) and any increases are implemented on 1 October.

There are different levels of National Minimum Wage, depending on the age of the worker:

- adults (people aged 22 and over) receive the full rate
- workers aged 18 to 21 receive "a development rate"

○ young people (those older than school leaving age and younger than 18 – you are under school leaving age until the end of the summer term of the school year in which you turn 16).

You are not entitled to receive the minimum wage if you are:
○ a worker under school leaving age
○ genuinely self-employed
○ some apprentices – see below
○ an au pair
○ in the armed services
○ a voluntary worker.

Apprentices under the age of 19 are not entitled to the National Minimum Wage. Also, apprentices who are 19 or over and are in the first 12 months of their apprenticeship are not entitled to the National Minimum Wage.

Health and safety

There are a number of laws and regulations which have been written to protect you at work. They also protect your colleagues and customers. The aim of health and safety laws is to avoid people getting hurt at work or becoming ill through work.

The **Health and Safety at Work Act 1974** (HASWA) is the main legislation covering health and safety in the workplace. Under this Act, employers and employees have responsibilities. For more on this, see Chapter 3, page 88.

There are many health and safety regulations and codes of practice which relate to different kinds of work and different sorts of workplaces, including:
○ Control of Substances Hazardous to Health (COSHH) 2002
○ Manual Handling Operations Regulations 1992 (amended 2002)
○ Health & Safety (First Aid) Regulations 1981.

If you are under 18 you will have further protection through the Management of Health and Safety at Work Regulations 1999: Provisions Relating to Young Persons.

These regulations aim to protect young workers, who are seen as being particularly at risk in the workplace. The reasons for this include:
○ lack of experience
○ lack of awareness of occupational risks to their health and safety
○ immaturity.

Investigate!
Find out what the current National Minimum Wage rates are.

Remember!
Many good employers pay well above the National Minimum Wage and their conditions of employment may include performance bonuses.

Remember!
For more information on health and safety, read Chapter 3.

Identify relevant qualifications, training and
experience for employment within the catering
and hospitality industry

These regulations state that:

o risk assessments must be carried out before a young person
  starts work
o young persons are not allowed to do certain work if a significant
  risk cannot be avoided
o the parent/guardian must be informed about certain aspects of
  the work
o students and schoolchildren under 18 years are covered by
  these regulations
o schools, colleges and individuals who arrange work experience
  schemes have duties under the HASWA 1974.

For further information, you can visit the Directgov website.

Did you know?

Where to get help

o The Advisory, Conciliation
  and Arbitration Service
  (Acas) offers free,
  confidential and impartial
  advice on all employment
  rights issues. You can call
  the Acas helpline on 08457
  474747 from 8.00 am to
  6.00 pm Monday to Friday.
o Your local Citizens Advice
  Bureau (CAB) can provide
  free and impartial advice.
  You can find your local
  CAB office in the phone
  book or online.

Try this!

Rights and responsibilities — understanding the difference

Copy each sentence and fill in the gap with the word **right** or **responsibility**.

1 Employees have a .... to an in-work rest break if the shift is
  more than six hours long.
2 Health and Safety is everybody's ....
3 If you are sick, it is your .... to tell your employer.
4 Employed people have a .... to a contract of employment.
5 Almost all UK workers have a legal .... to a minimum level
  of pay.

Legislation in the hospitality sector

In addition to the employment regulations we have already looked
at, the hospitality industry has a number of specific regulations
that all professional chefs should have a good understanding and
knowledge of. These include:

o The Food Safety Act 1990 (Amendment) Regulations 2004
o Food Safety (General Food Hygiene) Regulations 1995
o General Food Regulations 2004
o Control of Substances Hazardous to Health (COSHH) Regulations
  2002.

From 1 January 2006 the following European Union (EU) food
hygiene legislation has applied throughout the UK:

o Food Hygiene (England) Regulations 2005
o Food Hygiene (Scotland) Regulations 2005
o Food Hygiene (Wales) Regulations 2005
o Food Hygiene (Northern Ireland) Regulations 2005.

All food safety legislation is designed to protect the consumers from illness or harm.

Everyone who deals with food has a moral and legal responsibility to safeguard food and protect food from contamination.

Employers have a wide range of legal responsibilities. They must:
○ register their premises with local authorities
○ ensure their premises are designed, equipped and operated in ways which prevent contamination
○ have adequate facilities for washing and personal hygiene
○ ensure that staff are properly trained and supervised
○ operate a system of hazard analysis.

Employees' responsibilities in food safety controls include:
○ protect food from contamination
○ keep yourself clean and have good personal hygiene habits and practices
○ follow the instructions and rules for work
○ report all faults and potential food hazards to your supervisor.

> **Remember!**
> For further information on food safety, read Chapter 2 or visit the Food Standards Agency website.

Associations related to professional cookery

There are many organisations and professional bodies involved in the hospitality industry. The ones detailed below are specific to professional cookery and careers.

British Hospitality Association (BHA)

The British Hospitality Association is the national trade association for the hospitality industry. Established in 1907, it represents over 16,500 group and independent restaurants – including every motorway services operator – and over 18,000 contract catering units. The BHA promotes and protects the interests of all operators in the industry – from the largest international company to the smallest independent.

It also provides members with a wide range of services designed to keep them informed of industry issues, up to date with legislation, help grow their business and save them money and time.

Craft Guild of Chefs

The Craft Guild of Chefs is an association representing the interest of chefs. It aims to increase standards of professional cooking through greater awareness, education and training and to develop the careers of its members. This is achieved by helping members develop and maintain their knowledge, skills and ability by participating in craft skills competitions in the UK and internationally.

The association works with the industry, the education sector and the media to attain greater recognition for chefs and their profession. It promotes the use of British and European produce and manufacturers, many being affiliated to the Craft Guild of Chefs.

Springboard UK

Springboard UK is a young, dynamic organisation which promotes careers in hospitality, leisure and travel. It has a network of centres across the UK. Their specialist career service now provides well over 14,000 people with free advice each year. Every year Springboard UK holds its FutureChef schools competition, holding regional and national competitions for young chefs aged 12–16.

Institute of Hospitality

The Institute of Hospitality represents professional managers in the hospitality, leisure and tourism industries and has a worldwide membership. Its members come from all sectors of the industry, including hotels, contract catering and restaurants, as well as leisure outlets, theme parks and sports venues.

The Institute of Hospitality exists to benefit its members in their career and professional development, as well as continuing to improve industry sector standards.

North East Culinary Trade Association (NECTA)

NECTA promotes culinary and service excellence in the North East. The association works very closely with the local colleges and encourages chefs to enter competitions. Each year it holds a two-day competition to showcase the best students and chefs from the region.

The association propels careers, helps to strengthen the education of young chefs, and offers an early professional approach to the crafts skills within the industry.

British Institute of Innkeeping (BII)

BII is the professional body for the licensed retail sector and has a dynamic membership made up of licensees and other professionals from the sector. BII's awarding body, BIIAB, offers a wide portfolio of qualifications, including the market-leading BIIAB National Certificate for Personal Licence Holders, as well as staff and business development qualifications, and qualifications for cooking/catering.

People 1st

This is the government-funded Sector Skills Council for the Hospitality, Travel and Tourism Industry. It promotes skills training for businesses and it sets the National Occupational Standards. People 1st is at the forefront of developing the new Hospitality Diploma. One initiative it has launched with its business partners is the Skills Passport. This is a positive skills network with an online record of achievement for employers and career guide for employees.

Welsh Culinary Association

Formed in 1993, the Welsh Culinary Association exists to promote excellence in the art of professional cookery within Wales.

Beverage Service Association (BSA)

The Beverage Services Association is the trade association for companies supplying hot beverages, machines and related products to the Out of Home beverage market. Its aim is to raise and maintain the quality of beverages and the standards of service provided through education, training, information and communication. Its members range from large multinational companies through roasters, machine manufacturers, wholesalers and distributors, through to barista trainers and retail coffee shops.

Academy of Culinary Arts

The Academy of Culinary Arts is Britain's leading professional association of Head Chefs, Pastry Chefs, Restaurant Managers and suppliers. It is concerned with raising standards and awareness of food, food provenance, cooking and service, as well as running education and training programmes for the young chefs of the future.

Professional Association of Catering Education (PACE)

PACE is a professional association for people involved in delivering catering qualifications within educational institutions. PACE enables its regional and national network of members to speak with a single voice on issues such as curriculum development, teaching and learning technologies, and best practice. It runs an annual conference and promotes staff development and interchange within the industry.

National Skills Academy for Hospitality

The National Skills Academy was set up in 2009 to develop a set of nationally recognised standards against which all hospitality qualifications and learning opportunities in England can be measured. Its role is to identify, endorse and promote qualifications and learning opportunities that are delivered to the National Skills Academy standards.

Test yourself!

1 List five pieces of legislation that relate to employment rights and responsibilities.

2 What information can be found in a job description?

3 Name two chef associations.

Further information

You can find out more about the organisations mentioned in this chapter by visiting their websites. Links have been made available at www.heinemann.co.uk/hotlinks – just enter the express code 3729P.

Hospitality and catering companies

De Vere Hotels
Travelodge
Brewers Fayre
McDonald's
BaxterStorey

Information on qualifications and industry standards

Sector Skills Council (SSC)
Qualifications and Curriculum Authority (QCA)
UK Skills Passport
Office of the Qualifications and Examinations Regulator (OFQUAL)

Government websites

Directgov
Food Standards Agency

Professional associations

British Hospitality Association
Craft Guild of Chefs
Springboard UK
Institute of Hospitality
Welsh Culinary Association
British Institute of Innkeeping
People 1st
North East Culinary Trade Association
Beverage Service Association
Academy of Culinary Arts
Professional Association of Catering Education
National Skills Academy for Hospitality

Practice assignment tasks

Task 1

Produce a poster advertising the training course you are currently on. Give some details about the hospitality industry and the reasons why it is an attractive career.

Task 2

Produce an information sheet for anyone starting a new job in the kitchen. It should contain some rules of the establishment and include the following topics:

- health and safety
- food safety
- personal hygiene rules
- working hours and breaks.

Task 3

Research the career of a TV chef who has made it to the top of his or her profession. Discuss your choice with your tutor and prepare and present your findings in a five-minute talk to your colleagues.

Task 4

Decide what your career goal in the hospitality industry is going to be. Identify the training, qualifications, skills and the steps you need to take and how long it will take to reach your goal.

Food safety

2

This chapter covers the following outcomes from Diploma unit 202: Food safety in catering

- Outcome 202.1 Understand how individuals can take personal responsibility for food safety
- Outcome 202.2 Understand the importance of keeping him/herself clean and hygienic
- Outcome 202.3 Understand the importance of keeping the work areas clean and hygienic
- Outcome 202.4 Understand the importance of keeping food safe

Working through this chapter could also provide the opportunity to practise the following Functional Skills at Level 1:

Functional ICT: Developing and presenting – apply editing, formatting and layout techniques to meet needs including text, tables, graphics, records, numbers, charts, graphs and other digital content; combining information within a publication.

In this chapter you will learn how to:

- Identify the causes of food poisoning and ways to avoid it
- Identify allergens, food intolerances and contaminants
- Recognise good and bad practices in personal hygiene
- Report and handle illnesses and infections
- Identify correct cleaning procedures and practices
- Maintain surfaces and manage waste management
- Identify types of pest and signs of infestation and describe correct pest management and control methods
- Describe and carry out methods of food storage and stock control
- Manage temperature control
- Identify food safety procedures

Food poisoning

What is food poisoning?

If food is not prepared, stored or cooked correctly it becomes a **hazard** and those who consume it may become very ill or even die. This is why there are many laws and regulations controlling the provision of food. In the catering industry this puts a great responsibility on all employees whose job involves food preparation.

All the information that follows will help you understand what food poisoning is and how you can work safely to prevent its occurrence.

Food poisoning is caused by eating food contaminated with harmful **micro-organisms** (e.g. **bacteria**). These micro-organisms need food and water to survive. They have to multiply to a dangerous level to make a person ill. Food poisoning symptoms are usually fairly mild and short-lived.

A food-borne disease is passed on by the micro-organisms causing the illness being present in food or water. Food-borne diseases cause severe illnesses which can kill. Bacteria or viruses causing food-borne diseases such as typhoid and hepatitis can make a person very ill even when present in small numbers. Bacteria causing food-borne diseases do not become harmful only after multiplying in the food; they are very dangerous by themselves. Some of the symptoms of food poisoning and a food-borne disease are very similar.

Symptoms of food poisoning

The main symptoms are:
- abdominal pain
- diarrhoea
- vomiting (being sick)
- fever.

Other symptoms that may occur are:
- abdominal cramp
- difficulty in breathing
- nausea (feeling sick)
- flu-like symptoms
- rashes
- convulsions (fits).

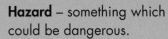

Definition

Hazard – something which could be dangerous.

Did you know?

Shigella bacteria cause **dysentery**. The bacteria are highly infectious and just a few can cause illness. Shigella bacteria do not multiply in food. The bacteria get onto the hands of food handlers from toilet seats, tap handles and nail brushes in washrooms and toilets. If the food handler does not wash their hands thoroughly the bacteria are transferred onto any food they touch. If an outbreak of dysentery occurs all the toilet and washroom areas must be thoroughly disinfected and the nail brushes sterilised. All staff must receive training in the importance of correct personal hygiene procedures.

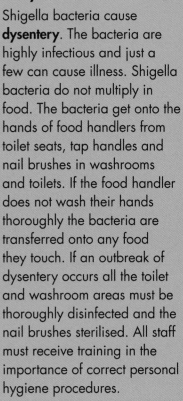

Definition

Bacteria – micro-organisms which cause disease.
Dysentery – a food-borne disease causing mild to severe diarrhoea and fever. It can be fatal.
Micro-organism – a very small life form which cannot be seen without a microscope.
Organism – any living animal or plant.

The time between consuming the food and experiencing the symptoms can be as little as one hour or as long as 70 days!

If you are suffering from food poisoning, the doctor will want to know what your symptoms are and how much time passed from the consumption of any suspect food to the symptoms appearing. This information often gives the first indication of the type of bacteria responsible for the outbreak. To find out the exact cause of food poisoning a **faeces** sample will have to be taken and sent to a laboratory for analysis.

People at risk from food poisoning

The majority of people who suffer food poisoning will have some very unpleasant symptoms for a few days and will feel rather weak and uncomfortable. They should make a full recovery within one to two weeks. Unfortunately, some sectors of the population may have a more severe reaction to the condition and need hospital treatment. Some people may even die from severe symptoms. Those most at risk are:

o babies and young children
o pregnant women and nursing mothers
o the elderly and infirm
o those already suffering from an illness or medical condition.

Some of those most at risk from food poisoning may be found:

o in hospitals
o in children's and old people's homes
o attending medical centres.

Any confirmed outbreak of a food-related illness causes severe problems for a business. Reports in newspapers and on the television and radio will stop many people from visiting a restaurant or take-away outlet. Many catering firms who have had an outbreak of food poisoning have had to close down, so the staff lost their jobs.

Causes of food poisoning

The most common cause is consuming a large number of the types of bacteria which cause illness. Other possible causes include:

o chemicals
o viruses which are present in some types of food, e.g. shellfish
o moulds
o physical contaminants.

Figure 2.1 The symptoms of food poisoning can be very unpleasant

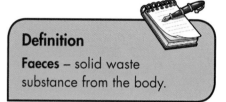

Definition

Faeces – solid waste substance from the body.

Micro-organisms

Bacteria

Bacteria are micro-organisms. They cannot be seen with the naked eye and cannot be tasted or smelt if they are on food.

Bacteria multiply by splitting into two. They can do this every 20 minutes. This means that after a few hours one bacterium can have multiplied to over one million. When there are about one million **pathogenic** bacteria per gram of a portion of food eaten, food poisoning can occur.

> **Definition**
>
> **Pathogen** – an organism that causes disease.

> **Did you know?**
>
> Certain types of bacteria are very useful to us. We use some types of bacteria to:
> o grow crops
> o digest food
> o treat sewage
> o create medicines
> o manufacture cleaning products
> o make food, e.g. yoghurt and cheese.

Figure 2.2 Bacteria can multiply very quickly

The types of bacteria that cause food poisoning are called pathogenic bacteria. Figure 2.3 shows common types of pathogenic bacteria.

Pathogenic bacteria	Where they come from
Salmonella	Raw meat and poultry, eggs and milk, pets, insects, sewage
Staphylococcus aureus	Human body (skin, nose, mouth, cuts, boils), milk
Clostridium perfringens	Human and animal **excrement**, soil, dust, insects, raw meat
Clostridium botulinum	Soil, raw meat, raw, smoked and canned fish
Bacillus cereus	Cereals (especially rice), soil, dust

Figure 2.3 Types of pathogenic bacteria

MORE TAKEN ILL IN E. COLI OUTBREAK

CAMPYLOBACTER BUG ON THE RISE

FOOD POISONING SHUTS SCHOOL

Girl, 5, struck down by E. coli

Figure 2.4 Food-borne diseases are widely reported

> **Definition**
>
> **Excrement** – solid waste matter passed out through the bowel.

Food-borne diseases are caused by micro-organisms which are found in food and water but do not depend upon them to survive. This makes them different to bacteria. Only a small number of these micro-organisms are needed to cause illness.

Figure 2.5 shows where food-borne diseases come from.

Micro-organism	Where they come from
Campylobacter	Raw meat and poultry, milk, animals
E. coli 0157	Human and animal gut, sewage, water, raw meat
Listeria	Soft cheese, **unpasteurised** milk products, salad, pâté
Shigella dysenteriae (Bacillary dysentery)	Water, milk, salad, vegetables
Salmonella typhi and paratyphi Typhoid/paratyphoid	Food or water contaminated by human faeces or sewage

Figure 2.5 Sources of food-borne diseases

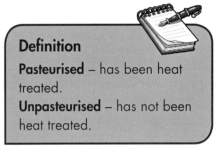

Definition
Pasteurised – has been heat treated.
Unpasteurised – has not been heat treated.

Spores

Some bacteria can form **spores**. A spore is a form of protective coating in which the bacteria can survive being cooked, dried and treated with cleaning chemicals. They cannot multiply when in this state, but when the conditions become more suitable, they start multiplying again.

Figure 2.6 Some bacteria can form protective spores

Conditions for bacterial growth

Bacteria multiply when they have ideal conditions to grow. These are:

- **Food**: Bacteria multiply on food, particularly protein-based food, e.g. meat, fish and dairy items.
- **Moisture**: Bacteria thrive in moisture, but cannot survive in food preserved by drying, salting or adding sugar.
- **Warmth**: Bacteria prefer body temperature but they are also happy at room temperature. In the fridge or freezer they do not die but become **dormant**, so they do not multiply. High temperatures of over 70°C for more than three minutes will kill most bacteria.

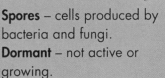

Definition
Spores – cells produced by bacteria and fungi.
Dormant – not active or growing.

- **Time**: In the best conditions the fastest time in which a bacterium can multiply is ten minutes. The average time for most bacteria is 20 minutes.
- **Oxygen**: Some bacteria need oxygen to multiply, and others prefer no oxygen. There are also types of bacteria that multiply regardless of whether there is oxygen or not.

High-risk foods

As the tables on pages 38 and 39 show, there are several types of food that can harbour the dangerous bacteria that can cause food poisoning. These are known as high-risk foods for these reasons:

- They are mainly ready-to-eat foods which will not be cooked further (cooking can make food safe to eat).
- They involve mixing and processing several ingredients. This increases the preparation time at room temperature. Time and temperature are needed by bacteria to multiply.
- Some dishes involve breaking down and mixing surface tissue with internal muscle. This happens with minced meat, poultry and fish. Few bacteria are found within the muscle and when this is cooked in a large piece, e.g. chicken breast, the bacteria on the outside surface are killed quickly. If the meat is minced, the outside surfaces – which contain more bacteria – are mixed in with the muscle areas.
- Some ingredients are sourced from high-risk areas, e.g. seafood from contaminated water.

The most common high-risk food categories:

- Cooked meats and poultry, plus pâtés and spreads made from these ingredients.
- Meat stews, gravy and meat-stock-based soups and sauces.
- Milk, cream and eggs – particularly items that involve raw or lightly cooked ingredients. Artificial creams and custards are included here.
- Shellfish and seafood including prawns, mussels, oysters both raw and cooked.
- Cooked rice that is not used immediately.

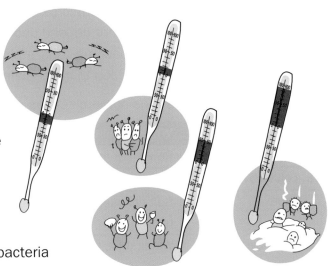

Figure 2.7 The effect of temperature on bacteria

> **Try this!**
> **Produce a booklet for staff training that details:**
> - *a table of the main micro-organisms*
> - *types of non-bacterial food poisoning*
> - *conditions for growth.*

Figure 2.8 Eating with your right hand

Viruses

A virus is a germ which causes disease. Viruses are even smaller than bacteria. Viruses multiply once eaten so only a few of these tiny micro-organisms are needed to cause illness. The most common food that can cause viral poisoning is shellfish which may have been grown in contaminated water and not been correctly cleaned before consumption. Viruses can be also passed from person to person via poor personal hygiene, e.g. not washing your hands after using the toilet.

Moulds

Moulds are multi-cellular organisms which will grow on food of all types – sweet, salty, acid or alkaline. They grow fastest at a temperature of 20–30°C, but can also grow slowly at temperatures as low as –10°C. Mould spores survive in the air, so even if they are destroyed by cooking it is virtually impossible to prevent them existing on food. Some moulds produce toxins which cause food poisoning symptoms and also may cause cancer. Moulds present on cereals, nuts, herbs, spices and milk can produce toxins in this way. Other moulds produce chemicals which are toxic to bacteria and help to destroy them, such as that used in penicillin.

Figure 2.9 Mould

Non-bacterial

Chemicals

Poisoning from chemicals is rare in the UK but it does happen occasionally. Some chemicals can get into food accidentally and can cause poisoning. These are examples:

○ **Cleaning chemicals** can cause poisoning if surfaces and equipment have not been rinsed properly. When the surfaces and equipment are used, the chemical residue can contaminate food.

○ **Pesticides** may be present from harvesting crops which have recently been sprayed with chemicals. In this case, poisoning can occur if the food is not peeled or washed properly.

○ **Metallic poisoning** can occur if food is poorly stored (e.g. leaving food in unlined tin cans in the fridge), or if food is cooked in unlined copper or aluminium pans, particularly acidic foods, e.g. fruit.

Toxins

Toxins forming in poorly stored oily fish, e.g. tuna, sardines and salmon, can cause severe illness. Shellfish, e.g. mussels, may become poisonous if they have fed on toxic **plankton**. This particular plankton only occurs at certain times of year in specific areas and so fishing is restricted during this season.

Incorrect cooking methods

Some food is poisonous if it is not cooked correctly. Red kidney beans can make people ill if they have not been boiled for at least ten minutes. (Tinned red kidney beans are safe as they have been thoroughly cooked as part of the canning process.)

Other food safety risks

Physical contaminants

Any item which is discovered in food when it is not supposed to be there is a foreign body. Foreign bodies found in food include:

○ pieces of glass, plastic and metal
○ mouse and rat droppings
○ gemstones and settings of jewellery
○ blue and natural-coloured plasters
○ strands of hair
○ flies, caterpillars and other insects

> **Definition**
>
> **Plankton** – a layer of tiny plants and animals living just below the surface of the sea.
> **Toxin** – a poison produced by bacteria.

Figure 2.10 Metallic poisoning can occur from poor storage

○ pen tops, drawing pins, paper clips
○ screws, nuts and bolts.

If such an item is found in food it is extremely unpleasant and upsetting for the consumer and embarrassing and inconvenient for the business. It is very probable that the presence of the foreign body breaks the law – either the Food Safety Act 1990 or HACCP procedures, see pages 79–82. If this happens, the catering organisation will have to look very carefully into its food safety system to find out where it failed.

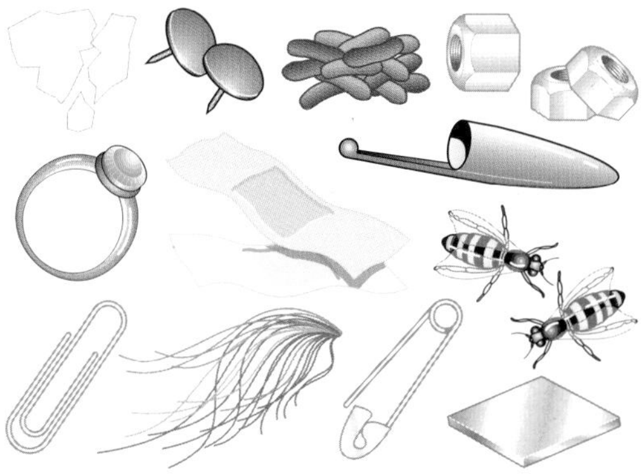

Figure 2.11 Foreign bodies that have been found in food

Allergies

An allergy is an intolerance some people have to certain substances, some of which may be types of food. An increasing number of people now suffer from mild allergic reactions to a range of food including:

○ wheat products (such as bread and biscuits)
○ dairy products (such as milk and cheese)
○ gluten (the elastic protein which is found in wheat flour).

Some symptoms of an allergic reaction can be very similar to that of a food-borne illness. It is important that they are not confused. An allergic reaction will only concern one person and usually occurs within a very short time of consumption. An incidence of food poisoning can affect a large number of people at the same time.

Symptoms of food allergies include:

○ vomiting
○ difficulty in breathing
○ diarrhoea
○ collapse
○ headache
○ rash.

The most dramatic reactions tend to occur in response to peanuts and shellfish.

Some allergic reactions are very severe, come on very quickly and can be fatal. This is why it is extremely important to inform customers of the precise ingredients in any dish they ask about.

Prevention of food poisoning

To try to prevent food poisoning:

- handle food hygienically (see pages 43–49, Personal hygiene)
- prepare food carefully
- store food in the correct manner
- keep all food preparation areas clean
- avoid cross-contamination (see pages 65–66)
- cook all food thoroughly.

Remember!

Always:

- keep yourself and your workplace clean at all times
- wear suitable, clean, washable protective clothing
- protect food from contamination at all times
- minimise the time that high-risk foods are left at room temperature
- keep hot food really hot at 63°C or above
- keep cold food in the fridge at below 5°C
- tell your supervisor your symptoms if you are ill
- take responsibility for working safely and hygienically
- follow all instructions and rules at work
- report all potential hazards.

Test yourself!

1 Which of the following is not a pathogenic bacterium?
   a Penicillin
   b Salmonella
   c Staphylococcus aureus
   d Bacillus cereus.

2 Which of the following describes the conditions necessary for most bacteria to reproduce?
   a Warmth, oxygen, food, moisture
   b Cool, oxygen, food, moisture
   c Warmth, carbon dioxide, food, dryness
   d Cool, carbon dioxide, food, dryness.

3 Which of the following is not a symptom of food poisoning?
   a Rash
   b Nausea
   c Sneezing
   d Abdominal pain.

4 Which Regulation concerns the safe system of food production?
   a COSHH
   b RIDDOR
   c HASAWA
   d HACCP.

5 Which of the following statements is true?
   a All pathogens cause illness
   b All moulds cause illness
   c All bacteria cause illness
   d All foreign bodies cause illness.

Personal hygiene

A high standard of personal hygiene reduces the risk of contamination of food and is a requirement under the Food Hygiene (England) (No2) Regulations 2005. Everyone who works in a job that requires them to handle food must:

- be in good health
- have hygienic personal habits
- wear the correct, clean, protective clothing
- be aware of the potential danger of poor hygiene practice.

Personal hygiene is very important when working in a catering environment. You need to be pleasant to work with (no body odour!) and feel comfortable in the kitchen. Make sure you wash your hair – if it feels sticky and heavy it will not be pleasant to work in a hot kitchen. Clean your teeth regularly – your colleagues will not want to work near you if you have bad breath! Keep your hands and nails clean and in good condition when working directly with food.

Figure 2.12 Would you want to eat at this chef's restaurant?

General health

It is important to remember that working in a catering kitchen can involve:

- standing up for long periods of time
- working in a hot, noisy atmosphere
- having to concentrate and multi-task for long periods of time
- starting work early in the morning
- finishing work late at night.

Bearing these points in mind make sure you:

- have sufficient sleep and relaxation during your time off
- eat regular, balanced meals – this is essential as it is too easy to "pick" which is not good for your digestion in the long term
- drink plenty of water during your shift at work, otherwise your concentration may be affected
- remember that healthy eating applies to staff just as much as to customers, see Chapter 4.

Clothing

Your uniform should fit correctly and be comfortable to wear. If your shoes are too tight and make your feet hurt, for example, you will not be able to concentrate properly. This could cause an accident if you are using dangerous equipment, e.g. knives or mixers.

It is important to wear the correct clothing in the kitchen, not only for health and safety but also to create a professional image. Customers, visitors and other members of staff are impressed by kitchen staff who are dressed in a clean, smart uniform. Kitchens may have "house rules" regarding correct dress but it will be a version of the traditional chef's whites.

Top marks!
Make sure your uniform is always pressed.

Hat This should be close-fitting and clean. It should be made of an absorbent material and washable or disposable. A hair net should be worn underneath if your hair reaches below the collar.

Jacket This should be made of an absorbent, thick but cool material (usually cotton mix). It should be double-breasted, so it can be fastened either way to give a double layer of material across the chest, and long-sleeved for protection.

Necktie This should be made of cotton, correctly tied and clean.

Apron This should be made of white cotton with long strings to tie in front. It may be bibbed. It should cover you from the waist to below the knee for protection, but should not be any longer as this would be a safety risk.

Trousers These should be cotton mix and loose-fitting for comfort. They should not be too long as this is a safety risk.

Shoes These should be comfortable, strong, and solid with protected toes. Clogs may be acceptable, trainers are not. Footwear must have non-slip soles and non-absorbent uppers. Socks (or tights) must be worn.

Figure 2.13 The correct clothing

It is important to remember the following aspects of good clothing practice.

o Clean, comfortable underwear is just as important as a clean uniform.
o Do not enter the kitchen in outdoor clothing; it will be contaminated.
o Do not wear your kitchen uniform outdoors for the same reason.
o Press studs or Velcro fastenings are more hygienic and easier to use than buttons.
o Change your uniform as soon as it gets dirty. This is usually every day for aprons and jackets. Trousers should be changed two or more times a week.
o If you are working for several hours in a cold area your supervisor may provide you with a body warmer to wear under a white coat.

You may need to wear gloves while at work. Types of gloves include:
o thin rubber or latex gloves for fine work with high-risk foods
o non-latex or vinyl gloves if the food handler has an allergic condition
o chain metal gloves to give protection from sharp knives
o thick, warm gloves to handle frozen items when taking stock from the freezer
o thick insulating gloves or a cloth to handle very hot items straight from the oven.

The advantages of wearing disposable gloves to work include the following.
o Using a fresh pair of gloves to handle food is more hygienic than using washed hands.
o Cross-contamination is reduced if a new pair of gloves is used for different food preparation processes.
o Strong smells cannot be transferred from one type of food to another.
o They give the wearer protection from damage by constant dampness, extreme cold and heat and rough surfaces, e.g. when peeling chestnuts.
o It is much more hygienic to cover a cut, burn or other condition (e.g. a boil) with a dressing and then to wear gloves too.
o Wearing gloves when preparing or serving food gives customers a more hygienic impression.

Did you know?

The most hygienic way of putting on your kitchen uniform is to put your hat on first to stop loose hairs falling onto your whites. When taking off your uniform, your hat should be removed last.

Figure 2.14 The correct order to put on your kitchen uniform

Try this!

Produce a presentation that outlines the training requirements of food handlers. Include recommendations for training staff in the following areas:
o *personal hygiene and presentation*
o *good hygiene practice*
o *reportable illnesses*
o *suitable dressings for wounds with an explanation of the risk of infection.*

However, wearing gloves has some disadvantages including:

o It can be difficult to grip certain items, e.g. fresh fish.
o Failing to use clean gloves can cause cross-contamination. It can take longer to complete a task.
o Having to keep changing gloves can be fiddly and time-consuming.
o Providing frequent changes of gloves is expensive.
o It can be easy to forget to use a fresh pair of gloves.

Personal habits

Hair: Wash your hair regularly and keep it under a hat. Longer hair should be tied back securely or contained in a net. This reduces the danger of flakes of skin or strands of hair falling into food. Beards and moustaches should also be covered. Do not touch your hair while working. When you have your hair cut, make sure you wash it again before you go to work.

Ears: Do not put your fingers into your ears while working in a kitchen. Earwax and bacteria can be transferred to food and work surfaces and equipment this way.

Nose: The pathogenic bacteria staphylococcus aureus, see page 36, is found in many adult noses and mouths. Sneezes and coughs can spread this bacteria over a wide area. This means that work surfaces, food and equipment can be contaminated very easily. A disposable handkerchief should always be used to catch a sneeze or blow your nose. Always wash your hands thoroughly after using a tissue. Nose picking is an extremely unhygienic activity as is wiping your nose on your sleeve, and neither should ever be carried out in a kitchen (or elsewhere!)

Mouth: Tasting food is essential but you must use a clean spoon each time. A spoon used for one taste should not be put back into the food for any reason without being thoroughly washed first. Spitting is extremely unhygienic – never do this. It is not acceptable to eat sweets or chew gum in the kitchen. Do not lick your finger and then use it to open bags, pick up small, light items or separate sheets of paper. All these activities can spread bacteria easily.

Neck: Do not wear strong perfume or aftershaves, deodorant or cosmetics as they can taint food.

Figure 2.15 Latex gloves for fine work, rubber gloves for handling wet food and chain mail for butchery

Remember!

Do not touch any part of any glassware, crockery or cutlery that may make contact with anyone's mouth. You would not like to drink out of a cup that someone's fingers had touched around the rim, would you?

Underarms: Daily bathing or showering removes the bacteria that cause body odour. Perspiration smells can be avoided by using a non-perfumed deodorant.

Hands: The most common method of contaminating food is by having dirty hands. Do not use your fingers for tasting. Keep your nails short and clean. Do not use nail varnish. Watches and rings (other than a plain wedding ring) are not allowed as bacteria can live in the food particles caught under them. Gemstones in jewellery may fall out and become foreign bodies in food. It is impractical to wear a watch because of the frequent use of water in the kitchen.

Keep your hair clean and tied back, wear a hat.

Do not touch your ears, do not wear earrings other than sleepers (maybe!)

Use a tissue to blow your nose and wash your hands afterwards.

Taste food with a clean spoon each time.

Do not wear strong perfume, cosmetics or jewellery.

Wash your underarms regularly, apply unscented deodorant.

Keep your nails short and clean, wash your hands frequently.

Cover cuts, burns and sores with a blue plaster dressing.

Change your underwear regularly.

Keep your feet clean and dry, wear clean, cotton socks.

Figure 2.16 Rules for good personal hygiene

Hand washing

Hand washing is one of the most important hygiene activities that all food handlers must carry out. Bacteria are transferred from dirty hands onto food all too frequently.

How to wash your hands properly:

1 Wet your hands with a non-hand-operated warm-water spray or fill the wash hand basin with hand-hot water and wet your hands.

2 Use a non-perfumed antibacterial liquid soap or gel to provide a good lather over the top and palms of your hands, between your fingers, around your wrists and lower forearms.

3 Only use a nailbrush to clean under your fingernails if it is disinfected regularly or is disposable.

4 Rinse your hands thoroughly with clean water.

5 Dry your hands well, preferably with disposable paper towels; hot-air dryers take longer and roller towels must be clean to be safe.

Wounds, illness and infection

Working in a kitchen with hot items, knives and dangerous equipment means it is likely that you will suffer a slight injury occasionally.

From a hygiene point of view it is essential that all wounds are covered. This is to:
o prevent blood and bacteria from the injury contaminating any food
o prevent bacteria from raw food infecting the wound.

Using a coloured waterproof dressing (blue plaster) keeps the injury clean and protects it. Blue is the best colour for a dressing in food areas as it is easily spotted if it falls off. Very few foods are blue!

Spots, blisters and boils are unpleasant skin conditions which can cause problems in food-handling areas because they will be infected with the pathogenic bacteria staphylococcus aureus (see page 38). If you have blemishes on your hands, work in suitable gloves (see pages 47–48). If they are on your face you must be very careful to avoid touching them with your hands while working. In severe cases your supervisor may give you non-food-handling tasks to carry out until the condition has cleared up.

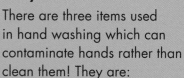

Did you know?
There are three items used in hand washing which can contaminate hands rather than clean them! They are:
o a dirty bar of soap used by many different people
o a non-disposable nail brush which is not disinfected very regularly
o a roller towel which is not changed very regularly.

Remember!
Always wash your hands:
o when entering the kitchen
o after using the toilet
o between each task
o between handling raw and cooked food
o after touching your face or hair
o after coughing, sneezing or blowing your nose into a handkerchief
o after any cleaning activity
o after eating, drinking or smoking during a break
o after dealing with food waste or rubbish.

Remember!
Always tell your supervisor straightaway if you are wearing a waterproof blue plaster dressing and it goes missing in food!

If you are ill and suffer any symptoms that could be from a food-borne illness you must let your supervisor know as soon as possible. The symptoms concerned include:

- diarrhoea
- vomiting
- nausea
- discharges from ear, eye and nose.
- colds and sore throats
- skin infections (e.g. eczema).

Remember!

Many people pick up "tummy bugs" while on holiday abroad. If you do so, you need to tell your supervisor before you return to work.

You should not work as a food handler while you display any of these symptoms. It is likely you will have to seek medical help if you suffer severe bouts of these illnesses. You may need clearance from your doctor before you can resume work as a food handler.

Your supervisor also needs to know about any similar symptoms suffered by the people with whom you live. This is because you may be a carrier of an infection without displaying any symptoms of the illness. If you are a carrier it means you can transmit the infection to others.

Certain illnesses legally need to be reported to the local health authority. Many of them are identified by the symptoms listed above. Your supervisor or doctor should arrange for this to be done if necessary.

Test yourself!

1 How often should you have a bath or shower during a working week?

2 How many occasions are there when you should wash your hands before resuming work?

3 What is a "carrier" of a food-borne disease?

4 When changing ready to start work, which item of kitchen uniform should you put on first?

5 State three advantages of wearing gloves to handle food.

6 Describe the correct procedure to follow when tasting food.

Cleaning

Cleaning is an essential process of removing dirt. It is vital to the safe operation of food businesses. Cleaning staff are employed in many establishments but it is the responsibility of all employees to make sure:

- all equipment and work areas remain clean
- the environment they work in is clean and safe.

Regular cleaning is vital in an area where food is handled for the following reasons:

- To reduce the danger of contamination of food from:
  - bacteria, by removing particles of food upon which they can feed
  - pests
  - foreign bodies.
- To create a good impression for:
  - customers
  - other staff and visitors
  - inspectors.
- To reduce the risk of:
  - accidents
  - equipment breakdown.

Marcus says:
Work in a tidy and clean manner and the cooking will be much simpler.

Methods of cleaning

A high standard of cleanliness is essential to keep the risk of food safety hazards low. Cleaning can reduce the risk of food safety hazards because it:

- removes food particles upon which bacteria can feed
- reduces the risk of contamination of food which is being prepared or stored
- reduces the danger of pests, e.g. insects, rats and mice, coming into the kitchen
- helps to prevent accidents by providing a clean work area
- encourages safe working methods
- helps keep the area pleasant to work in.

Cleaning has to be carried out in all areas of the kitchen. These include:

- **surfaces**: floors and worktops
- **equipment**: manual or electrical machinery
- **utensils**: hand-held kitchen tools.

The COSHH Regulations (see page 102) cover cleaning because there are several potential hazards which could occur. These include:

o Using dirty cloths to clean, which spreads bacterial contamination.
o Using the same cleaning equipment to clean raw food preparation areas as well as those for preparing cooked food and causing cross-contamination (see pages 67–68).
o When cleaning has been carried out very poorly and contamination remains.
o When there is no separate cleaning equipment for cleaning toilet and changing room areas and the kitchen so cross-contamination is likely.
o Using cleaning chemicals incorrectly, leaving a residue over food preparation areas, which will cause chemical contamination (see page 42).
o Storing chemicals in food containers, which could result in contamination.
o Pest infestation (see pages 60–63).

Cleaning products

o **Water** is the most effective cleaning agent. It can be used hot or cold and also under pressure. When used in the form of steam it can also disinfect. Water leaves no residue and is very environmentally friendly. It is also used for rinsing.
o **Soap** is made from fat and caustic soda. Soap can leave a scum on surfaces, so it is not suitable for kitchen cleaning. Disinfectants are sometimes added to soap for hand washing.
o **Detergents** are chemicals manufactured from petroleum. They break dirt up into fine particles and coat them so they are easy to remove. Detergents can be in the form of powder, liquid, foam or gel. They usually need mixing with water before use.
o **Disinfectants** are chemicals that will reduce the numbers of micro-organisms to a safe level if left in contact with the surface for a sufficient amount of time. It is better to apply the chemicals with a spray rather than a cloth. Their efficiency is affected if the surface that is being treated is not clean.
o **Sanitiser** is a mixture of detergent and disinfectant chemicals. It is often used in sprays for hard surface cleaning. It needs to be left in contact with the surface to be cleaned for a sufficient amount of time to be effective. Always read the manufacturer's instructions.

○ **Bactericides** are substances which have been specifically formulated to kill bacteria.

○ A **steriliser** is a piece of equipment that usually uses extremely hot water or steam to kill all the micro-organisms on a surface. Alternatively, sterilisers may use strong chemical disinfectants or bactericides. It is difficult to successfully sterilise equipment in a normal catering situation.

What to disinfect	Example	When to disinfect
Food contact surfaces	Chopping boards, containers, mixers	Before and after each use
Hand contact surfaces	Refrigerator handles, taps, switches	At least once per shift
Contamination hazards	Cloths and mops, waste bins and lids	At least once per shift, cloths and mops after each main use

Figure 2.17 Disinfection frequency table

> **Remember!**
> Remember that the COSHH Regulations control all the chemicals used in cleaning.

When using any type of cleaning chemical:
○ Always follow the manufacturer's instructions correctly.
○ Store chemicals in their original containers, away from food and in clean, cool, dry conditions.
○ Never decant a chemical into a different container which is not labelled correctly.
○ Always wear any recommended personal protective equipment when preparing and using the product.
○ Never mix chemicals.
○ Always dispose of chemicals safely. Check the instructions before you pour any chemical down a drain.

Cleaning equipment

To clean effectively you need suitable equipment. This is likely to include:
○ small equipment, e.g. cloths, brushes, mops and buckets
○ large equipment, e.g. dishwashers, jet washers, wet and dry vacuum cleaners.

Small equipment should be colour-coded so that it is only used in the correct areas and for the correct job. Red equipment could be used in raw food preparation areas, and yellow in cooked food preparation areas for example. A blue set of equipment could be reserved for cleaning changing-room areas and this should be stored separately.

Cloths frequently spread more bacteria than they clean away. All reusable cloths should be changed every few hours in a shift as they will contain constantly increasing numbers of bacteria at room temperature. Reusable cloths should be washed and disinfected thoroughly before being dried ready to use again. It is more expensive but much more hygienic to use disposable cloths. These are available in a range of colours to help with coding and controlling where they are used. Disposable cloths should be thrown away as soon as they are dirty.

Energy used in cleaning

Cleaning is an expensive process. As well as specialist chemicals and equipment it also requires energy. The energy used does not only involve plugging a machine to an electrical socket! Effective cleaning usually involves two or more of these energy sources:

○ **Physical energy**: carried out by people using pressure and movement on surfaces (also known as elbow grease!)
○ **Kinetic energy**: produced by machines using their weight in conjunction with movement, e.g. a floor cleaner.
○ **Agitation**: provided by liquids being constantly moved against a surface, e.g. in a washing machine or when cleaning tubes or pipes.
○ **Thermal energy**: using high and low temperatures combined with pressure to remove dirt, e.g. in a steam pressure cleaner or when freezing a skirt to remove chewing gum.
○ **Chemical**: Using a chemical reaction between two substances to loosen and remove dirt, e.g. washing powder and water.

Figure 2.18 Colour-coded kitchen equipment

 Investigate!
Some materials will be damaged by usual cleaning methods and therefore need special attention. Find out how the following materials should be cleaned:
○ cast iron
○ copper
○ aluminium.

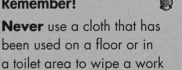 **Remember!**
Never use a cloth that has been used on a floor or in a toilet area to wipe a work surface.

Six stages of cleaning

The main stages of thorough cleaning apply to each area. Before starting to clean, switch off and unplug electrical machinery and dismantle any items as required.

1 **Pre-clean** to remove any loose dirt and heavy soiling, e.g. soak a saucepan, sweep the floor or wipe down a mixer.
2 **Main clean** by washing the item with hot water and detergent. Use a suitable cloth or brush to remove grease and dirt.
3 **Rinse** with hot water only to remove the detergent and any remaining dirt particles.
4 **Disinfect** with extremely hot water (82°C) or steam in a controlled area, e.g. in a dishwasher. Where this process is not safe or practical use a chemical disinfectant. Apply it to the appropriate surface and leave it for the length of time stated on the instructions.
5 **Final rinse** to remove all cleaning chemical residue.
6 **Dry** – air drying is the most hygienic, otherwise use paper towels or clean, dry cloths.

When cleaning is finished, put the equipment back together correctly and safely. Put it in the right place ready for use.

Figure 2.19 Cleaning a slicing machine

Cleaning schedules

A cleaning schedule forms part of the HACCP procedures (see page 79) and may be used together with checklists to ensure a thorough job is done.

A cleaning schedule is a written plan that tells everyone in the kitchen:
o what items and surfaces are to be cleaned
o where they are to be cleaned
o who is to carry out these tasks
o how often the cleaning is to be carried out
o when the cleaning should be done
o how long it should take to clean correctly
o what chemicals and equipment are needed to clean it
o what safety precautions should be taken when cleaning, e.g. wearing goggles and gloves, putting out warning signs
o the method of cleaning that should be used.

Frequently used items and work areas may have to be cleaned after each task in preparation for the next. It is the responsibility of all food handlers to carry out this clean-as-you-go system correctly. It is particularly important when you are preparing raw foods. You must disinfect the work area thoroughly once you have cleaned it, to prevent cross-contamination.

Remember!

A cleaning schedule forms part of the HACCP procedures and may be used together with checklists to ensure a thorough job is done.

Investigate!

How frequently are the following cleaning tasks carried out at your workplace?

○ **Cleaning the ovens**

○ **Washing down the walls**

○ **Cleaning out the refrigerators**

○ **Cleaning the bin area.**

Cleaning schedule and checklist

Area/item of	Frequency	Responsiblity	Cleaning materials	H&S precautions	Method of cleaning	Checked by
Walls	Daily	Kitchen porter & 2nd chef	Detergent & cloth	Ladder to be used to reach areas above shoulder height	1) Pre-clean 2) Clean, apply detergent with hand-held spray, leave for 2 mins 3) Rinse 4) Air dry	
Floors	Daily	Kitchen porter	Detergent & mop & bucket	Hazard notices to be put out in entrances to the area being cleaned	1) Pre-clean 2) Clean, apply detergent with mop 3) Rinse 4) Air dry	
Work surface	Daily	Chefs	Sanitiser & cloth	None required	1) Pre-clean 2) Apply sanitiser with trigger spray, leave for 2 mins 3) Wipe over 4) Air dry	
Oven	Weekly	Kitchen porter	Oven cleaner	Rubber gloves, overall, mask & goggles	1) Ensure oven is turned off & cool 2) Pre-clean 3) Clean, apply oven cleaner, leave for 30 mins 3) Rinse 4) Air dry	
Fridges	Weekly	Kitchen porter & 2nd chef	Hot water & detergent	None required	1) Pre-clean 2) Clean, apply detergent with hand-held spray, leave for 2 mins 3) Rinse 4) Air dry	
Bins	Weekly	Kitchen porter & 2nd chef	Hot water & detergent	Gloves	1) Pre-clean 2) Clean, apply detergent with hand-held spray, leave for 2 mins 3) Rinse 4) Air dry	
Windows	Monthly	Kitchen porter	Hot water & detergent	Ladder to be used to reach areas above shoulder height	1) Pre-clean 2) Rinse 3) Air dry	
Ceiling	Monthly	Kitchen porter	Detergent & cloth	Ladder	1) Pre-clean 2) Clean, apply detergent with hand-held spray, leave for 2 mins 3) Rinse 4) Air dry	
Freezer	Monthly	Kitchen porter & 2nd chef	Hot water & detergent	Gloves	1) Pre-clean 2) Clean, apply detergent with hand-held spray, leave for 2 mins 3) Rinse 4) Air dry	

Figure 2.20 Example cleaning schedule and checklist

Hygienic work surfaces and equipment

It is very difficult to maintain good standards of work and hygiene in a food production area if the working area and equipment are unsuitable. All equipment and work surfaces should be specifically produced and designed for catering kitchens.

All surfaces that come into contact with food should be:

- easy to maintain, clean and disinfect
- made from a safe, **non-toxic** material that is **inert** and will not react with any food or chemical
- smooth and **impervious** to water, i.e. waterproof
- designed to avoid any joins or seams where food particles could lodge
- resistant to corrosion, e.g. rusting or pitting
- strong enough to support heavy weights and heat resistant so hot pans can be put on it.

Stainless steel has all these qualities. It is the most commonly used material in modern catering kitchens.

For reasons of health and safety and to follow the HACCP procedures, it is important to act when you notice any damage to surfaces or equipment in the kitchen.

Definition

Non-toxic – not poisonous or harmful.
Inert – has no reaction with any other substance.
Impervious – does not allow water to pass through it.

Waste management

Every catering establishment wants to manage waste carefully for several reasons:

- All food thrown away represents lost income to the business.
- All businesses have to pay to have their waste removed, so large amounts of waste can increase this cost.
- Reducing the amount of waste produced helps the environment.
- Waste can attract pests which can be a food safety hazard.

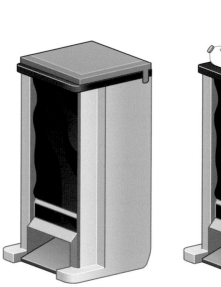

Figure 2.21 Kitchen waste bins should be emptied regularly

In every kitchen there should be sufficient waste bins provided at suitable points. The bins should:

○ have tight-fitting lids
○ be lined with a polythene disposable sack (if appropriate)
○ not be overfilled
○ be emptied regularly
○ be cleaned regularly
○ not smell
○ not be left in the kitchen overnight.

The bagged waste from kitchen bins should be transferred to a large lidded bin in the outside refuse area as soon as necessary. The bags should be tied securely to prevent any spillages. This will help to reduce the hazard of pest infestation. The outside refuse area should be kept clean for the same reason.

Recycling waste

Many establishments are now trying to recycle as much material as possible. Food waste may be kept apart as it can be collected separately. Individual bins should be provided for paper, cardboard, glass and plastic to allow recycling systems to be used. In large businesses this type of waste may be crushed by compactor machines to take up less space before binning. Waste oil may be collected separately from the main rubbish collection as it can be recycled. Eventually it may be used as fuel for cars.

Figure 2.22 A well-organised outside bin area

> **Remember!**
> Some waste can be dangerous, e.g.
> ○ broken glass can cause injury
> ○ fat and oil can leak out of containers and make floors slippery.

> **Remember!**
> Waste oil should **never** be poured down drains. It should be put in a suitable container (often the drum in which it was delivered).

Figure 2.23 Used oil can be poured into a suitable container ready for recycling

Pest control

Pests are responsible for the majority of closures of food establishments by the Environmental Health Officer. Pests are also responsible for large amounts of food being wasted by infestation or contamination. Staff and customers become very upset if they find any type of pest on the premises. Under the HACCP procedures a catering business is expected to have effective pest control methods in place.

Pests live in or near catering premises because these provide:

○ **food** in store rooms, waste areas, poorly cleaned production areas

○ **moisture** from dripping taps, outside drains, **condensation** droplets

○ **warmth** from heating systems and equipment motors, e.g. refrigerators

○ **shelter** in undisturbed areas, e.g. the back of store cupboards, behind large equipment.

By removing as many of these conditions as possible, pests may be put off living in the area and look elsewhere.

> **Definition**
>
> **Condensation** – a coating of tiny drops formed on a surface by steam or vapour.

Signs of infestation

How can you tell if there is a pest infestation in your workplace? Look for:

○ dead bodies of insects, rodents and birds

○ droppings, smear marks

○ eggs, larvae, pupae cases, feathers, nesting material

○ paw or claw prints

○ unusual smells

○ scratching, pecking or gnawing sounds

○ gnawed pipes, fittings or boxes

○ torn or damaged sacks or packaging

○ food spillages.

Pests cause hazards in the following ways:

○ Bacterial contamination from pathogenic bacteria found:

   – on the surface of the pest's skin

   – in pest droppings.

○ Physical contamination from fur, eggs, droppings, urine, saliva, dead bodies, nest material.

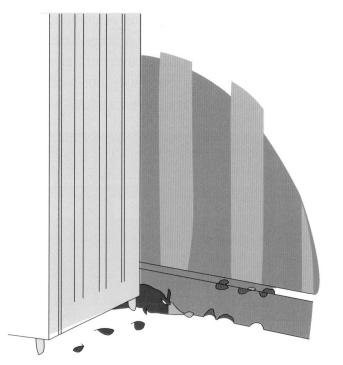

Figure 2.24 Evidence of infestation

- Chemical contamination from using strong chemicals to kill the pests which then gets into food.
- Cross-contamination which occurs when a pest transfers pathogenic bacteria from one area to another, e.g. a fly landing on raw meat and then moving on to a cooked chicken.

Types of pests

Insects

Flies are one of the most common insect pests. They are usually found in places which have not been cleaned thoroughly and where rubbish is allowed to gather. A female housefly can lay up to 600 eggs in her life. An egg takes about two weeks to go through the maggot stage and become a fully grown fly.

Cockroaches are one of the oldest types of insects, said to date from prehistoric times. They do not usually fly and only come out when it is dark. Their eggs take around two months to hatch. They can live for up to a year. Cockroaches can be detected by their droppings or their unpleasant smell.

Weevils are very tiny insects that live in dry goods, e.g. flour, cereals and nuts. They can only be seen with the naked eye if they are moving. It is possible to spot an infestation if there is tunnelling or speckling in the commodity.

Ants are attracted by sweet items which have not been stored securely. They usually nest outdoors, and follow set paths to food sources.

Rodents

Rats commonly get into buildings through drains or holes but they also burrow under walls. Rats are a particular hazard as they can transmit Weil's disease, and a worm-type parasite as well as food poisoning bacteria. They also bite. The Norway rat is the most common in the UK. It usually lives outside.

House mice are the main problem in buildings. They can climb very well and cause considerable damage by gnawing to keep their teeth short. Like rats, their teeth grow throughout their lives and unless they wear them down, their teeth will pierce through their heads! Mice dribble urine nearly all the time and leave droppings at frequent intervals. They breed very quickly – a pair of mice can have 2,000 offspring in one year!

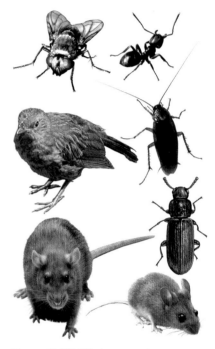

Figure 2.25 Kitchen pests

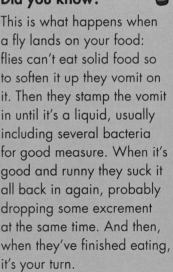

Did you know?

This is what happens when a fly lands on your food: flies can't eat solid food so to soften it up they vomit on it. Then they stamp the vomit in until it's a liquid, usually including several bacteria for good measure. When it's good and runny they suck it all back in again, probably dropping some excrement at the same time. And then, when they've finished eating, it's your turn.

Birds

Pigeons, starlings and seagulls can be a problem in outside waste areas where bins are allowed to overflow and are not kept covered. Once in the area, birds may then get into a building through doors and windows and will often try to nest in roof spaces. As well as contaminating food with feathers and droppings, birds can block gutters with nests and spread insect infestation.

Pets

Domestic pets, e.g. cats and dogs, are classed as pests and should not be allowed to enter catering premises.

Preventing pest infestation

It is almost impossible to prevent pests entering a building. It is possible, however, to discourage them from staying! There are some ways of preventing pests:

- Regular thorough cleaning of areas, e.g. changing rooms and food stores, particularly in corners where pests may be able to hide unnoticed.
- Clearing up any spillages thoroughly and promptly.
- Not allowing waste to build up and keeping bins covered at all times.
- Keeping doors and windows closed, using self-closing doors or using insect screens across openings.
- Using bristle strips and kick plates on doors that are ill-fitting to prevent gnawing damage and rodent access.
- Moving cupboards and equipment as far as possible to clean behind and under them regularly (see Lifting, carrying and handling on pages 97–98).
- Removing any unused equipment and materials from the area.
- Ensuring food storage containers are properly closed when not in use.
- Checking all deliveries – of all items, not just food – for signs of infestation.
- Storing and rotating stock correctly.

Pest control management

Most businesses use specialist pest control companies to monitor and control pest infestation in their premises. They agree a contract which specifies the number of visits per year by a pest control specialist.

The pest control contractor will inspect premises looking for evidence of infestation by any type of pest. They will then deal with any pests they discover. Finally, they will complete a report describing what action they have taken. A copy of the report is left on the premises.

A pest control contractor may:
○ lay bait and set baited traps
○ use sticky boards
○ install electric ultraviolet insect killers
○ spray an insecticide chemical over an area.

The contractor will leave instructions regarding the treatments used. It is important not to touch or move any items that have been left to catch pests. Any sprayed areas must be left untouched for the instructed period of time.

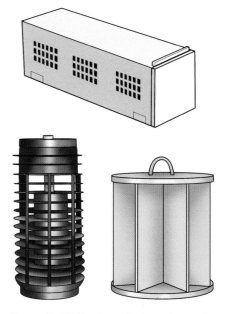

Figure 2.26 Pest control equipment

Test yourself!

1 What is the **most** important reason for cleaning?
   a To make a good impression on customers
   b To keep the work area pleasant
   c To reduce the danger of contamination
   d To prolong the life of equipment.

2 Which one of the following is the correct order for the six-stage cleaning process?
   a Pre-clean, clean, rinse, disinfect, rinse, dry
   b Pre-clean, rinse, clean, disinfect, rinse, dry
   c Pre-clean, disinfect, rinse, clean, rinse, dry
   d Pre-clean, rinse, clean, rinse, disinfect, dry.

3 Which one of the following kills bacteria?
   a Detergent
   b Disinfectant
   c Soap
   d Warm water.

4 Where might you find an infestation of weevils?
   a Flour
   b Fish
   c Fruit
   d Fennel.

Food storage and stock control

A considerable range of ingredients is used in the average catering kitchen. If you were to list all the food items used in your workplace it could run into hundreds! Some of these commodities can be stored for very long periods of time before use, e.g. dried fruit. Other food items will only remain safe to prepare and eat for a very short time, e.g. fresh mussels which must be stored in a refrigerator.

Correct delivery and storage of all foods is required under the HACCP procedures and appropriate records should be kept, for example, of temperatures on delivery.

Receiving stock

Food items are delivered to a catering business in one of three temperature ranges:

○ ambient/room temperature for fresh, dried or tinned items

○ chilled/refrigerator temperature for high-risk fresh or processed foods

○ frozen/freezer temperature for high-risk items that are in longer term storage.

Figure 2.27 Accepting a delivery of food items

Checking a food delivery

If you receive a food delivery at your workplace you need to check the following.

The **vehicle** delivering the items:

○ Is it suitable?

○ Is it clean inside?

○ Is it refrigerated for the delivery of chilled items?

The **temperature** of the delivered items:

○ Are chilled items below 5°C?

○ Is frozen produce kept below −10°C?

○ Use a temperature probe to check if necessary. If the temperature is too high reject the goods.

The **packaging**:

○ Is it clean and undamaged?

○ Is there any sign of mould or other spoilage?

○ Are any containers dented, bulging or leaking?

○ Are the items labelled with:
  – the name of the company?
  – description of the food?
  – product code?
  – ingredient list?
  – use by date?
  – weight?
○ Is the "best before" or "use by date" still several days in the future?
○ Do the items delivered match the delivery note provided in terms of:
  – amounts of each item? (e.g. 1 x 25kg bag)
  – specification of each item? (e.g. King Edward potatoes)

If you have to reject a delivery make sure:
○ The delivery person has agreed to return the item to the supplier.
○ The item being returned is recorded on either the delivery note or a separate return slip.
○ The delivery person signs the delivery note or return slip, as you may do if requested.
○ You give your copy of the delivery note or return slip to your supervisor as soon as possible. You need to make sure that your employer does not pay for goods that have been rejected and returned.

Stock rotation

It is very important to use ingredients in the same order that they have been delivered. This is because:
○ food loses quality the longer it is kept
○ food will have to be wasted if it is not used by the "best before date"
○ food thrown away is money wasted for the business.

Storage systems must ensure that stock is used in the correct rotation. When putting food away it is very important that:
○ older stock of the same item is moved to the front so that it is used first
○ new stock is never mixed up with old stock on shelves or in containers.

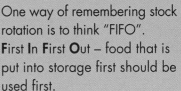

Did you know?
One way of remembering stock rotation is to think "FIFO".
First In First Out – food that is put into storage first should be used first.

Try this!
Produce a flow diagram of the key stages of food receipt and storage to include:
○ *key checks that need to be made on receipt of goods*
○ *stock rotation systems*
○ *food types and storage conditions*
○ *temperature for food storage.*

Storing stock

A delivery must be put into the appropriate storage as soon as possible after arrival.

Frozen and **chilled** items must be put away first. Prompt storage is necessary because:

○ frozen items must not be left in warm conditions where they could start defrosting

○ chilled items must not be allowed to warm to an unsafe temperature at which bacteria could grow. This is especially important with ready-to-eat items, e.g. salads.

Packaged items should have storage instructions included on the label. These should be followed exactly.

Fresh items must be put into cool storage to preserve their quality ready for preparation.

Dry goods should be taken to the stores area where they should be entered on to the stock record to prevent theft.

Your employer may have a system for date coding all items delivered. A date sticker may have to be attached to the items as they are put away. As you put new stock away, move the old stock to a position where it will be used first. This is called stock rotation. See page 65 for more information. Handle all items carefully. Do not attempt to lift heavy items on your own (see pages 97–98).

Some items may need to be removed from the original external packaging before storage, e.g. if a cardboard box is breaking or there is not enough space to store an item in its full packaging. Care must be taken to transfer any important information, e.g. use by dates, onto the replacement container. Your workplace should have a system for this.

Some businesses ensure stock rotation of short life items by marking the item with a coloured sticker to indicate the day of delivery. This encourages the use of food in the correct order.

Did you know?

In many countries it is now the law to label food with a date after which it is not assured of being safe to eat. It is an offence to change this date without re-treating or processing the food appropriately. Highly perishable foods (those that spoil quickly) must be marked with a "use by" date. Less perishable items (which are preserved in some way) are marked with a "best before" date. These dates indicate that the food will be in its best condition before this date. If consumed after this date it may have deteriorated in quality but it will not be a health risk.

Figure 2.28 Date code deliveries

Try this!

Imagine you have been asked to put away a delivery of fresh, whole chickens. The box they have been delivered in is very weak and flimsy. Describe exactly what you would do to make sure the chickens were stored safely.

What is cross-contamination?

Bacteria cannot move by themselves and so are only able to contaminate food by being transferred onto it by something or someone else. This is known as cross-contamination and is one of the main factors in outbreaks of food poisoning.

Types of cross-contamination

There are three main types of cross-contamination:

○ **Direct**: when contaminated food comes into direct contact with another food item and bacteria are transferred from one item to the other.

○ **Indirect**: when contaminated food comes into contact with a surface which then comes into contact with another food item, which then becomes contaminated.

○ **Drip**: when a contaminated item (usually raw meat or poultry) is stored above other food and the juices from the contaminated item drip down and contaminate the food underneath.

Illness will result if the newly contaminated food item is not cooked thoroughly before service.

The most common type is indirect cross-contamination. The main sources are:

○ hands of staff working in food production areas
○ cloths and equipment used by staff in these areas
○ infestation of pests in the kitchen (see pages 60–63)
○ poor storage of food.

Hands: if hands are not washed thoroughly between one job and another then cross-contamination can occur very easily (see Personal hygiene on page 45). There is a particular risk in the following situations:

○ If raw food is prepared, followed by cooked food.
○ If food preparation is resumed directly after a visit to the toilet or a smoking break.

Cloths and equipment: if cloths are not changed or cleaned regularly then cross-contamination can occur. Cloths can carry large amounts of bacteria and have been known to spread more over a surface than were present in the first place!

Equipment: this must be cleaned thoroughly after each use and checked for cleanliness before being used again. Some pieces of equipment may only be used for specific types of foods or in certain areas of the kitchen. Large catering operations may have completely separate preparation areas for certain food, e.g. a meat kitchen, a vegetable kitchen and so on. Most establishments have a separate pastry area.

Infestation of pests: cross-contamination can occur by an insect or animal touching the surface of a raw food product and then one that has been cooked, thus transferring bacteria from one to the other. Pests can also transfer bacteria by leaving fur or droppings on food. (Further information on pests can be found on pages 60–63.)

Poor storage of food: this can result in cross-contamination. If food is not put into suitably sized containers and covered, spillages may result. This could involve some of one item falling into another. Apart from being very messy and wasteful, this can become a food safety hazard, e.g. if an uncooked chicken defrosting on the top shelf of a refrigerator drips liquid onto an uncovered trifle on the shelf below, it is highly likely that salmonella bacteria will be transferred from the chicken to the trifle.

Figure 2.29 Flies cause cross-contamination

Methods of preventing cross-contamination

Cross-contamination can be prevented by breaking the chain of raw items getting into direct or indirect contact with other foods. Identify where there are weaknesses in the workflow and storage systems which may allow cross-contamination to take place.

Ways in which cross-contamination can be prevented:

- Use colour-coded systems for food types or store them in separate areas, e.g. a separate refrigerator for raw meat.
- Have separate preparation areas for raw and cooked items.
- Colour code equipment so that it is only used for either raw or cooked food preparation.
- Store food at the correct temperature, package it correctly, label it fully and use it in order.
- Organise the work area to prevent raw and cooked produce coming into contact.
- Ensure all staff wash their hands thoroughly at the appropriate times (see page 50).
- Use disposable cloths for one purpose only. Sometimes these are colour coded.

> **Remember!**
> Chopping boards may be colour coded to reduce the risk of cross-contamination. The following code is commonly used in the industry:
> o red – raw meat
> o brown – vegetables
> o blue – raw fish
> o white – bakery, dairy
> o yellow – cooked meat
> o green – salad, fruit
>
>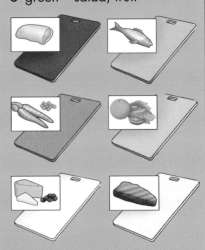
>
> *Figure 2.30 Colour-coded chopping boards*

Identification of spoiled food

Food that is no longer suitable to eat may:
- be discoloured at the edges or in patches throughout
- show mould growing on the surface
- have a different, often unpleasant smell
- feel different in texture, e.g. soft, pulpy, dry, cracked and wrinkled
- taste different, e.g. bitter sour, with an aftertaste.

Storing food

All the methods of storing food are intended to keep the food safe from contamination and to reduce the speed at which spoilage occurs. When storing food, it must be kept covered, cool and dry.

There are three main areas where food is stored in the kitchen:
- dry stores
- refrigerator
- freezer.

These may be free-standing or walk-in units.

Follow these general food storage rules:
- Always protect food from contamination by keeping it in suitable containers.
- Store all food items off the floor on shelves or pallets.
- Do not overload shelves.
- Leave space between items for air to circulate.
- Keep storage areas clean, dry and free from debris at all times.
- Rotate stock correctly (see page 65).
- Report any signs of pest infestation (see page 60).

Figure 2.31 A well-organised dry stores area

Dry storage

- The store should be cool and well-ventilated.
- Flours and cereals may be stored in wheeled bins to protect them from pests. The bin must be fully emptied and cleaned before new stock is added.
- Shelves should not be overfilled and old stock must always be put in front of new.
- Move items from flimsy bags or unsuitable containers, make sure the description label with the "use by" date is transferred.
- Cleaning products should not be stored with food.

Did you know?

A blown tin has both ends bulging as the contents have spoiled and gases have been produced in the process.
The contents of these tins are not safe to eat and must be discarded. Be careful! The pressure built up inside the tin from the gases may cause the tin to explode.

Keep the following items in the dry store:

- Dry foods, e.g. flour, sugar and dried herbs.
- Canned and bottled items (unless the label specifies they need to be refrigerated).

Fruit and vegetable storage

- Fresh fruit and vegetables should be stored in a cool, dry place.
- Root vegetables store best in a dark area.
- Loose soil around fresh vegetables should not be taken into the kitchen.
- Fresh fruit and vegetables are often stored in a refrigerator if there is space, in a safe position.

Temperature and conditions for food storage

High-risk foods and those which will spoil quickly need to be stored in a refrigerator. This is because most pathogenic and food spoilage bacteria multiply very slowly or not at all between 0°C and 5°C – the temperature of a refrigerator.

All industrial refrigerators should defrost automatically. If ice is allowed to build up inside the unit it will reduce its efficiency.

Refrigerators

When separate refrigerators are not available for raw and high-risk foods then these items have to be positioned carefully in one unit. Raw food should **always** be stored below other food so that no blood or juices can drip down and contaminate items on the lower shelf.

Take care with strong-smelling foods (e.g. strong cheese and fish), as they can taint more delicate items (e.g. milk and eggs) and make them taste very strange. All items in a refrigerator should be covered, e.g. in a container with a fitted lid or covered with waxed paper, cling film, greaseproof paper or foil. Do not put food directly in front of the cooling unit if possible as this can affect how efficiently the refrigerator operates.

The following food should be refrigerated:

- raw meat, poultry, fish and seafood
- cooked meat, poultry, fish and seafood
- meat, poultry and fish products, e.g. pies and pâtés
- the contents of any opened cans in suitable containers
- milk, cream, cheese and eggs, and any products containing them (e.g. a flan)

Remember!
Remember to rotate the goods so that the oldest goods are used first. Although goods in the dry stores last a long time they do gradually deteriorate in quality.

Remember!
Even if you are in a hurry do not add new goods to a container already holding old goods.

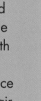

Did you know?
Opened cans of food should never be left in a refrigerator. As well as the danger of a cut from the sharp, exposed lid of the tin, if the juices inside the tin are acid (e.g. as with tinned fruit) they can react with the lining of the tin once exposed to the oxygen in air. This reaction can taint the food and give it a metallic flavour which is unacceptable. Some tins now have a plastic coating on the inside to stop this. It is still best to change the container of opened tinned items to be stored in the fridge.

- prepared salads
- fruit juice
- spreads and sauces
- any other item labelled for refrigeration.

Try this!

What problems can you identify with this refrigerator?

Freezers

Food is frozen to make it last longer without spoiling. It also keeps it safely, as pathogenic bacteria cannot multiply in temperatures below −18°C. However as soon as the temperature rises bacteria may start reproducing. Food that has been allowed to thaw should not be refrozen. This is in case the number of bacteria present have been able to reach a dangerous level and cause food poisoning. If a thawed item has been cooked it may be refrozen. This is because the cooking process will have killed any pathogenic bacteria present.

Storing foods inside a freezer

When loading a freezer with frozen food remember to:

- make sure all items are well wrapped
- label items clearly and include the date
- stack items close together to maintain the temperature
- place raw food below high-risk foods
- put stock with the shortest shelf life at the front.

Storage conditions required by different foods

An alternative way of stopping spoilage is to preserve the food. There are several methods of preservation that can delay the process or prevent it altogether. These include:

- **Heat treatment** by cooking, canning, bottling, sterilising, pasteurising and ultra-heat treatment (UHT). The amount of heat

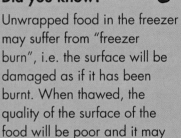

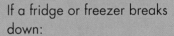

and the length of heat treatment will increase the storage time. UHT products will keep for several months, canned goods will keep for several years.

- ○ **Low temperatures** used in the chilling or freezing of food.
- ○ **Dehydration**, i.e. the drying of fish, meat, fruit, vegetables, soups, stocks and beverages. This process excludes water. Dehydrated items stored in airtight containers will last a considerable period of time.
- ○ **Chemical preservation** by salting, pickling and curing (using sodium nitrate and nitrite salts). This method also alters the flavour of the item. It is often combined with the canning or bottling processes.
- ○ **Vacuum packing** is used mainly for meat, fish and poultry. This process removes oxygen from around the food and greatly extends the shelf life. The items should remain in chilled storage.
- ○ **Smoking**, used particularly for fish, poultry and meat including ham and sausages. This process imparts a strong flavour to the food. Smoked items last longer than non-smoked items but still have to be kept in the refrigerator.
- ○ **Irradiation** is a process that kills pathogenic bacteria and spoilage organisms. It works by subjecting the food to a low amount of radiation. It does not kill spores and toxins.

Thawing and defrosting food

Some food can be cooked straight after being removed from the freezer. If this is the case there will be appropriate instructions on the packet. Otherwise the item must be allowed to thaw before cooking. This is especially important with raw meat and poultry.

The rules for thawing food:
- ○ Always keep thawing raw meat items well away from other food.
- ○ Thaw items in a cool room, thawing cabinet or in the bottom of a refrigerator.
- ○ Always thaw items on a tray where juices can collect safely.
- ○ Once the item is thawed keep it in the refrigerator and cook it within 24 hours.
- ○ If using a microwave oven to defrost an item be aware of cool spots where it may remain frozen.
- ○ Never refreeze an item that has been thawed.

Did you know?

Some ingredients in dishes do not freeze well. Sauces which are to be frozen should not be made with wheat flour because once defrosted they will separate if not used within a few weeks.

Did you know?

Some tinned foods have been opened after hundreds of years and the contents have still been edible (although not very nice to eat!)

Figure 2.32 Fruit that is canned or frozen lasts much longer than fresh fruit

Figure 2.33 Is your Christmas turkey safe?

Food storage and temperature control documentation

Under the HACCP procedures (see page 79) it is important to record readings and actions taken while preparing food. These procedures provide protection for the catering business and its employees in the event of a food safety issue.

The Environmental Health Officer visits all catering businesses regularly to check that food is being prepared according to the Regulations. The Officer will expect to see evidence of how food safety is being maintained. They will expect to see records of a variety of monitoring procedures, including:

- temperature records of all refrigerators and freezers
- pest control reports
- probe temperature records of reheated foods and those held at hot temperatures
- cleaning checklists and schedules
- delivery monitoring forms recording temperature of foods at time of delivery.

If there was an outbreak of food poisoning in a restaurant, the manager should be able to prove that all the food safety procedures have been carried out correctly. This process is known as showing **due diligence**. The Environmental Health Officer may decide that the blame for the outbreak is not with the restaurant and investigate other possible causes, e.g. the food suppliers.

Did you know?

Thawing large frozen turkeys has to be carried out very carefully to avoid outbreaks of food poisoning. A 9kg turkey will take several days to thaw. Great care has to be taken to make sure the inside of the bird is defrosted. If not it will not cook to a safe temperature and bacteria will continue to reproduce.

Definition

Due diligence – that every possible precaution has been taken by the business to avoid a food safety problem.

Test yourself!

1 What is the maximum acceptable temperature for a chilled food delivery?
   a 3°C
   b 5°C
   c 7°C
   d 9°C.

2 What is the correct order in which the following delivered goods should be put away?
   a Frozen, chilled, fresh, tinned
   b Chilled, fresh, tinned, frozen
   c Fresh, tinned, frozen, chilled
   d Tinned, frozen, chilled, fresh.

3 What does FIFO stand for?

4 What is the term that describes food damaged by the freezer?

5 Define the term "cross-contamination".

6 How would you identify spoiled food?

Temperature control

Cooking and reheating food

It is always important to cook food correctly. The choice of method should suit the food to be cooked and the time and temperature at which the food is cooked is important to ensure that all the harmful bacteria that may be present are destroyed. This must be achieved without spoiling the quality of the item that is to be served to the customer. Overcooked food may be very safe but may also be **inedible**! Some food is cooked for only a short time, such as a rare steak.

To make cooking as safe as possible, remember these points:

○ Heat items as quickly as possible to reduce the time spent in the temperature danger zone when bacteria will reproduce quickly.

○ Cut large joints of meat and poultry into smaller portions where possible to ensure even cooking all the way through.

○ Cook stuffings separately (they often do not reach the required temperature quickly enough and have caused many outbreaks of food poisoning in the past).

○ Stir stews and casseroles regularly during cooking to keep the temperature even throughout.

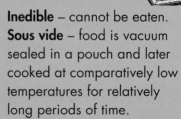

Definition

Inedible – cannot be eaten.
Sous vide – food is vacuum sealed in a pouch and later cooked at comparatively low temperatures for relatively long periods of time.

Remember!

All food must be heated to at least 75°C and that temperature held for at least two minutes to make it safe. In Scotland food must be heated to at least 82°C for at least two minutes. No food should be reheated more than once.

Chilling or freezing food

If food has been cooked and is not for immediate consumption it should be cooled as quickly as possible. Ideally this should be carried out in a blast chiller. Large production kitchens may operate a large cook-chill operation producing hundreds of chilled meals every day. Some cook-chill systems also use the **sous vide** method for preservation of food in vacuum-packs. This type of production involves specialist equipment. See also Refrigerated storage on page 70.

Harmful bacteria may be present in cooked food as a result of spores not being destroyed in the cooking process. They may also have been transferred onto the cooked food from another source, e.g. dirty equipment. Bacteria will then remain in the food either reproducing at room temperature or dormant in the refrigerator or freezer.

Figure 2.34 A blast chiller

Many catering premises now use blast chillers to reduce the temperature of cooked food as quickly as possible to make it safe.

Cooked food must not be cooled in a refrigerator or freezer where other food is being stored. If a hot item is put into this environment to cool down quickly it will raise the temperature of the surrounding air. This will result in the other chilled food becoming warm. Bacteria may then start reproducing in the food being stored. The warmth may also cause frozen food to start defrosting. Condensation may then occur and drip liquid onto food and contaminate it.

When cooling cooked food remember:
○ The smaller the size of the food item, the more quickly it will cool.
○ Shallow, flat containers have a greater surface area to allow faster cooling.
○ The greater the difference in temperature, the faster cooling will take place.

If food is to be frozen rapidly, specialist equipment is needed to carry out this procedure safely. Blast freezers cool food down to –18°C in 240 minutes.

If freezing food you must remember to:
○ reduce the temperature as quickly as possible
○ keep the thickness of the food to be frozen as even and thin as possible
○ wrap the food thoroughly
○ label the food clearly.

Report any spoilage to your supervisor, and ensure it is disposed of correctly (see pages 58–59).

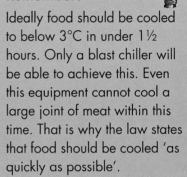

Remember!
Ideally food should be cooled to below 3°C in under 1½ hours. Only a blast chiller will be able to achieve this. Even this equipment cannot cool a large joint of meat within this time. That is why the law states that food should be cooled 'as quickly as possible'.

Remember!
Frequent opening and closing of the door of a refrigerator will cause the temperature inside to keep rising and falling.

Figure 2.35 A shallow, flat container allows faster cooling

Try this!
If an item is frozen in a standard freezer it will take much longer to freeze and the ice crystals that form within the item will be much larger. This will cause the texture of the item to be poor. Freeze a strawberry in a domestic freezer and then let it thaw! What happens to the strawberry?

Holding hot and cold food for service

Hot food

Hot cupboards and counter service equipment are designed to store food for a few hours at a safe hot temperature. The heating elements in this equipment are not sufficiently powerful to raise the temperature of the food quickly. This could mean that pathogenic bacteria could survive and reproduce to a dangerous level during the slow heating process.

The following rules apply when using hot holding equipment:
○ Always preheat the equipment before use.
○ Do not use the equipment to reheat food.
○ Check the equipment regularly if hot water is used; if it needs topping up use hot water (not cold).
○ If heated lights are used, keep the food fully within the lit areas.

When hot food is out on display and cannot be kept above 63°C it can only be put out for one continuous period of up to two hours. After this period of time the food must be thrown away. This is because it will have been at a temperature at which bacteria can multiply rapidly for too long and may no longer be safe to eat.

Cold food

Food which is to be held for service at room temperature has to be treated very carefully. This is because the temperature at which it has to be kept is ideal for bacteria to multiply rapidly. However, if the food were held at a lower temperature it could be unpleasant to eat. Imagine eating a sandwich which has been taken straight out of a refrigerator!

Cold food in a display cabinet or vending machine must be kept at below 8°C and ideally at below 5°C. Where this is not possible, cold food can be put out on display at room temperature for only one continuous period of up to four hours. After this time it must be thrown away. The length of time the food is left out must be recorded so it is never left out for too long. Different establishments use different systems to record this information. It is very convenient when the meal service time lasts four hours as the food put out at the beginning and left unsold can be thrown away when service finishes.

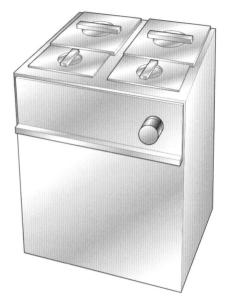

Figure 2.36 A bain-marie, one type of hot holding equipment

Did you know?

To ensure that all heat-resistant spores are destroyed by cooking, a temperature of 75°C must be reached for 30 seconds minimum. In Scotland it must reach 82°C. Such intense heat may damage the quality of the food. It is also possible to destroy spores by heating food at a lower temperature for a longer period of time.

How to use a temperature probe

Some food may reach the required temperature on the outside but still be a very different temperature in the middle. This is where a temperature probe is needed to check that the internal temperature has reached the necessary level.

A temperature probe is a type of thermometer on a long stick that is used to take the core temperature from the middle of food. It is particularly useful when:

○ reheating food ready to serve on a counter
○ testing to see if the inside of a whole chicken is cooked
○ measuring the temperature of a joint of meat which is being roasted in the oven.
○ checking to see if a hot item has cooled down sufficiently to be put in the refrigerator.

Figure 2.37 Use a temperature probe to measure the temperature of a joint of meat

Temperature probes are usually digital and can be battery operated. It is important to keep them very clean. They should always be sterilised before and after each use, otherwise they could transfer dangerous bacteria from one food to another.

Temperature probes need to be checked regularly to make sure they are working correctly. If they are not accurate they should not be used until they have been repaired or replaced.

Test yourself!

Complete the following statements:

1 The transfer of bacteria from raw to cooked food is called _____ _____ .

2 The person authorised to enter food premises to inspect them for food safety is called an _____ _____ _____ .

3 The main law controlling the hygienic supply, preparation and service of food is called the _____ _____ _____ .

4 To make it safe, all raw food should be heated to _____ °C for _____ minutes.

5 To find out if food being heated is the correct temperature all the way through a _____ _____ needs to be used.

6 The _____ of bacteria may survive high temperatures.

Food safety procedures

To ensure that all food served to the public is safe, there is a range of laws and regulations which need to be followed by food handlers and food business operators. Each catering organisation has to produce a policy document giving details of the standards it is setting and the training it undertakes to give all the catering staff. A detailed set of records has to be kept on a day-to-day basis in a catering kitchen to prove that the correct procedures are being followed. In this way customers should be confident they will not be made ill by eating food produced by the establishment. Environmental Health Officers regularly inspect all the hygiene, health and safety aspects of businesses to make sure the standards are met.

Key requirements of food safety legislation

Food safety laws require all catering businesses to ensure:
o All their food production and service staff practise a high standard of personal hygiene, see page 45.
o All their staff have regular training in all hygiene, health and safety matters relating to their workplace, see Chapter 3.
o All their staff comply with the rules and regulations of their organisation, particularly regarding the preparation and service of food.
o All their staff obey the requirements of the food safety legislation which relates to them. This should be explained clearly to staff by their employer and training records should be kept.

It is very important that all required records, e.g. temperature records, are accurately kept. They may be needed as evidence if there is a food safety incident. If an organisation is investigated but can show that it has kept all the records correctly and has high food safety standards it may be given a lower penalty if it is prosecuted, or not prosecuted at all. This defence is called "due diligence" (see page 73).

Did you know?
The Basic Food Hygiene test makes sure food handlers know the main principles of food safety. Some food handlers take the Intermediate Food Hygiene examination. Supervisors may take the Advanced Food Hygiene qualification.

Case study – A due diligence defence

A customer complained that he had been made ill by eating mussels at a seafood restaurant. The Environmental Health Officer visited the restaurant and inspected the way in which the mussels had been prepared and stored, both before and after cooking. The Officer checked the refrigerator temperature and the delivery temperature records and the quality checks that had been carried out. The Food Hygiene Certificates of the staff were presented to indicate that they were all trained in hygienic work practices. The Environmental Health Officer also studied the kitchen layout and the workflow system to try to find out if cross-contamination could have occurred during the preparation and service of the mussels. As the Officer was satisfied that every possible precaution had been taken the restaurant was able to offer the defence of due diligence and was not prosecuted for making the customer ill.

HACCP practices and procedures

In every business that produces, serves or sells food it is vital that there is an organised system to reduce all risk of food safety hazards.

The HACCP procedures require there to be a **documented** system highlighting all areas where special attention should be paid to food safety. The system should cover all food used on the premises and follow the route from the delivery of the raw materials through to the consumption, service or sale of the items.

The stages a food safety management system should cover are:
o quality, packaging and temperature of the food at delivery
o packaging, temperature, location and method of storage
o method of preparation
o type and length of storage between preparation and cooking
o method of holding hot food after cooking
o method of cooling and storing after cooking
o method of reheating cooked food
o method of serving.

The HACCP system exists to identify food safety hazards. Once a hazard has been identified then the risk it poses is analysed and a solution to reduce the risk put into place. The system is very logical and methodical and looks in detail at each stage of the food production process in each catering organisation. It can involve a large number of checks to be carried out and records to be kept.

Definition
Documented: making a detailed record of information.

Did you know?
The Hazard Analysis and Critical Control Point (HACPP) system is an internationally recognised way of managing food safety and protecting consumers. It is a requirement of EU food hygiene legislation that applies to all food business operators.
The HACCP procedures were first developed in the 1960s to ensure that astronauts going up in space had food to eat that was absolutely safe.

Step	Hazard	Action
1 Purchase	High-risk (ready-to-eat) foods contaminated with food-poisoning bacteria or toxins.	Buy from reputable supplier only. Specify maximum temperature at delivery.
2 Receipt of food	High-risk (ready-to-eat) foods contaminated with food-poisoning bacteria or toxins.	Check it looks, smells and feels right. Check the temperature is right.
3 Storage	Growth of food poisoning bacteria, toxins on high-risk (ready-to-eat) foods. Further contamination.	High-risk foods stored at safe temperature. Store them wrapped. Label high-risk food with the correct "sell by" date. Rotate stock and use by recommended date.
4 Preparation	Contamination of high-risk (ready-to-eat) foods. Growth of food-poisoning bacteria.	Wash your hands before handling food. Limit any exposure to room temperatures during preparation. Prepare with clean equipment and use this for high-risk (ready-to-eat) food only. Separate cooked foods from any raw foods.
5 Cooking	Survival of food-poisoning bacteria.	Cook rolled joints, chicken, and re-formed meats e.g. burgers, so that the thickest part reaches at least 75°C. Sear the outside of other, solid meat cuts (e.g. joints of beef, steaks) before cooking.
6 Cooling	Growth of food-poisoning bacteria. Production of poisons by bacteria. Contamination with food-poisoning bacteria.	Cool foods as quickly as possible. Don't leave out at room temperatures to cool, unless the cooling period is short, e.g. place any stews or rice, etc. in shallow trays and cool to chill temperatures quickly.
7 Hot-holding	Growth of food-poisoning bacteria. Production of poisons by bacteria.	Keep food hot, above 63°C.
8 Reheating	Survival of food-poisoning bacteria.	Reheat to above 75°C.
9 Chilled storage	Growth of food-poisoning bacteria.	Keep temperatures at right level. Label high-risk ready-to-eat foods with correct date code.
10 Serving	Growth of disease-causing bacteria. Production of poisons by bacteria. Contamination.	COLD SERVICE FOODS – serve high-risk foods as soon as possible after removing from refrigerated storage to avoid them getting warm. HOT FOODS – serve high-risk foods quickly to avoid them cooling down.

Figure 2.38 Critical control points – Department of Health

Several systems of HACCP have been developed for use in the catering industry:

o Codex HACCP
o Assured safe catering
o Safer food better business.

Try this!

Produce a report that outlines the HACCP practices and procedures required to maintain food safety in a typical kitchen environment. Identify the:

o hazard analysis at all stages of food production
o control points and critical control points
o control limits
o corrective action
o audit and verification documentation
o key safety records
o reporting procedure.

Many small catering businesses will use one of these systems successfully. Larger catering companies may decide to develop their own. A HACCP system must include:

- an analysis of the possible hazards at all stages of food production
- identification of the points at which these hazards can be controlled
- identification of the most important critical points at which the hazards must be controlled
- the maximum and minimum limits at which the hazard must be controlled
- the ways in which the hazard can be reduced or removed
- the records that are needed to show how this process is being carried out.

HACCP monitoring

One of the key procedures in the HACCP system is **monitoring**. To be able to check condition, it has to be measured against a standard that has already been set. For example, if your speed of work was being monitored, it would be measured against an average that had been worked out in advance. This would be obtained by watching and timing a range of people all carrying out the same task.

In a catering kitchen there are many types of monitoring that take place:

- The Head Chef monitors the standard and amount of work produced by the kitchen staff.
- Refrigerator and freezer temperatures are monitored and recorded several times each day.
- Cleaning is monitored daily by supervisors to make sure standards of hygiene are being maintained.
- Contractors regularly monitor a range of equipment in the kitchen including:
  - pest control equipment
  - alarm systems
  - fire-fighting equipment
  - microwave ovens and other cooking equipment, e.g. steamers
  - refrigerators and freezers
  - dishwashers
  - extraction systems.
- Deliveries are checked for quality, temperature, best before dates and correct weight.

Definition

Monitoring – regularly checking condition and progress.

Fridge temperatures

Week commencing: _____

	Time	Signed	Time	Signed	Time	Signed
MON	Temp		Temp		Temp	
TUE	Time	Signed	Time	Signed	Time	Signed
	Temp		Temp		Temp	
WED	Time	Signed	Time	Signed	Time	Signed
	Temp		Temp		Temp	
THURS	Time	Signed	Time	Signed	Time	Signed
	Temp		Temp		Temp	
FRI	Time	Signed	Time	Signed	Time	Signed
	Temp		Temp		Temp	
SAT	Time	Signed	Time	Signed	Time	Signed
	Temp		Temp		Temp	
SUN	Time	Signed	Time	Signed	Time	Signed
	Temp		Temp		Temp	

Comments

_____
_____
_____

Figure 2.39 Temperature control record sheet

○ Rotation of stock is monitored frequently to make sure the oldest products are used first.

○ The amount of wasted food thrown away may be checked very regularly in some kitchens.

○ The presentation standard of the food produced is monitored, often by checking against prepared photographs in standard operating procedures.

The process of monitoring can take several forms, including:

○ completing a checklist

○ recording specific information on a chart

○ filling in particular sections on a schedule

○ carrying out spot checks

○ questioning staff and contractors

○ observing work practices and work areas

○ taking samples – of food or **swabs** of work surfaces and equipment

○ weighing items.

> **Definition**
>
> **Swab** – a sterile piece of cotton used to take a sample for chemical analysis.

Figure 2.40 Completing a checklist

Try this!

Which monitoring processes would you use for the following situations?

○ *Keeping the results of refrigerator temperature checks.*

○ *Making sure all areas of the staff changing room have been cleaned thoroughly.*

○ *Checking that a meat delivery is correct.*

○ *Finding out if there is any evidence of mice in the dry stores area.*

Action to take when monitoring reveals a problem

The purpose of monitoring and checking is to spot a potential problem or risk before it becomes a serious hazard. If checking is carried out regularly then any difference in results should show up very quickly.

The action taken depends on the type of problem. Urgent action is necessary if the problem concerns a possible food safety hazard.

Figure 2.41 shows the type of action that may be necessary to prevent food becoming a hazard.

Problem	Possible action to be taken
Poor standard of work produced by kitchen staff	Retraining and closer supervision by Head Chef.
Refrigerator temperature rises significantly	Check that the refrigerator is not defrosting automatically. If this is not the case: o move items to another refrigerator with the correct temperature o unplug the refrigerator if possible o put an "out of order" notice on it o tell your supervisor as soon as possible.
A mouse is spotted in the corner of the kitchen	o Tell your supervisor as soon as possible. o The pest control contractor will be called out immediately. o Kitchen staff will need to look out for evidence of mouse infestation. o Make sure that no food crumbs are left around or any food left uncovered in kitchen and stores areas.
Microwave does not heat the food properly	o Check the portion of food is the correct size for the time allowed. o Test the microwave by heating a cup of water. o If it does not perform as it should, unplug the equipment so it cannot be used. o Put an "out of order" sign on the machine. o Tell your supervisor. o An engineer should attend to rectify the problem.
Chilled produce is delivered in a van that is not refrigerated	o Check the temperature of the delivered items. If over the safe limit of 8°C, refuse the delivery. o Tell your supervisor, as this may have been a problem before and the supplier may be changed.
Out-of-date salad items are found at the back of the refrigerator during a stock take	o Tell your supervisor, as stock figures will be affected.
A large amount of raw vegetable waste is found in the bin	Head Chef to retrain staff in efficient preparation methods.
A large amount of cooked waste is found in the bin	Head Chef will investigate and take action. Possible reasons: o incorrect portion size o quality of food poor.
The plated food items do not look like the prepared photographs	Head Chef will investigate and take action. Possible reasons: o poor quality food used o staff not trained correctly.

Figure 2.41 Action to take when monitoring reveals a problem

The relative importance of different hazards

It is important to be able to identify which situations require urgent action and which problems can be solved a little later on.

All circumstances which put any person in danger should be dealt with immediately. These include any:

- fire or security alert
- accident to any person in the area
- foreign body found in food
- equipment found in a dangerous condition
- floor surface found in a dangerous condition
- food left in an unsafe condition
- food stored in an unsafe condition.

Try this!

Put the following incidents in the order you would deal with them if they all happened together. Then state the action you would take in respect of each hazard.

- *A carton of cream is past its "use by" date in the refrigerator.*
- *There is a pool of water around the door of an upright freezer and the contents are thawing.*
- *A chef cuts their finger and needs a plaster.*
- *A fly falls in a pan of soup on the stove.*
- *A frying pan overheats and catches fire on the stove.*

Figure 2.42 Can you spot all the things that have gone wrong?

Identifying types of food safety hazard

Food safety hazards can come from the most unlikely sources – some of them quite unexpected. When trying to identify possible food safety hazards you need to be very open-minded.

Figure 2.43 shows the questions you need to ask when trying to identify food safety hazards:

Question	Possible answers
Where could harmful bacteria be found in the workplace?	o Poor cleaning of equipment. o Insect or rodent infestation. o Poor hygiene practices of staff – not washing hands sufficiently, staff being ill and still coming to work.
How is cross-contamination caused?	o By using the same chopping boards for raw and cooked foods. o By storing raw food above cooked food in the refrigerator. o By food handlers not washing their hands thoroughly in between dealing with raw and cooked foods.
What other possible ways are there for food to be contaminated in the workplace?	o Cleaning chemicals getting into food from poor storage or not rinsing properly. o "Foreign bodies" getting into food from breakages not being cleared away carefully.
Which high-risk foods come into the kitchen in an uncooked state?	o Chicken o Eggs o Meat o Vegetables o Rice. These are high-risk due to the food poisoning bacteria or toxins that may be found in them in their raw state.
Is it possible for harmful bacteria to be able to multiply to a dangerous level?	o Is any food cooked and then left out at room temperature for a long time before being put in the refrigerator? Is there a better procedure that can be used? o Is any high-risk raw food left out for a long time at room temperature? Can this be avoided? o Is there ever a significant delay between cooking food, keeping it hot and it being served? Is there an alternative to this practice?
Is a probe used correctly to ensure thorough cooking and reheating of food?	If no, what happens instead?
Is food ever served before it has been reheated properly?	If yes, why and how can this be avoided next time?

85

Is frozen food sometimes not defrosted in time?	If yes, what happens?
Does the correct equipment exist in the kitchen for certain processes? Is it used when it should be (e.g. a blast chiller used to chill food quickly)?	If the equipment is not available, what happens?
What happens when demand is unpredictable? How is extra food provided at short notice?	Is there a stock of stand-by items kept in a freezer? How long does it take to get this ready for service?
What happens when food has to travel some distance between preparation and service? Does this happen when the food is hot or cold?	Is specialist equipment provided? If not, how is the food kept free from contamination and at the correct temperature?

Figure 2.43 Identifying food safety hazards

It is very important to report all possible hazards to your supervisor. The situation may result in:

o a serious safety hazard (food or health and safety)
o a high level of wastage leading to shortages and inaccurate stock records
o a repair or service call-out to fix or maintain a piece of equipment or to maintain the hygiene of the premises
o the identification of a need for staff training.

> **Try this!**
> Look at the table above. Now think about your workplace. Make a similar list that identifies risk areas that exist with present work practices. This is the first stage of the HACCP procedures for creating a food safety management system.

Key elements of a food safety policy

Current food safety legislation recommends that all catering organisations have a food safety policy. This document describes how the business provides training and maintains standards to keep within the food safety laws. A policy will include:

o standards of personal hygiene required by all food handlers (see page 45)
o procedures for reporting sickness and accidents within the workplace (see page 117)

- requirements for pest control measures within the building (see page 63)
- minimum acceptable standards of cleaning and disinfection in food production areas (see pages 52–57)
- requirement for all visitors to the production areas to wear suitable protective clothing. This is usually a white coat and hat but sometimes gloves, hairnets and special footwear are also provided.

Records and reporting procedures

Under the HACCP legislation there is a requirement to keep records relating to the hazard analysis and monitoring process. The type and number of records kept will depend on the size and type of catering operation. The most common types of records and reporting systems are:

- training records for the use of dangerous machines, cleaning procedures, hygiene requirements, etc.
- pest control records (see page 63)
- temperature records for freezers, refrigerators, hot and cold holding equipment, cooling food, etc.
- accident report forms (see page 117)
- sickness records of any notifiable illnesses (see page 51)
- customer complaints regarding possible food safety issues
- maintenance record of equipment which could affect food safety.

Test yourself!

1 Which of the following is an example of monitoring food safety?
  a Taking fridge temperatures
  b Writing weekly menus
  c Washing the kitchen floor
  d Calculating food cost.

2 What is the process of collecting information to prove food safety called?
  a Assessing hygiene methods
  b Monitoring bad practice
  c Copying clear records
  d Demonstrating due diligence.

3 Which of the following is not an example of a HACCP record?
  a Staff rota
  b Temperature chart
  c Cleaning schedule
  d Equipment checklist.

4 Complete the table below indicating the conditions and location where you would store the following items and which you would put away first:

Item	Order of storage	Location	Conditions (e.g. temperature)
Fresh fish			
Tinned tomatoes			
Dried basil			
Fresh garlic			
Chilled potato salad			
Frozen peas			

Health and safety

3

This chapter covers the following outcomes from Diploma unit 103: Health and safety awareness for catering and hospitality

- Outcome 103.1 Be able to demonstrate awareness of health and safety practices in the catering and hospitality workplace
- Outcome 103.2 Be able to identify hazards in the workplace
- Outcome 103.3 Be able to follow health and safety procedures

Working through this chapter could also provide the opportunity to practise the following Functional Skills at Level 1:

Functional Maths: Representing – solve simple problems involving ratio, where one number is a multiple of the other

Analysing – use simple formulae expressed in words for one or two step operations

In this chapter you will learn about:

- The meaning of health and safety
- Why it is important to keep yourself and others safe at work
- The common causes of accidents and how to avoid them
- How to lift objects safely
- How to deal with hazardous situations
- The use of personal protective equipment (PPE)

Awareness of health and safety

Most accidents are a result of human error. Over 3,000 accidents occur in the hospitality industry each year. **Health** and **safety** laws aim to try to reduce this figure. When you are working with other people and dealing with members of the public, it is particularly important to behave in a safe and hygienic manner.

Everybody in a workplace should be able to carry out their tasks without causing any accident or injury to themselves or others. Members of the public using the building should also be safe. A law called the Health and Safety at Work Act 1974 was brought in to make sure that everyone works safely and carefully. This law has meant that most people now take much greater care to work in a safe manner. The result is that there are fewer accidents in the workplace.

Under the Health and Safety at Work Act, both employers and employees are responsible for keeping a workplace safe. They all have a duty to themselves, each other and any visitors, customers and guests who come to the premises. If they fail to carry out this duty they could be personally **liable** and could be fined or imprisoned!

> **Definitions**
> **Health** – good condition of the body and mind, with no illness or disease.
> **Safety** – freedom from danger or risk of injury.

Common causes of accidents

Common causes of accidents include:
○ lifting and carrying heavy or awkward objects
○ stacking and storing objects carelessly
○ slipping and falling in work areas
○ working in a rush
○ not concentrating when using equipment and machinery.

To avoid accidents you must be alert and be able to look ahead to notice any possible danger. The safety of you and your colleagues in a catering kitchen may be affected by:
○ being short of sleep
○ being under the influence of alcohol or drugs
○ having long hair which is not tied back correctly
○ wearing jewellery.

Long hair or jewellery could get caught in machinery or cause hygiene problems by falling into food which is being prepared.

> **Definition**
> **Liable** – legally responsible.

Figure 3.1 Lack of concentration is a common cause of accidents in the catering industry

Even though you wear the correct uniform and work as safely as possible, it is quite likely you will injure yourself at some time while working in a professional kitchen. The most common injuries are slight cuts and burns.

Reasons why accidents happen in the workplace

There are three main types of reasons for accidents happening in the workplace.

People

People at work can be easily distracted and forget to work safely. This can be due to:

○ working in a careless way
○ being new to the job and lacking experience
○ having to work under pressure
○ being unable to concentrate due to personal reasons
○ not being trained correctly.

Surroundings

The workplace environment can cause problems such as:

○ poor levels of lighting in work areas, on stairs or in corridors
○ very high or low working temperatures – e.g. at the stove or in the freezer
○ trying to concentrate in a noisy area – e.g. with loud machinery working
○ poorly maintained flooring, which could cause someone to slip or trip.

Equipment and substances

Examples of equipment and substances that might cause problems include:

○ machinery at high temperatures and pressures – e.g. steamers and ovens
○ strong chemicals such as oven cleaners – e.g. if they are incorrectly diluted or used in an incorrect way
○ poor extraction systems
○ large amounts of dusty ingredients, such as flour
○ chemical reactions.

Did you know?

Slips and trips account for more than half of all accidents reported in the catering industry.

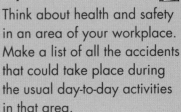

Top marks!

Think about health and safety in an area of your workplace. Make a list of all the accidents that could take place during the usual day-to-day activities in that area.

Effects of an accident in the workplace

When an accident happens at work it is not only the person involved who may be affected. Accidents can result in:

○ wasted materials – e.g. burned food or broken glass
○ wasted time – e.g. delays in replacing food or equipment
○ increased workload for others – e.g. if an accident victim cannot return to work quickly
○ disruption in work flow – e.g. if an area of the kitchen cannot be used for some time
○ loss of revenue – e.g. if fewer dishes can be produced
○ increase in costs – e.g. if an additional member of staff has to be brought in to cover.

> **Did you know?**
> The most common hazards in the catering industry which break the Health and Safety at Work Act are:
> o missing guards on food slicing machines
> o trailing cables
> o insecure wiring on plugs
> o faulty microwave seals
> o broken or worn steps
> o poor lighting of work areas.

Figure 3.2 What effects of the accident can you spot in the picture?

Benefits of good working methods

It is very important to work in a safe and hygienic way for several reasons:

○ it avoids injuring yourself or others
○ it is usually quicker and easier
○ it is more professional.

To reduce the risk of accidents, you should follow any guidelines given to you about safe working practices. By working safely both the employee and employer can benefit from:

○ less time and money lost from illness and injury
○ the business having a good reputation for health and safety
○ fewer extra costs from covering employees who are off sick.

If health and safety regulations are not met, you or your employer could be fined and your workplace may be closed down until safety improvements have been made.

Responsibilities of employers

The Health and Safety at Work Act makes sure that employers do not put their staff in dangerous situations where they could hurt themselves or others. Under this Act, employers must:

- keep all their staff safe while working
- provide safe equipment, tools and surroundings in which to work
- train staff how to work in a safe and hygienic way
- train staff how to use chemicals safely
- train staff to look after the equipment they use
- produce a policy document telling everyone how to behave safely
- provide first aid equipment and help
- keep an accident book and use it correctly.

Figure 3.3 All chefs need to know the health and safety laws

Responsibilities of employees

While at work, employees must:

- take reasonable care of their own safety and the safety of others
- work in the way required by the employer, especially regarding safety
- tell their supervisor if they see anything that they think may be unsafe and could cause an accident.

Failing in the duty of health and safety

If an employer does not look after the health and safety of their staff, this could result in an accident. If a serious accident happens, the employer will be interviewed by an inspector from the Health and Safety Executive or the local council. The inspector will want to investigate how the accident happened. They will ask many questions and want to watch how people work in the area. If the inspector decides that the employer has failed in his or her responsibility to look after the employees, the inspector has the power to:

- give verbal or written advice about improvements needed in the workplace
- issue a notice requiring improvements to be made

- prevent the use of dangerous equipment
- **prosecute** either the business or an individual for breaking health and safety law.

If an employee causes an accident at work, this should be investigated by the employer. Depending on how serious the accident is, the employer may:

- give the employee a verbal warning
- give the employee a written warning
- require the employee to leave their job
- refer the incident to the Health and Safety Executive, who may decide to prosecute the employee.

If there is a prosecution under the Health and Safety at Work Act, either the employer or the employee may be found guilty. The punishment may be up to two years in prison, a fine of an unlimited amount, or both. This means that a serious health and safety problem – e.g. a major accident – could be very expensive and also give the person responsible a criminal record.

If a business is prosecuted under the Health and Safety at Work Act it can result in:

- bad publicity for the organisation
- the business may be fined a large sum of money
- the business may have expensive legal costs to pay
- the business may have to pay compensation to the injured person.

It may also mean:

- shortages of staff if an employee was injured
- staff being disrupted and upset by health and safety investigations
- staff feeling greater stress in the workplace
- everyone feeling very sad if someone has been killed or badly hurt in the accident.

> **Definition**
> **Prosecute** – to bring a criminal case against someone who has broken the law.

> **Did you know?**
> **Store fined £15,000 after worker falls in kitchen**
> A national store was fined £15,000 after an accident in its store in Gateshead. A catering assistant slipped and fractured her skull in the wash-up area of the store's cafeteria kitchen. The floor had become wet and contaminated with food. Four similar accidents had taken place in the kitchen over the previous 12 months. The victim spent a total of 11 days in hospital and she is unlikely ever to return to work. The shop has since replaced the flooring in the kitchen.

> **Did you know?**
> **London restaurant fined £15,500 for health and safety breaches**
> A restaurant in London was fined more than £15,500 after a child fell down an open cellar hatch and severely injured his head. The delivery hatch had been left open on the pavement outside.

Test yourself!

1 Copy and complete the sentences.
   a The _____ and _____ at Work Act requires all staff to work safely in the kitchen.
   b All _____ are responsible for the safety of themselves and others.
   c _____ must ensure that their staff are trained correctly in operating machinery.

2 List three effects that an accident at work may have on the other members of staff.

3 List three common causes of accidents in the workplace.

4 What is the maximum punishment (penalty) for an offence under the Health and Safety at Work Act?
   a Unlimited prison sentence and unlimited fine.
   b Two years in prison and unlimited fine.
   c Unlimited prison sentence and £200,000 fine.
   d Two years in prison and £200,000 fine

Identify hazards in the workplace

There are many hazards in a working kitchen. They include slippery floors, items falling from work tables, pans catching fire and heavy items which need lifting. It is important to be able to recognise a situation in which an accident could easily happen and know how to prevent it.

Slips, trips and falls

Slips, trips and falls make up over 50 per cent of the major reported accidents in the hospitality industry. Some of the main reasons for these accidents are:

- spillages on the floor not cleaned up properly
- floor left wet without a danger sign
- worn-out floor surface
- people rushing around in the kitchen
- uneven floors and awkward steps in older buildings
- constantly slippery floor in an unventilated walk-in refrigerator
- failed light bulbs not being replaced in dimly lit areas
- people working in a hurry and not following safety rules
- kitchen staff wearing unsuitable footwear at work
- items left on the floor in busy work areas
- kitchen staff working when they are too tired or feeling unwell.

Ways of reducing the danger from slips, trips and falls include:

- always thoroughly clean up spillages straightaway
- always put out wet floor signs as soon as possible
- report worn floor surfaces for urgent repair
- do not rush around the kitchen
- get uneven floors and awkward steps repaired, or at least fitted with handrails, signs and good lighting
- improve ventilation in areas with constantly slippery floors
- replace failed light bulbs very promptly
- follow safety instructions at all times
- always wear non-slip footwear to work in the kitchen
- never leave items on the floor
- do not work when feeling unwell or too tired.

> **Definitions**
>
> **Hazard** – anything that can cause harm – e.g. a knife, a slicing machine or a slippery floor.
>
> **Risk** – the chance of harm being done. A risk usually involves a hazard – e.g. the risk of slipping when walking across a wet floor.

Figure 3.4 What is the cause of this accident and how could it have been avoided?

Lifting, carrying and handling

It is very easy to hurt yourself if you do not know how to lift and move items safely. It is not just heavy items that can cause problems when moving them about. Many back injuries and strains to hands, wrists, arms and necks are caused by frequent or awkward body movements. Bruising can occur if an item falls against you. It is also possible to break bones when trying to move an awkward, heavy item and you can cut yourself if the item has sharp edges.

Here are some guidelines for carrying and moving items safely.

○ Be very careful when moving pots containing hot liquids. Do not have them too full.
○ When taking items out of ovens, be careful not to burn anyone who is passing by when turning round.
○ Do not overload trolleys or trucks.
○ Always make sure you can see where you are going.
○ Stack heavier items at the bottom and lighter items at the top of a pile.
○ Do not stack shelves too high.
○ Use steps with great care. Ask someone to hold the steps at the bottom if possible.

The Manual Handling Regulations advise that you should:

○ avoid lifting or moving heavy items if there is a safer way – such as using a trolley
○ if possible, make heavy, large loads into loads that are smaller and lighter
○ make awkward loads easier to get hold of
○ change the layout of a work area to reduce the need for lifting or moving items
○ wear suitable protective equipment such as gloves and steel-capped footwear when moving heavy items.

Figure 3.5 Careless handling and lifting can lead to problems

If you have to lift, carry or handle items, you can reduce the risk of injury by finding out:

○ what the item is and where it is to be moved to before starting to shift it

○ if more than one person is needed to lift it – in some cases you may need more than just one person to help you

○ the best way of holding the item

○ the shortest, safest route to carry the item.

You may also need to find out if the item to be moved is very hot or very cold so that you can protect your arms and body as necessary.

Lifting a heavy object

Correct training is required to lift a heavy object safely. A few guidelines follow.

○ Keep your muscles relaxed as tense muscles strain easily.

○ Plan what is to be carried and to where.

○ Check the route is clear, doors open, ramps in position, lights on.

○ Get help if the object is likely to be heavier than you can easily handle.

○ Position your feet carefully on each side of the object to keep your balance.

○ Use one hand to support the weight of the item, the other to pull the item towards you. This way your body can take part of the weight. Use your whole hand to lift, not just the tips of your fingers.

○ Do not twist to change direction as you are lifting or carrying. Move your feet using lots of small steps.

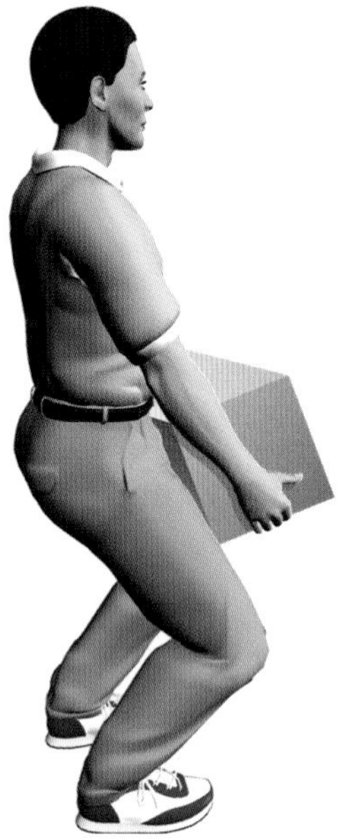

Figure 3.6 Lifting a heavy object safely

Try this!

Practise lifting a medium-sized, empty box following the guidelines above to avoid straining yourself.

Accidents from machinery or equipment

Equipment can be either manual or electrically operated. Machinery needs electricity to work. Training must be given in the operation of equipment and machinery. All electrical items have to be checked regularly.

Ways in which you can be injured by equipment include:
○ entrapment – e.g. getting your finger stuck in a mincing machine
○ impact – e.g. dropping a heavy saucepan on your foot
○ contact – e.g. touching a hot pan on the stove with your hand
○ ejection – e.g. not fitting a processor lid correctly and it flying off during use
○ faulty equipment – e.g. using a mixer with a faulty on/off switch
○ inappropriate use of equipment – e.g. using a knife blade to open a tin.

Knife care and safety

Types of manual equipment include:
○ knives
○ mandolins (see page 159).

Poor knife techniques and untidy work methods are often a cause of accidents in the kitchen. Follow these rules to work safely.
○ Store your knives in a specially designed area when not in use, e.g. in a box, case, wallet or on a magnetic rack. Storing loose knives in a drawer can damage the blades and cause injury.
○ When moving knives, transport them in the appropriate box or case. Never leave them loose. This avoids accidents in the workplace. It also stops you getting into trouble with the police when carrying your knives to and from work.
○ When carrying a knife, always point it down and hold it close to your side. Work colleagues can be unintentionally stabbed if this rule is not followed!
○ If passing a knife to a colleague always offer it to them handle first.
○ Never leave a knife on a work surface with the blade upwards.
○ Never leave a knife hanging over the edge of a work surface.
○ Never try to catch a falling knife – let it come to rest on the ground before you pick it up.
○ Never use a knife as a can opener or screwdriver.

Figure 3.7 A mandolin

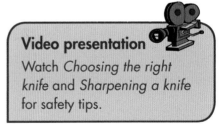

Video presentation
Watch *Choosing the right knife* and *Sharpening a knife* for safety tips.

○ Do not use a knife which is blunt or has a greasy, loose or damaged handle. It can easily slip and cause a serious cut.

○ Always use the correct knife for the job.

○ It is recommended that you use colour-coded knives to prevent cross-contamination. See Chapter 2.

○ Only use a knife on a chopping board which has a damp cloth underneath to prevent slippage.

○ When wiping a knife clean after use, wipe from the blade base to the tip with the sharp edge facing away from your body.

○ Never leave a knife in a sink. Wash it and remove it immediately.

Figure 3.8 A set of chef's knives. Always take care when handling these

Electrical equipment

Electrical equipment includes:

○ slicing machines

○ mixers

○ mincers

○ blenders.

These are known as "prescribed dangerous machines" and have special regulations relating to their use.

All electrical equipment should be tested regularly by qualified electricians. They will ensure that the cables are not damaged and the correct fuses and circuit breakers are fitted. No item of electrical equipment should be used if it has a damaged flex or is faulty. It should be removed from the work area if possible and have an out of order sign attached to it until it can be checked and repaired by a qualified person.

Rules for operating machinery

○ Always follow the manufacturer's instructions.

○ Never operate machinery if the safety guards are not in place. Many machines will not work unless correctly and fully assembled. However, some older models may work without the safety equipment being fitted – be very careful with these.

○ If the machine does not work properly, seek help from your supervisor.

○ Ensure that the correct attachments are being used on the equipment for the task to be carried out.

Remember!

Take great care when operating machinery. No one under the age of 18 may clean, lubricate or adjust a machine if they will be at risk of injury from a moving part.

○ Never push food against a cutting blade with your hands – use a proper plunger or the handle supplied. (Many chefs have lost fingers by not following this rule!)

○ If using a spoon do not let it touch any moving parts. If it does the spoon and the machine will be damaged.

○ Do not use faulty machinery. Label it "out of order" and unplug it or partly dismantle it so it cannot be used. Report the problem to your supervisor so a repair can be arranged.

○ Do not overload electrical sockets. This may cause a fire or cause fuses to blow and could affect everybody working in the building.

○ To avoid electric shock, do not operate electrical equipment with wet hands, near sinks or any other sources of water.

○ Keep your hands away from sharp blades. Wait for them to stop rotating after switching the machine off before starting any other activity, e.g. cleaning.

○ Make sure the power is disconnected before starting to clean electrical machinery.

○ Do not use machinery if the plug or flex is damaged in any way.

Remember!

Before using any type of machinery or equipment the member of staff must be trained in the correct procedures. They must be fully instructed about any danger and be supervised adequately by someone with knowledge and experience of the machine.

Many serious accidents in the workplace involve machinery. It is important that all machinery is correctly set up, maintained and only used by people who have received full training. There are a number of chefs in the industry who no longer have a full set of fingers and thumbs due to poor health and safety practices in the kitchen.

To avoid accidents when using machinery and equipment at work it is important to follow these guidelines.

○ Do not try to use any item of equipment or machinery until you have been fully trained by the appropriate person.

○ Make sure you are wearing any personal protective equipment (PPE) required – e.g. the correct type of gloves, goggles, apron, etc.

○ Work carefully and safely. Do not try to rush or take short cuts in the process.

○ If the machine does not work correctly do not continue to use it. Make sure it cannot be used by someone else and report the fault to your supervisor as soon as possible. (See page 107.)

Hazardous substances

Any substance that is not in the appropriate place or is not being used correctly may become a hazard. In catering, the types of substances that may become hazardous include:

- cooking oil, gels or spirits which may:
  - overheat and catch fire
  - be spilled on the floor and make it very slippery
- cooking gas cylinders which may:
  - overheat and explode
  - leak and cause an explosive fire
- cleaning chemicals, which may:
  - be used incorrectly – e.g. not **diluted** enough and damage the surface being cleaned
  - cause burns if not used with the appropriate personal protective equipment – e.g. goggles and gloves
  - be mixed together and give off dangerous fumes which can be breathed in
  - be stored in an unlabelled container and mistaken for another liquid – this could result in the chemical being swallowed by accident.

To reduce risks from hazardous substances the following rules must be observed.

- Everyone working in the area must be trained in the use of these substances.
- The appropriate protective equipment should be worn when using them – e.g. gloves, goggles and masks if necessary – and suitable signs should be displayed.
- The work method used must always be safe and carried out in a suitable area – e.g. cleaning chemicals should be used in a well-ventilated area, a fryer should be refilled with oil only when cold.

The special regulations regarding chemicals (COSHH) state that:

- chemicals that may be dangerous to people must be clearly identified
- these chemicals must be stored, issued and used safely
- training must be given in the use of these chemicals
- suitable personal protective clothing must be provided for use with the chemicals.

Definition

Dilute – to add extra liquid (usually water) to make the solution weaker.

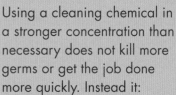

Did you know?

Using a cleaning chemical in a stronger concentration than necessary does not kill more germs or get the job done more quickly. Instead it:

- wastes the cleaning chemical (which can cost quite a lot of money)
- might damage the surface on which it is being used
- will need more rinsing off after use (which makes the job take longer in the end).

When using any type of chemical:

o always follow the manufacturer's instructions carefully
o never mix one chemical with another
o never move any chemical from its original container into an alternative one which is incorrectly labelled or has no label at all
o never use food containers to store a cleaning chemical
o always store chemicals in the correct place.

Definition

Caustic – a substance that will stick to a surface and burn chemically. It is used for heavy-duty cleaning.

Did you know?

In a bar some cleaning fluid was kept in an unlabelled, clear glass bottle. This bottle was placed near some fruit squash. A young child in the bar with her family wanted an orange drink. The member of staff poured her a measure of squash and then topped it up with what looked like water from the clear glass bottle. Instead of water the liquid was an extremely strong, **caustic** chemical. The little girl had to be rushed to hospital for emergency treatment.

Figure 3.9 Never pour a liquid into an unlabelled container

Top marks!

Investigate the range of Health and Safety signs that are found in kitchens and surrounding areas. Either photograph or draw examples of the signs and label where they were. Include the symbols found on cleaning chemical containers as well as other equipment. Write the meaning of each sign next to it.
Build up a collection of all the different types in a book. Test your colleagues to see if they can identify them all and know what they mean!

Fire and explosions in the workplace

Fire is very dangerous and can easily become life-threatening. It is very important that you know what to do in the event of a fire. Respect fire and treat it with the utmost caution. Explosions are not as common in a catering environment but when they do occur can cause serious injury.

Fires can be started in kitchens quite easily. Hot stoves are left on for long periods of time and hot fat in fryers can overheat and catch fire. There is a large amount of electrical equipment which can develop a fault and start a fire. Over 28 per cent of fires on catering premises start in the kitchen and are caused by cooking procedures.

Explosions can be caused by fuel or **flammable** vapours becoming ignited. Gas or electrical stoves and boilers not working correctly are all possible sources of an explosion. Small explosions may also be caused by **blown cans** and fermented ingredients in bottles and jars where gases have built up and created pressure inside.

Other causes of fires and explosions include:

○ gas leaks – from a fractured pipe or gas burner left on but unlit

○ build up of gas – from a gas leak which is not attended to straightaway

○ smoking – putting a **smouldering** cigarette or a lighted match on or near a flammable substance

○ forgetting about a food or liquid on the stove – this may become overheated and then catch fire

○ using a blow torch carelessly and allowing the naked flame to ignite other items.

Definitions

Flammable – describes a substance or material that can catch fire easily.

Blown can – a can which has not been properly sealed during the canning process and has bulging ends. The contents are dangerous and should not be eaten.

Smoulder – to burn slowly with a red glow and not much smoke.

Did you know?

Many fires on catering premises have been started by a spark from the stove being sucked up the extraction canopy. When the canopy is dirty and coated with a layer of grease a fire can easily start. Because the smoke gets sucked up through the extraction system, no one may be aware there is a fire until it has spread to a dangerous level. Some commercial insurance companies will not insure catering premises unless the kitchen canopy is professionally cleaned very regularly.

Figure 3.10 A fire can start when a spark from the stove is sucked into a dirty extraction canopy

How to reduce the risk of fire and explosions

Working carefully and being observant are the main ways of reducing the risk of fire and explosions. Good working practices include:
○ keeping hot work areas clean of fat and grease
○ never overfilling fryers and frying pans
○ keeping walls and canopies around stoves clean
○ not allowing cloths to dangle over stoves
○ not overloading electrical sockets
○ never leaving electrical or gas appliances on unattended.

How can a fire start?

Fire needs three things to burn. As soon as one is removed, the fire will go out.

Fuel: fire has to be fed with fuel. A fuel is any substance that will burn – e.g. gas, electricity, cloth, oil or wood. Once the fuel has been used up the fire will go out.

Oxygen: fire requires oxygen to keep going. Oxygen is found in air, so if the source of air is removed the fire will go out. This is why a fire blanket can put out a fire.

Heat: fire creates heat. If the heat of the fire is removed the fire will go out. This is how many fire extinguishers work.

A fire can be put out by:
○ starving it of fuel
○ smothering it by removing air
○ cooling it by taking away the heat.

How to deal with a fire

A fire can easily start in a kitchen, so it is important to know what to do if it happens. Sometimes a drop of grease will catch fire on the stove and go out by itself almost at once. This is not an emergency. However, if it does not go out and gets bigger it could become dangerous.

Figure 3.11 The three things that fire needs

Remember!
The thick, toxic smoke given off by a fire kills and injures more people than the flames. It is very important to keep fire doors closed to stop smoke spreading. Thick smoke can make it impossible for people to escape from a burning building.

You should only tackle a fire if you feel confident to do so. If you are going to try to put out a small fire, you need to know which extinguisher to use for which type of fire. If you use the wrong one by mistake it could make the fire much worse.

Once you have used a fire extinguisher you must let your supervisor know as it has to be refilled as soon as possible. Extinguishers must be checked every year to make sure they are full and work properly.

In some situations it may be appropriate to try to put out a fire that has just started, but you must act speedily!

Figure 3.12 Types of fire extinguisher

Situation	Response
A person's clothes catch fire	Quickly wrap them in a fire blanket or wet tablecloth (or similar) and lay them on the floor. This excludes air and heat from the fire so it should go out. Do not take off the blanket or tablecloth. Call for a first aider to attend the scene.
A pan of fat catches fire	Turn off the gas or electricity and quickly cover the pan with a lid or fire blanket and leave it where it is. Use an oven cloth if possible to protect your hands. The fire should go out by itself after a few minutes as the air has been removed. Do not try to move the pan. Do not put water on this type of fire as it will make it much worse immediately.
An electrical appliance catches fire – e.g. a mixer	Turn off the electricity at the plug and use a carbon dioxide extinguisher. This gas cools the fire and removes the oxygen. It does not conduct electricity and is safe to use on electrical machinery. Do not use any other type of extinguisher in this situation.

Figure 3.13 Action to take to put out different types of fire

If a fire starts that cannot be put out easily:
- raise the alarm by operating the nearest fire alarm or shouting "Fire!"
- follow the procedure you have rehearsed in your fire training.

Try this!
Imagine a fire has broken out. Without asking for help, see if you can answer these questions following the procedure you have been taught to follow in the event of a fire.
- *Where is the nearest fire extinguisher?*
- *Where is the nearest emergency exit point?*
- *Where do you have to assemble outside?*

Afterwards, answer the questions again with the help of someone who knows the correct answer. Were you right?

Remember!

Emergency escape routes must always be kept clear and unlocked. Never leave anything in front of an emergency exit. Most deaths in fires occur because people cannot get out of the building.

How to deal with electricity

Electricity is very useful as a source of power. Many jobs in the kitchen would be much more time-consuming and tiring without electricity – e.g. washing pots, mixing ingredients and chopping ingredients very finely. However, electricity must be treated with care as it can be extremely dangerous. If an electrical machine is faulty it can start a fire or give anyone trying to use it an electric shock. Electricity can generate a great deal of heat which can burn, and if electricity comes into direct contact with water the shock caused can kill.

Did you know?

All electrical equipment in the workplace has to be tested once a year to make sure it is safe. This is known as PAT (Portable Appliance Testing). When this check has been carried out, a sticker should be attached to the equipment with the initials of the tester and the date.

How to prevent danger from electricity

As long as manufacturer's instructions are followed when using electrical equipment, there should be no danger from injury. If an electrical machine does not work as expected – e.g. a blender motor makes a loud noise and smoke, or you see sparks inside a microwave – immediately stop using the item, unplug it and make sure it is not on fire. Place an "out of order" notice on the appliance and report the fault to a supervisor. The appliance should not be used again until it has been checked by a qualified electrician who is happy that it is safe and working correctly. Any piece of equipment that has a damaged flex or exposed wires should not be used until it has been repaired.

If an electrical socket fails to work, the socket should be taped over and an "out of order" sign placed beside it to stop anyone trying to use it. It should be reported in the same way.

If an electrical light fails, do not try to change the bulb yourself. Make sure that a member of staff who has been suitably trained carries out this procedure. Replacing it with a bulb of the wrong wattage could cause the fitting to overheat.

Figure 3.14 It is essential to follow the correct procedure when dealing with faulty machinery.

Dealing with an accident involving electrical equipment

○ Do not touch the injured person. This is very important if you think the person may have received an electric shock. If you touch them you will get an electric shock too.
○ Visually make sure that they are in no further danger.

Did you know?

A circuit breaker is a special device that is used between an electrical socket and an electrical appliance. If a piece of electrical equipment is faulty it will automatically turn it off before there is any danger of electric shock.

- If there is any machinery involved, immediately turn off the power at the plug or the main switch.
- Contact your supervisor and get the help of a first aider.
- If this is not possible:
  - telephone 999 (free call – even from a locked phone)
  - ask for the ambulance service
  - give your telephone number so you can be called back
  - give the location of the accident
  - describe what has happened and give details of the injuries as clearly as you can
  - follow any instructions given over the phone – this may involve giving some first aid, getting information from the injured person or going to a meeting point to wait for an ambulance.

How to treat a casualty while waiting for help

- Talk to the person and reassure them. If you do not know them, find out their name and where they live. Be kind and considerate.
- Tell them that help is on the way.
- If they feel cold, cover them with a blanket or any available clothing. Try not to cover a major burn.
- Do not move the person unless they are in danger of further injury.

Evacuation procedure

If you have to leave the kitchen as the result of an emergency, remember to do the following.

- Turn off all the power supplies (gas and electricity). Some kitchens are fitted with a red button which automatically turns off all power supplies. In kitchens which do not have a red button, you will need to turn off all the appliances individually.
- Close all the windows and doors in the area.
- Never stop to gather personal possessions.
- Leave the building by the nearest emergency exit. Do not use a lift.
- Assemble in the designated area away from the building.
- Answer a roll-call of names so that everyone knows you have left the building safely.

> **Remember!**
>
> **See it! Sort it!** If you see a hazard that could cause an accident in your work area, don't just ignore it – do something to put it right to stop someone having an accident. Either:
> 1 make the hazard safe – as long as you can do so without risking your own safety
> 2 report the hazard to your supervisor as soon as you can, making sure no one enters the area without being aware of the danger.

Figure 3.15 Taking a roll call

Try this!

The table below includes some situations in which the Health and Safety at Work Act was not followed. Read the situations and answer the question for each situation.

Situation	Question
A kitchen porter kept a very strong oven cleaner in a plain white spray container under the pot wash sink. He had been trained how to use the cleaner. While the kitchen porter was on holiday the trainee chef was asked to clean the oven. She tried to use the same oven cleaner, but she had not been shown how to use it. She got the chemical on her hands, which started to blister and sting. She was taken to hospital, but the doctors had trouble knowing how to treat her because they did not know which chemical she had been using.	1 What went wrong here?
A dinner for 500 guests is held every year in the exhibition hall of a large conference centre. All the equipment and prepared food needs to be transported 300 metres from the kitchen to the hall. Last year the staff had to carry everything on trays and in large containers. Some items were so heavy that two people had to share the load. After the event, one of the chefs had to have time off work with a strained back.	2 How can this situation be avoided this year?
A young chef was asked to clean the meat slicing machine after use. He had not yet been trained how to do this but thought it should be easy enough. He took the machine apart as much as he could but then cut his hand on the sharp blade he had exposed.	3 Why was this a dangerous thing to do?
Some hot fat fell onto the solid stove top in a busy kitchen during service. The fat caught fire and spread over the cooker. The chef at the stove turned off the equipment and looked for a fire blanket to put over the flames. The case on the wall where the fire blanket should have been was empty. By the time the chef had found a foam fire extinguisher the flames had spread up the wall of the kitchen. The fire brigade had to be called to put the fire out.	4 How could this incident have been avoided?
The kitchen porter cleans the wall tiles behind the cooker once a week. He uses a very strong degreaser spray and he always wears goggles, mask, gloves and overalls to carry out the task safely. One day the strap of his goggles broke and he asked the chef for a replacement, but the chef forgot. When the kitchen porter started to clean the wall tiles, without wearing the goggles, he suffered damage to his eye from the chemical spray and had to be treated in hospital.	5 What should have happened here?

Figure 3.16 It is essential that safety equipment is kept in the right place and is in good condition

Test yourself!

1 What type of extinguisher would you use for each of these
   three types of fire?
   a Paper in a waste bin.
   b A frying pan of burning oil on a stove.
   c An electrical food mixer smoking and starting to burn.

2 Write down four safety points to follow when using electrical
   equipment.

3 Write down four safety points to follow when using knives.

4 What action should you take if you notice each of the
   following situations?
   a The handle of a floor mop has fallen across the corridor,
      blocking the way. It had been left leaning against the wall.
   b Some boxes stacked up on a high shelf are leaning to one
      side and looking as if they will soon fall down.
   c A corner of vinyl flooring has come unstuck and is likely to
      cause someone to trip over it.

Following health and safety procedures in the workplace

It is very important that everyone at work tries to work in a safe manner. Working safely helps to prevent accidents which may result in injuries to people and damage to equipment. A bad accident may mean that anyone injured might not be able to continue with their job and their health could be affected in the long term – e.g. serious injury to an arm or leg. Working safely also helps everybody to work fast and efficiently so that they can get their tasks completed to a good standard in plenty of time for service.

Many accidents can be avoided if you remember:
- clean up spillages immediately
- place a warning notice next to a slippery surface
- do not place items in corridors and walkways for any reason
- take care when lifting and carrying items
- use a trolley or sack truck whenever possible to transport large, heavy or awkward items
- get help if you cannot manage to move or clear away an item easily
- keep your work area clean and well organised
- plan the movement of all items in advance
- do not rush around the kitchen
- consider others working around you
- report unsafe equipment and surroundings.

Personal protective equipment (PPE)

In some work areas staff have to be provided with personal protective equipment to use. This is often called PPE for short. PPE is necessary where the type of work carried out means that unavoidable hazards still exist. The type of equipment involved includes:
- aprons
- overalls
- gloves
- footwear, such as boots with steel-capped toes
- goggles
- ear protectors
- face masks.

Responsibilities of employers and employees

Employers must make sure that appropriate protective equipment is available for certain tasks and that staff understand how to use it and why. The correct equipment should always be worn for the task, no matter how short a time the task will take. A stock of replacement equipment should be kept available and ready to use.

Employees must make sure they wear the protective equipment correctly to carry out the tasks necessary. If the protective equipment they are trying to use is broken or not available, they should contact their supervisor for replacements. Staff should not carry out the job without wearing the protective equipment necessary.

Safety signs

A sign is usually the best way of informing people of hazards. You could write a temporary sign yourself if there is no alternative. Better still, use a sign provided by your workplace.

Many safety signs use visual symbols which can be understood by everyone, including people who cannot read English. Signs that are in frequent use – e.g. signs for fire exits – are produced in colours that can be seen by colour-blind people.

Some hazards are temporary so the signs warning about them should also be temporary – e.g. a wet floor sign can be moved out of the way when the floor is dry. Other signs are there because of a permanent hazard – e.g. a low beam may have a permanent sign nearby warning everyone to mind their head.

Did you know?

Two good ways in which you can warn other people about hazards are:

o block the route past the hazard

o use a sign.

Figure 3.17 Blocking entry is one way of warning people about a hazard

DANGER!

Figure 3.18 Usually the best way of warning people about a hazard is to use a sign

Commonly used hazard warning signs

The colour and shape of the sign shows the type of hazard involved.

Hazard warning signs are yellow triangles. They are used where there is a risk of danger – e.g. "Mind your head", "Caution hot surface".

Prohibition signs are red circles with a line through the picture. They tell you something you must not do in the area – e.g. "No smoking"; "No mobile phones".

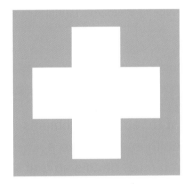

Mandatory signs are blue circles with a white picture or writing. They tell you what you must do – e.g. "Shut the door"; "Wear safety gloves".

Emergency safety signs are green with a white picture or writing. They give information about how to escape the building or where first aid equipment is – e.g. "Emergency exit" or "First aid box".

Fire fighting information signs are red with white symbols or writing. They tell you what to do in case of fire or where fire equipment is – e.g. "Fire extinguisher".

The following signs should be displayed on the containers of hazardous chemicals.

Corrosive – could burn your skin.

Poison – may kill you if swallowed.

Irritant – may cause itching or a rash if in contact with skin.

Investigate!

- ○ Which chemicals used in your workplace display these symbols?
- ○ What are these chemicals used for?
- ○ What type of protective equipment should you wear when using them?

Reporting health and safety incidents

It is important to report all problems relating to health and safety to a supervisor. You must do this so that any dangers can be put right quickly to avoid an accident happening and somebody getting hurt.

There are four main types of health and safety problems that can occur in a catering environment. The following are problems that need reporting to a supervisor.

Figure 3.19 Making your supervisor aware of a problem means that it can be fixed quickly

114

Buildings and equipment

This includes any hazards to do with the building
you are working in and the equipment you use.
For example:

- a failed light bulb on a staircase leaving it poorly lit
- a broken guard on a slicing machine
- trailing wires across a floor.

Ill health

Some health problems need reporting to a supervisor. In the
catering industry great care must be taken not to pass on
infectious diseases to other staff or customers. This means that
anyone suffering from any of the following conditions must let their
supervisor know:

- skin infections such as dermatitis, eczema and psoriasis
- notifiable diseases such as dysentery, typhoid, hepatitis,
  tuberculosis, upset stomach and food poisoning.

Illness may be brought on by activities at work – e.g. a new cleaning
chemical may react with your skin and make it sore, itchy or cause
a rash. If this happens your employer may provide you with gloves
to wear when you use this chemical in the future.

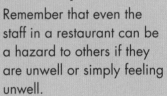

Marcus says:
Remember that even the
staff in a restaurant can be
a hazard to others if they
are unwell or simply feeling
unwell.

Environmental

Working conditions that are difficult, distracting and very
uncomfortable should also be reported to your supervisor as they
could make an accident more likely. Such conditions may include:

- continuous loud noise
- prolonged intense heat or cold.

Personal

Working in a busy kitchen with the stress of service can cause
some people to get agitated and become aggressive to their
colleagues. In extreme cases some kitchen staff may throw things
at other members of staff or be very rude to them. This behaviour
is not acceptable and should be reported as soon as it happens so
it can be dealt with.

Try this!

1 What types of hazard exist in a catering kitchen? (Think of your own workplace.)

2 Look at the picture below. How many accidents can you see waiting to happen?

3 Group the hazards according to the type: Buildings and equipment; Ill health; Environmental; Personal.

Figure 3.20 Spot the hazards in this kitchen and write them down

Reporting incidents

An incident is any event that does not come in the normal routine. Incidents can be pleasant, such as a visit from an inspector that is very positive and complimentary. Incidents can also be very unpleasant if they create damage, injury or problems in the workplace – e.g. a fire, an accident or a fight.

Most incidents in the workplace that cause problems need to be reported. An investigation may then take place to see if the same incident can be avoided in the future. Reports and investigations can also provide information for statistics produced by the health and safety industry – e.g. the number of serious accidents in the catering industry which required an injured person to be treated in hospital.

Types of incident in the workplace that require reporting include:
- accidents of any type
- spillages of chemicals or dangerous substances such as hot oil
- arguments that include verbal abuse or assault
- dangerous work practices
- theft – e.g. of cash, food, equipment or personal property.

Reporting accidents

All accidents should be reported to your supervisor. Every
workplace must have an accident book, and all accidents must be
recorded in it. This is part of Health and Safety law.

Try this!
Try to remember an accident that you have seen or one that happened to you. Then
answer these questions.
- *What happened?*
- *How many people did it involve?*
- *What pieces of equipment (if any) were involved?*
- *Did it involve any problems with the building (e.g. the floor)?*
- *How was the accident dealt with?*
- *Who dealt with it (e.g. the manager or head chef)?*
- *What did they do?*
- *Did the accident result in any changes in the area afterwards – e.g. a change
  in the position of some equipment or a different floor surface being laid?*

The key information that has to be recorded about an accident is the:
- date and time of the incident
- full name and occupation of the person involved
- type of injury
- location of the accident and what happened
- names of any witnesses to the accident
- name and job title of the person completing the report
- time and date the report was made.

A serious accident has to be reported to the Environmental Health
Officer of the local council. This may be done by phone at first and
then followed up in writing. A serious accident means: broken bones,
loss of a limb or eyesight, electric shock or any other injury which
involves the person being kept in hospital for more than 24 hours.

Accident report

Details of person involved
Name: John Smith   Occupation: Chef
Type of injury: Serious burn

Incident details
Location: Kitchen
Date: 20/11/06   Time: 19.45
Details of witness: Bob Jones, Samantha Rice, Faye Lemon

Description of what happenend:
While handling a heavy pot of boiling stock the chef slipped and
spilt the contents on his arm. He sustained heavy burns and was
sent to hospital.

Report completed by: Sarah Jane Smith
Job title: Chef
Date and time of report: 20/11/06 20.30

Figure 3.21 An accident report form

Try this!
Use a blank accident form to report the following incident.

Beryl Smith worked in the pot wash. She came to work on Monday morning as usual. After her morning break she slipped on some grease. This had dripped onto the floor from a saucepan left on her table which had tipped onto its side. She fell down, banged her head on the leg of the table and cut her ear. Martin Newman, the chef, is a first aider. He treated the cut, which soon stopped bleeding. He got Beryl to sit in the office for a while to make sure she had no ill-effects from banging her head. After about 15 minutes Beryl felt able to carry on with her work. The grease on the floor was cleared up by the kitchen porter while Beryl was being looked after.

Test yourself!

1 Name four types of personal protective equipment (PPE) that may be used in a kitchen.

2 State four kitchen tasks that may need the use of PPE.

3 Describe the colour of the following signs:
   a A sign telling you to do something – e.g. "Wear protective goggles"
   b A sign warning about a danger – e.g. "Slippery floor"
   c A sign guiding you to a way out – e.g. "Fire exit"
   d A sign telling you not to do something – e.g. "No smoking"

4. Match these signs to the written warnings.
   a Danger   b No entry   c Now wash your hands   d Emergency exit.

i    ii    iii    iv

Further information

To be able to keep a workplace healthy and safe it is important to keep up to date with new work practices and modern developments and improvements in machinery and equipment.

Possible sources of this type of information may come from:
- manufacturer's instructions that come with the equipment
- safety magazines (new regulations and safety equipment)
- British Safety Council
- Royal Society for the Prevention of Accidents
- Health and Safety Council newsletter (published by the Health and Safety Executive)
- local authorities or councils (advice given by Environmental Health Officers and Health and Safety Inspectors)
- trade press such as *Caterer and Hotelkeeper*.

Useful organisations

- St John Ambulance
- Health and Safety Executive
- Royal Society for the Prevention of Accidents
- Institute of Hospitality

You can find out more about these organisations by visiting their websites. Links have been made available at www.heinemann. co.uk/hotlinks – just enter the express code 3729P.

Practice assignment tasks

Background information

You have been asked to look after a new member of staff who is just starting work in the kitchen. It is important that they are aware of health and safety procedures and can work safely.

Task 1

You need to prepare a short presentation about safe work practices in the kitchen. Your session should include the following.

○ Information about what staff and managers have to do to keep within the health and safety law.
○ Explanations of the terms used in health and safety, e.g. hazard, Environmental Health Officer, PPE, PAT, Manual Handling, etc.
○ How health and safety procedures can help people at work.
○ What can happen if health and safety procedures are not followed in the workplace.

Task 2

Put together a presentation covering as many different health and safety signs as you can. Include the meaning of each sign. You can either draw the signs or take photographs of them to include in your presentation. Write a short quiz for your new member of staff to help them identify the signs which will be important for them.

Task 3

Prepare a list of examples of hazards in the kitchen for the new member of staff. Make sure you cover all the risks in the table below. Suggest at least one cause of each possible accident and two ways of reducing the risk. The first one has been done as an example.

Possible accident	Cause(s) of accident	Ways of reducing the risk of accident.
1 Slipping on floor	Oil spilt on floor	○ Putting out a danger sign ○ Cleaning up the oil quickly
2 Hurting your back		
3 Getting a headache		
4 Getting an electric shock		
5 Damage to your eyes from chemicals		
6 Cutting your finger badly		
7 Breathing in fumes		
8 Severe fat burn on hand and arm		

Healthier food and special diets

4

This chapter covers the following outcomes from Diploma unit 104, Introduction to healthier food and special diets

- Outcome 104.1 Be able to demonstrate awareness of healthier food
- Outcome 104.2 Be able to identify the need for special diets

Working through this chapter could also provide the opportunity to practise the following Functional Skills at Level 1:

Functional English: Speaking and listening – prepare and contribute to a formal discussion of ideas and opinions, make different kinds of contributions to discussions

In this chapter you will learn about:

- The benefits of healthy food
- Types of healthy food
- The consequences of not using healthy ingredients
- Why it is important for caterers to offer healthier options
- Where you can find more information about government initiatives
- What the current nutritional guidelines recommend
- How to change dishes and menus to make them healthier
- How to identify groups of people who may need a special diet
- How to offer the correct nutrients to vulnerable groups of people
- How to offer people on special diets the correct food to meet their needs

Demonstrate awareness of healthier food

Most foods in their basic form are healthy if they are eaten in the correct proportions. Cooking methods such as deep fat frying can make foods less healthy.

Food groups

There are four main food groups, as follows.

Carbohydrates

These are made up of three groups:
○ starches such as bread and potatoes
○ sugars such as pure sugar and sweets
○ fibre (sometimes called unavailable carbohydrates) such as wholemeal bread, brown rice and the skin of a jacket potato.

Protein

Protein is found in meat, fish and eggs, as well as nuts and pulses. Protein is the body builder and helps with the growth and repair of the body.

Fat

Fat is found in butter, cheese and dairy products. It should be eaten in limited quantities and added as little as possible when cooking.

Vitamins and minerals

These are found in all foods in small quantities. Some foods are especially high in particular vitamins and minerals.

○ Liver, cheese and eggs are a good source of vitamin A – this gives us healthier skin.
○ Oranges, blackcurrants and strawberries are a good source of vitamin C – this is good for the body's defences against disease.
○ Calcium is found in milk and dairy products and aids the growth of teeth and bones.
○ Iron is found in red meat and eggs and is good for the blood.

Remember!

There are three types of carbohydrate: starch, sugar and fibre (or unobtainable carbohydrate).
Try and remember these like this:
starch – the good carbohydrate
sugar – the bad carbohydrate
fibre – the ugly carbohydrate

Figure 4.1 The good, the bad and the ugly carbohydrates

What is a balanced diet?

A balanced diet means eating a range of foods each day in the correct proportions. The body needs a variety of different foods to be able to work well and we need different foods to stimulate our taste buds and make the foods we eat interesting. It is important to understand the correct proportions of food groups needed to enjoy a healthy and balanced diet.

The largest parts of the diet should be made up of carbohydrates such as fruit and vegetables and starchy foods. Smaller amounts of proteins are needed – meat, fish and dairy products or nuts or pulses for vegetarians. Only a very small amount of foods high in fat and sugar should be included. Many of the foods we need have been available for many years – there is nothing new about a healthy diet.

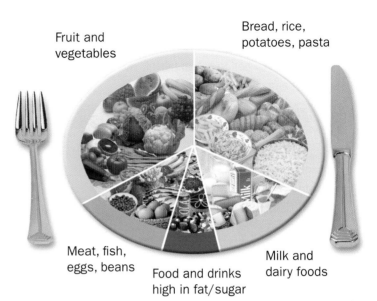

Fruit and vegetables

Bread, rice, potatoes, pasta

Meat, fish, eggs, beans

Food and drinks high in fat/sugar

Milk and dairy foods

Figure 4.2 The proportions of different types of foods needed to give a well balanced diet

Benefits of a healthy balanced diet

The benefits of a healthy balanced diet are better health and fitness with less risk of serious illnesses, such as heart attacks, diabetes and cancer. A well balanced diet will improve energy levels and give an overall improvement to the quality of life.

Many customers are now more aware of foods that are good for them and will be looking for these items on the menu. It is a good idea to describe these items as a healthy option but you must be sure that the cooking method also reflects a benefit to health. There is nothing new about healthy foods but the wider choice of foods and cooking methods available today can reduce the health benefits of the food we serve to customers.

Additional benefits of a healthy diet are that with less illness there will be fewer people needing hospital care. A caterer who can provide healthy options can also be making a contribution in this way to the whole country.

Did you know?
Bananas have been available for over one million years and give an excellent source of potassium which is very good for a healthy heart.

Try this!

Use a table like the one below to make your own Food Diary. Write down everything that you had to eat and drink yesterday — don't cheat, don't miss anything out and don't add anything extra in.

Time of day	Food	Drinks
Breakfast		
Mid morning		
Lunch time		
Afternoon		
Evening meal		
Supper		
Improvements needed		

Figure 4.3 Food diary

Now look at the table and highlight all the **healthy** things you had to eat or drink. Remember that drinks are just as important to a healthy lifestyle. In small groups discuss your food diary and see how it compares to other people in your group. Make suggestions for changes either to your diary or to others. Fill in the last box with any improvements you think you could make.

Healthy food options

Unrefined ingredients

Over many years foods have become more **refined** – e.g. white flour is often used instead of wholemeal, white rice instead of healthier brown rice.

Refined food is usually not as good for us as unrefined food. Brown rice has only the very hard outer layer of the husk removed, whereas white rice has been polished and the valuable fibre and Vitamin B content has been removed. Fibre is needed to aid digestion and prevent constipation. Brown rice may take a little longer to cook but the benefits to health outweigh this.

The same is true for flour used to make bread – wholemeal and whole grain options are much healthier and add texture and flavour to the bread.

Definition

Refined – describes food that has been processed to make it look or taste more appealing.

Fruit and vegetables

Fruit and vegetables should be a large part of all diets. The government's "five a day" campaign encourages us to eat at least five portions of fruit and vegetables every day. Fruit and vegetables are full of vitamins and are a good source of fibre. They help to maintain a healthy body weight. Fruit and vegetables can reduce the risk of heart disease and some types of cancer.

Reduced fat

It is not just the main ingredients of the food that matter but also what is added during cooking. Fat is used in a lot of food preparation and there are different types of **fat** and **oil** available.

Saturated fats such as butter and lard are bad for the heart. Saturated fats come mainly from animal fats and dairy products but can also come from palm oil and coconut oil – these should be used sparingly in recipes that claim to be for healthy eating.

Unsaturated fats can be broken down into two groups:
- polyunsaturated fats such as vegetable oils, corn oil, sunflower oil and fish oil
- monounsaturated fats such as olive oil, rapeseed oil, walnut oil and avocado oil

Unsaturated fats are better for the body than saturated fat and monounsaturated fat is especially good – it is even thought to benefit the heart by lowering cholesterol.

The body needs a certain amount of fat to give the vital organs, such as the kidneys, protection. Rather than using butter, the fat needed can be supplied from alternatives such as lower-fat spreads, olive oil spreads and the natural oil in some types of fish, e.g. mackerel.

Definition
Fat is solid, whereas **oil** is liquid. Both are classed as "fats" when talking about nutrition.

Healthy eating
Try using herbs as flavourings rather than adding high levels of salt and fats.

Try this!
Select a menu from your establishment and think about the food groups involved. Try to think of a healthier alternative for each item on the menu.

Now write a few sentences saying why you made your choices.

Many cuts of meat have a lot of fat on them – pork chops are a very good example. This does not mean that the meat cannot be used as part of a healthy menu, it just needs a little work prior to cooking. The fat can be trimmed off and the meat will then be much healthier – see Figure 4.4.

The **marbling** of fat in the meat will always remain – but this is not a problem as it helps to keep the meat tender when it is cooked. Without the marbling of fat through good-quality meat, the meat would dry out during cooking and become tough and tasteless.

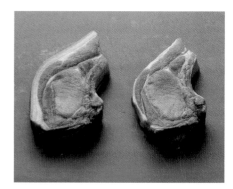

Figure 4.4 Trimming fat makes the meat healthier

Pulses

Pulses are an excellent source of protein for vegetarians and **vegans** who may otherwise lack protein that others get from meat. Pulses are the seeds of a plant and are stored dry. They include lentils, split peas, beans and chickpeas. Pulses need to be soaked before cooking. This is best done overnight. They may be used as the main ingredient of a dish or added to soups. Pulses do not contain saturated fats and are therefore a good ingredient in a healthy diet.

Definitions

Marbling – the thin white lines of fat running through the lean part of the meat.

Vegan – a strict vegetarian who will not eat anything that comes either directly (such as meat) or indirectly (eggs or dairy products) from an animal.

Consequences of poor diet

There can be serious consequences from eating a poor diet and we hear a lot about this in the media. For most people, a diet high in fat will mean an increase in weight, leading to obesity, higher risk of heart disease, low energy levels and poor skin and hair. It is always best to aim for a well-balanced diet combined with a reasonable level of exercise to maintain a healthy body.

Low immune system

Our body's immune system protects us from disease. It can be affected if the diet lacks proteins and minerals. Proteins are the "body builders" of our diet and are needed for growth and regular maintenance of the body. Vegetarians and vegans need to be particularly careful to ensure that there is enough protein in their diet.

Obesity

Obesity is a major threat to the health and well-being of our nation. We all have a responsibility to provide a healthy and well-balanced diet that will improve this situation and encourage healthy eating habits. Someone who is obese is very overweight and is putting their life in danger.

Obesity is a major cause of heart disease – if someone is very overweight their body has to work harder to cope with the strain and this puts stress on their heart. Arteries that carry the blood round the body become lined with fat and prevent them from working well. The diagram in Figure 4.5 shows a healthy artery and an artery blocked by fat where the opening is almost closed. Obesity is linked to several types of cancer, especially those of the digestive system such as stomach and bowel cancers.

As providers of food, caterers must take on a responsibility to provide healthy options and not load dishes with unnecessary fats and sugars.

Lack of energy

Excess weight will also cause energy levels to be reduced and it is then always tempting to eat something high in sugar or fat for a quick energy boost. The problem with these foods is that they only provide a very short burst of energy and do not provide the energy that the body requires over a long period of time. They also tend to leave excess fat in the body and increase the person's weight problem.

Skin problems and poor general health

A fatty diet can lead to poor skin condition and greasy hair – but there is no firm link to fatty foods being the cause of teenage acne. However, a healthy balanced diet will almost certainly improve a person's general health and allow the body to fight the acne and skin problems. Unhealthy diets that lack fresh fruit and vegetables can also cause brittle nails.

Reduced bowel function

It is important to include enough fibre in the diet to encourage healthy bowel function. Many foods can provide this much-needed fibre, but in many cases the food is refined and the fibre is removed prior to service. For example, jacket potatoes are an excellent source of fibre because the skins are left on. A less healthy option would be creamed potatoes, which have had the skin containing most of the fibre removed and also fat added.

Look back at Healthy food options on page 124 for more information.

Definition
Obesity – being very overweight.

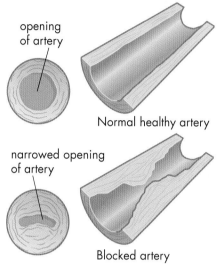

opening of artery

Normal healthy artery

narrowed opening of artery

Blocked artery

Figure 4.5 A healthy artery and an artery blocked by fat

Changing dishes to make them healthier

Caterers are now being asked for healthier choices on their menus. Customers are more aware of the health issues linked to food and diet and it is important for catering establishments to respond to this.

Here are some of the ways in which dishes can be adapted to make them healthier.

- Reduce salt and add flavour from herbs and spices.
- Reduce the amount of fat and use unsaturated fat instead of saturated fat.
- Add green vegetables that are cooked in a healthy way, such as steaming.
- Take out the vegetables that are cooked with additional fat or use a lower-fat cooking option.
- Reduce the sugar and rely more on the natural sugars from either fresh or dried fruit.
- Use less refined food – e.g. use brown rice instead of white, or potatoes in their jackets.

You can find out much more information about diet and nutrition on the internet.

Identify the need for special diets

Not everyone needs the same type of diet. As a caterer you must be aware of this and be prepared to provide suitable food for all your customers.

Some groups of people have special dietary needs because they are classed as vulnerable, for example:

o pre-school children (under 5 years old)
o pregnant women
o older people
o people who are unwell.

Other groups of people need special diets because of their beliefs or culture, or because they are allergic to certain foods.

Marcus says:

Be aware of the many different diets and allergies that can affect your diners. If you have been given the information, remember to use it!

Vulnerable groups

Pre-school children

Make food tempting to a child by arranging it on the plate to form a picture such as a face or a spaceship. This will encourage the child to try new and different-flavoured foods. If the child is very resistant to new foods you can introduce these gradually. For example, wholemeal bread could be brought in gradually by mixing white and brown bread in a checker board of mini sandwiches.

Food should be cut into small pieces so that a young child does not run the risk of choking on the food. Most children of this age will still be eating with their fingers and the small pieces will be easier to pick up. It is not your responsibility as a caterer to supervise a young child eating, but it is worth noting that they should not be left on their own when they eat. Choking can kill a young child very quickly.

Figure 4.6 How you arrange food on the plate can make it more appealing to a child

Dietary and nutritional requirements of pre-school children

Pre-school children need high-energy foods with plenty of vitamins and minerals. At this age children grow rapidly so they need a lot of calcium to strengthen their bones and teeth.

It is also important to get young children into good eating habits as this will last a lifetime. If they are given very sugary foods when they are little they will develop a taste for these that will be difficult to break. High sugar levels in sweets and drinks are also a major cause of tooth decay in young children.

Young children can also be anaemic and lack iron in their blood, so it is important that at least one iron-rich food is served daily. Red meat is a good source of iron. Pulses also contain iron, so for vegetarian children serve peas, beans or lentils. Dark green vegetables such as spinach and broccoli are also very good sources of iron, but make sure that they are not overcooked.

You should take care not to give a diet that is too high in fibre, as a small child's digestion may not be able to cope with this. As a general rule a child should have their age plus 5 grams of fibre a day. So, for example, a 4-year-old needs about 9 grams of fibre a day.

Always try to offer foods that do not contain too many additives, such as artificial flavourings and colourings, as these can cause **hyperactivity** in young children. Try to rely on the natural sweetness in fruit rather than adding sugar to a dish. Choose foods that have natural colour to make them attractive to the child.

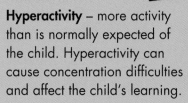

Definition

Hyperactivity – more activity than is normally expected of the child. Hyperactivity can cause concentration difficulties and affect the child's learning.

Try this!

The table in Figure 4.7 shows some of the foods to avoid for young children and ideas to replace them. Copy and complete the table. Think of some good substitutes for the last three items and add your own ideas at the bottom.

Food and drink to avoid	Good substitutes
Fizzy drinks	Fresh fruit juice and water
White bread	Wholemeal bread
Tinned vegetables	Fresh vegetables
Burgers and sausages	Lean meat and chicken
Tinned fruit	
Fruit drinks	
Ready meals	

Figure 4.7 Healthy food alternatives for young children

Expectant mothers

During pregnancy the unborn baby is completely dependent on the food it gets from its mother. So the mother's diet is vital for the health of her baby. It is important that an expectant mother does not put on too much weight as this can affect her health and that of her unborn baby. It is not true that a pregnant woman should "eat for two". Even in the final three months of pregnancy a woman only needs 200 calories a day more than normal to maintain a healthy weight.

Dietary and nutritional requirements of expectant mothers

An expectant mother needs a diet rich in iron, calcium and folic acid. Folic acid is particularly important in the first 12 weeks of pregnancy. Fresh vegetables and fruit are good sources of folic acid. They should be cooked simply without the addition of fats.

There are also key foods to avoid during pregnancy. These include liver and any products containing liver. This is because liver contains high levels of vitamin A and this can harm the unborn baby.

Many pregnant women complain of indigestion because the baby is pressing on their digestive organs. For this reason rich and spicy foods should be avoided. Unpasteurised cheese is also not recommended.

Figure 4.8 Pregnant women need a special diet

Older people

Generally as people get older their muscle mass decreases and they are not as strong as they were when they were younger. However, this can vary greatly depending on how active a person is. Some older people remain very active, regularly taking part in sport, gardening or dancing. Others may lead a quieter lifestyle, perhaps reading, watching TV or carrying out hobbies from their armchair. It is important to know the activity level of the older person you are catering for when you plan their menu.

Older people are also more vulnerable to disease and infections because their immune system is not as strong as in younger, fitter adults. This means that they are also more likely to get food poisoning, so you must take particular care with food hygiene.

Older people often have smaller appetites than when they were younger, and they usually feel less thirsty as well. An older person may not have such a good sense of taste or smell and so food needs

Did you know?
Folic acid helps to prevent problems like spina bifida in the baby.

to be appetising to encourage them to eat. Some older people have dentures, and this can make chewing food quite difficult. Soft foods offered in small portions can help with this problem.

Dietary and nutritional requirements of older people

Older people should be encouraged to drink plenty of fluids, but not excessive alcohol. Offer smaller portions with a variety of fresh foods to stimulate a low appetite level. Make sure that the food provides a good source of nutrients and that cooking methods do not reduce the natural nutrition the food has to offer.

Vitamin D is important in the diet of older people. It occurs naturally through exposure to sunlight, but older people with frail skin may not want to be out in the sun for long periods of time. Foods rich in vitamin D are oily fish such as mackerel, sardines and salmon.

Always include fibre-rich foods as the bowel function can also be weakened in an older person, causing constipation and making it uncomfortable for them to go to the toilet. Include lots of fresh fruit and vegetables to give a range of vitamins and minerals.

Osteoporosis affects one in five women over 50 years of age. It causes bones to become brittle and break easily. This is a painful illness and can restrict the quality of life of the sufferer. A diet rich in calcium will assist the person to a healthier lifestyle.

People suffering from ill health

When a person is ill their immune system has a lower activity level and their body is less able to defend itself from infection. A healthy diet is vital to encourage recovery. Many people do not feel like eating when they are ill, so it is your responsibility to prepare and serve food that will not only help to repair their body but encourage them to eat.

Dietary and nutritional requirements of people with ill health

Always try to select dishes that have a high nutritional value, are easily digested and look appealing. Spicy and fatty foods should be avoided, but do make sure that the meals are still tasty and appealing. Always ask for feedback on the meals served to people who are ill and learn from what they tell you.

Figure 4.9 Food being served to an older person

Definition

Osteoporosis – the loss of bone mass. It can be treated with hormone replacement treatment and is helped by a calcium-rich diet.

Remember!

A sick person may be in bed with little opportunity to move around. They do not want indigestion to cope with as well as their existing illness. They may dream of cream cakes but these may not be the best food to aid recovery!

Figure 4.10 What an ill person dreams of eating is not always what is best for their recovery

Try this!

Select one of the vulnerable groups from this section and plan a birthday party menu that meets the nutritional requirements of the group and looks attractive, interesting and is full of healthy options. You may wish to prepare some of the dishes and arrange a tasting session with your friends. If you have selected a group that may not be able to eat with a knife and fork, make sure that you try eating the food with your fingers or with just one hand.

Other special dietary needs

Other groups who may require different diets are:

○ vegetarians
○ vegans
○ cultural and religious groups
○ diabetics
○ people with allergies or food intolerances.

Vegetarian

A vegetarian generally avoids all products which need an animal to be killed to produce them. A person may be vegetarian because they are against any suffering caused to animals, for religious reasons or they just may not like meat. A vegetarian will not eat meat, fish or chicken but usually will eat milk, butter and free range eggs. Some vegetarians will eat any types of cheese but others will want special vegetarian cheese that has been hardened without the use of animal **rennet**.

Definition

Rennet – a product produced from a calf's stomach used to harden cheese. A vegetarian may well refuse cheese made with rennet.

Dietary and nutritional requirements of vegetarians

When planning a vegetarian menu always be aware that it is very easy to load dishes with dairy products and fats. Include nuts, pulses and soya products in your menu, with a wide range of fresh vegetables and fruits. Make sure that there is a balance of healthy and tasty ingredients on offer in your dishes.

Try this!

Select one item from your regular menu and adapt it for a vegetarian.

Vegan

A vegan is a very strict vegetarian who will not eat any animal-based products, including milk, cheese, butter, eggs and honey. Often a vegan will not wear wool or leather and will not use cosmetics or soaps that may contain animal products.

Dietary and nutritional requirements of vegans

The protein needed for a healthy vegan diet must be supplied entirely from pulses, beans, nuts and cereals. These do not have as much protein in them as meat and so a variety of these ingredients will be needed. Extra bulk can be gained from carbohydrates such as potatoes and rice.

The cereals will also provide some of the calcium that is missing when dairy products are removed from the diet. Less calcium in the diet can be a particular problem if the vegan is very young and the bones are still growing. It is important to remember when cooking for a vegan that no animal fats must be used in the cooking process – only vegetable-based oils and spreads can be used.

Figure 4.11 A vegan diet includes fruit, vegetables, pulses, beans, nuts and cereals

Cultural and religious diets

The cultural and religious beliefs of many people are vital to their way of life and must be respected by the caterer. When preparing food for a customer with a particular belief you should never feel afraid to ask them for advice. Usually they will be only too happy to help you. We all have a right to our own beliefs and customs and we can learn much from each other about customs that may be new to us.

Dietary and nutritional requirements of people with cultural or religious diets

The chart in Figure 4.12 provides a guide to the different foods that may or may not be acceptable to different customers. It provides just a basic guideline and covers only some religious groups.

Food	Orthodox Hindus	Non-orthodox Hindus	Sikhs	Muslims	Jews
Alcohol	No	Yes	Some	No	Yes†
Beef and Offal	No	No	No	Yes*	Yes†
Lamb and Offal	No	Yes	Yes	Yes*	Yes†
Pork, Ham and Bacon	No	No	No	No	No
Poultry	No	Yes	Yes	Yes*	Yes†
Eggs	Some	Yes	Yes	Yes	Yes†
Milk and Milk Products	Yes	Yes	Yes	Yes	Yes†
Oily Fish	No	No	Yes	Yes	Yes†
White Fish	No	Yes	Yes	Yes	Yes†
Shellfish	No	Some	Yes	No	No
*All meat must be Halal – this means ritually slaughtered. †All food must be Kosher – the meat and poultry must be ritually slaughtered; fish must have fins and scales; milk and meat products must be prepared and eaten separately.					

Figure 4.12 Foods that may and may not be acceptable to different customers

Diabetic

There are two types of diabetes. Type 1 diabetes requires the person to inject insulin every day as their body no longer makes insulin for them. Type 2 diabetes is more common and does not need injections but the person may take tablets to control the condition. Both types require a regular diet of healthy food.

Dietary and nutritional requirements of diabetics

A diabetic person needs a diet high in fibre and low in fat that is also rich in nutrients.

Diabetes can also be linked to heart disease and high blood pressure, so a low salt diet is very important. Try not to season food with salt but use herbs in cooking to add flavour.

The other thing you must be aware of is the need for control of alcohol.

Food allergies and intolerance

Food allergies and intolerances can affect people in many different and very severe ways. They are due to the body's immune system reacting to the chemicals in certain foods. In all cases these foods **must** be avoided. It is essential that there is no possibility of cross-

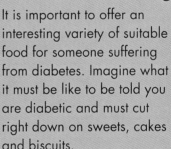

Remember!

It is important to offer an interesting variety of suitable food for someone suffering from diabetes. Imagine what it must be like to be told you are diabetic and must cut right down on sweets, cakes and biscuits.

135

contamination in the food preparation area as some allergies are so severe that even the smallest amount of an intolerable food can make a customer very ill.

As with all of the special diets that you have learned about in this chapter, it is important that you continue to offer an interesting and varied diet so that the customer does not feel they are being left out and not getting the delicious meal that their friends are enjoying.

Investigate!

Look at the Food Reactions and Allergies website for much helpful information on food intolerance and additives. Go to www.heinemann.co.uk/hotlinks and enter the express code 3729P.

Dietary and nutritional requirements of people with allergies and intolerances

The foods to be especially careful about are:
- cows' milk – dairy intolerance is often linked to eczema
- gluten in wheat and barley – intolerance can cause a bowel disorder called coeliac disease
- soya products – allergy to soya can give skin rashes but is not generally very serious
- nuts, especially peanuts – nut allergies are often in the news as they can be very severe, especially in children – they can cause anything from a tingling in the mouth to severe shock and death
- shellfish (particularly clams, lobster, prawns and shrimps) – allergies can put the body into severe shock and immediate attention is needed – generally only adults are affected
- fish – allergies produce similar reactions to shellfish and affect both adults and children
- fruits – can cause problems, especially grapefruit which is one to avoid if the customer is diabetic
- spices – can cause a reaction in some people, especially hot spices like chilli.

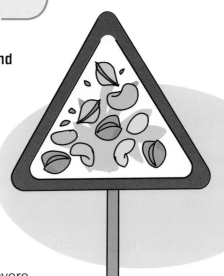

Figure 4.13 Nut allergies are particularly dangerous

Top marks!

List some examples of healthy and less healthy dishes with details of their ingredients. You should provide references for your information as this is good practice and will also encourage others to find out more.

Further information

It is essential to keep up to date with information and the following websites will give you excellent sources of information. Links to these websites have been made available at www.heinemann. co.uk/hotlinks – just enter the express code 3729P.

The Food Standards Agency
The British Nutrition Foundation
The Department of Health
Five a Day Campaign
Department of Environment, Food & Rural Affairs
Schools Food Trust
Food in Schools
BBC Healthy Living
Diabetes UK
British Heat Foundation
Coeliac UK
Food Reactions and Allergies
The Vegetarian Society
The Vegan Society

Test yourself!

1 Give three benefits of a healthy diet. You can include pictures to illustrate your answer.

2 Name a healthy alternative to each of the following:
   - chips
   - sherry trifle
   - chocolate bar.

3 Name three vulnerable groups of people and explain why they are vulnerable.

4 Plan a packed lunch for an elderly person going on a coach trip.

Practice assignment tasks

Task 1

Choose a main course dish that you know how to cook. Think about how each ingredient works in the dish and suggest how you could replace it with a healthier option if necessary. Do the same for the methods used to cook the dish and suggest ways in which these could be made healthier.

Task 2

Once you have decided on the changes that you plan to make, try out your dishes to check that your ideas work. Take photographs to remind yourself of what the different versions of the dish look like. Ask other people to taste your dish to see which options they prefer. Record their comments in a table or chart to help you to remember what people thought about each different version. Think about the side dishes that you may serve with your main dish and prepare these too.

Task 3

Once you have tried out several different options, think about how you might advertise the final version of your dish to make it a top-selling menu option. Finally cook the dish and use this as your "model" in your advertising on the menu.

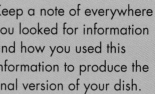

Top marks!

Keep a note of everywhere you looked for information and how you used this information to produce the final version of your dish. Always keep all your rough notes so that your tutor can see the "journey" that your dish has taken.

Task 4

Produce a wall chart that could give information about special dietary needs to be used in a hospital kitchen. Include at least two types of vulnerable people and two groups who need to follow a special diet. Make sure the chart is interesting and informative, easy to read from a distance and gives clear and concise information and reference sources.

Introduction to kitchen equipment

5

This chapter covers the following outcomes from Diploma unit 105: Introduction to kitchen equipment

- o Outcome 105.1 Be able to use large and small items of equipment and utensils
- o Outcome 105.2 Be able to use knives and cutting equipment

Working through this chapter could also provide the opportunity to practise the following Functional Skills at Level 1:

Functional English: Writing – write clearly and coherently, including an appropriate level of detail; present information in a logical sequence; use language, format and structure suitable for purpose and audience and possibly, if investigating costings, scaling recipes involves N1.2 ratio and proportion

and Functional Skills in:
- o Mathematics
- o English
- o ICT

In this chapter you will learn how to:

- o Select equipment and utensils safely
- o Use equipment and utensils correctly and safely
- o Identify the hazards involved in using, cleaning and storing equipment and utensils
- o Carry out routine care and storage of equipment and utensils
- o Identify the different types of knives and cutting equipment and utensils
- o State the importance of correct and safe use of knives and cutting equipment
- o Identify age restrictions in the use of cutting equipment

Use large and small items of equipment and utensils

In a professional kitchen you will find a wide variety of large and small equipment. The equipment will have been purchased and positioned to suit the menu and the type of operation it is expected to serve.

In this section we will identify and explain the various types of large and small equipment used in most commercial kitchens.

Large equipment

A lot of professional kitchens have a central range under an extractor fan canopy where the majority of the large cooking equipment is positioned. Most large equipment uses electricity or gas as its main power source, although oil and solid fuel equipment (such as wood-burning pizza ovens) is also available.

The following points need to be considered:
- fuel type
- menu
- available space
- energy efficiency
- ease of cleaning – e.g. is an oven self-cleaning? Is a fryer self-filtering?

Ovens

Conventional oven

This is the basic oven, which uses either gas or electricity. It is usually situated beneath a solid top or six or four ring hob. A gas oven will have a pilot light that is lit manually and it will also have a manual temperature control.

Fan-assisted convection oven

Convection ovens have the advantage of an electric fan or blower to circulate the hot air inside the sealed oven space. The advantage of this type of oven is that it will provide a more even and constant temperature through the oven and will allow the food to be cooked evenly in any part of the oven. The heat is used more efficiently, so the cooking temperature can be lower and the cooking time is often less. This means that energy savings can be made.

Figure 5.1 A central cooking range

Figure 5.2 A convection fan oven

Chefs like convection ovens as the quality of the food is retained – food shrinks less, the surface colour and texture change rapidly and more flavour and moisture are retained (especially in meats).

Combination (steam/dry heat) oven

This type of oven can be programmed to be a dry oven or a steamer or a combination of both. These ovens are usually more complicated to operate and staff need to be trained to use them.

These ovens are automatic and can be programmed to produce exact cooking times using either of the cooking methods or a combination of the two. They are widely used in the catering industry for baking, roasting and steaming and are especially used in banqueting operations or industrial catering to reheat foods.

Figure 5.3 A combination steam/dry heat oven

Microwave ovens

In professional kitchens, microwave ovens need to be more hard-wearing than the ones used by most people in their homes, because of the increased use they will have. They come in different sizes with varying levels of power and functions, including defrosting and browning. Microwave ovens cook and heat food using high-frequency power. The microwaves disturb the molecules in the food, causing friction and heat.

Figure 5.4 A commercial microwave oven

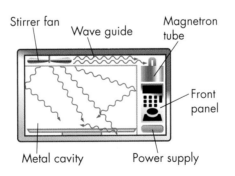

Figure 5.5 How a microwave oven works

Top marks!

Compare the advantages and disadvantages of using gas or electricity as the source of energy for your major kitchen equipment.

Hobs

Induction hobs

This type of hob has only recently been developed to meet the needs of a modern kitchen. They have a copper coil beneath a ceramic plate. This reacts with the metal in the base of the saucepan and produces heat directly in the pan. If the pan is removed detectors automatically turn off the power, which saves energy.

The advantages of induction cookers include: easy to clean, energy efficient, safer to use as only the pan gets hot.

Figure 5.6 An induction hob and how it works

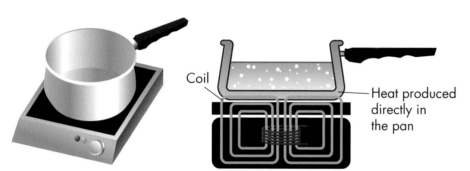

Solid top

A solid top hob supports a number of different-sized pots and frying pans. The heat is concentrated in the middle and rear, where the main gas burner is sited. This area is used for rapid heating. Pans are moved away from this area once the required heat is reached. The best way of using this type of hob depends on the method of cooking different foods, and you will learn from experience how to do this.

Figure 5.7 A solid top hob

Open range

Open ranges have a number of gas burners (four, six or eight) that can be used for rapid heating and boiling. Some open ranges have large gas burners and tops that are used for wok cooking.

Both the solid top and open range usually come with a thermostatically controlled oven and shelves.

All burners can be lit using manual or electric spark ignition buttons.

Figure 5.8 An open range hob

Grills

Also known as a salamander, the grill is heated from above using gas or electricity with one or more rows of heating elements or jets.

Char grills

Char grills cook food such as steaks on a grill but above variable heat gas heated steel bars. It is a similar cooking method to a barbecue but is used indoors. It is now a popular method of cookery as the food that is cooked in this way remains moist and is a healthy method of cooking.

Figure 5.9 A grill

Steamers

Modern steamers can be used for a number of cooking methods in addition to steaming, including stewing, poaching, braising and roasting. In modern commercial kitchens, a combination steamer/oven is most often used – see Figure 5.3.

Fryers

As the range, convenience and variety of pre-prepared foods has been developed deep fat fryers have become one of the most used items of equipment in catering kitchens. A fryer is essentially a pot filled with oil. The cooking oil can be heated by gas or electricity and there is a thermostatic control to prevent overheating and the cooking oil catching fire.

Fryers can be manual or programmable, freestanding or tabletop. Modern fryers can have additional functions such as computer control programs that automatically switch the fryer on and off, calculate the exact time and temperature of the cooking process, and even basket lifting when the food is ready.

Remember!

Safety when using fryers
You must be extremely careful to ensure food is cooked at the correct temperature and that the fryer is regularly cleaned, maintained and the thermostat tested. Staff who are responsible for the operation and cleaning must be properly trained and aware of the dangers of hot cooking oil to themselves and others.

Figure 5.10 A modern, freestanding deep fat fryer

Did you know?

10,000 tonnes of used cooking oil are produced in the UK every week! Used cooking oil must be disposed of safely through recycling. This will be closely monitored by local environmental health officers and local authorities. Waste cooking oil is classed as a hazardous substance and its disposal is strictly regulated. It must never be put down drains or sinks as the oil will build up causing blockages in the sewerage system and any food waste in the oil will attract pests, especially rodents.

The "duty of care" standards regulated by the European Union and enforced in the UK are:

1 Waste oil is collected on a regular basis by a licensed contractor.
2 Any waste collected will receive an official receipt known as a "Controlled waste transfer collection note".
3 Waste oil must be removed in containers with lids.

Investigate!
Find out a use for used cooking oil.

Cold holding equipment

Refrigerators

High risk foods and those that spoil quickly need to be stored in a refrigerator. Most professional kitchens have more than one refrigerator to keep raw and high risk foods separate. Types of refrigerator include: large walk in, stand alone, counter table and display cabinet models. All types are produced specifically for the catering industry to comply with current legislation. They have digital temperature-monitoring displays operating at 0–5°C and sound an alarm if anything malfunctions.

Remember!
See Chapter 2 for further information on the cold storage of food.

Freezers

Freezing allows food to be kept longer without spoiling. There is a vast amount of frozen food available which allows the caterer to offer a wider menu choice. Modern freezers come in a variety of models, including: walk in, vertical stand alone and chest freezer models. They operate below –18°C.

Figure 5.11 A commercial fridge and freezer – both with digital temperature displays

Hot holding equipment

Hot cupboards, hot plates and counter service equipment are designed to store all types of cooked food for up to four hours at a safe, hot holding temperature of 63°C and above. The heating elements are not powerful enough to heat the food quickly and should not be used for this purpose.

Bain marie

A bain marie is one type of hot holding equipment that keeps food at a safe hot temperature. Again, it should not be used to reheat food.

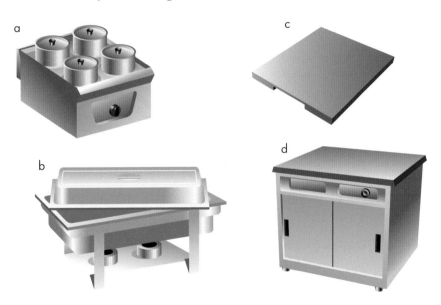

Figure 5.12 a) a bain marie, b) a chafing dish, c) an aluminium hot plate, d) a hot cupboard

Did you know?

Chafing dishes are mobile bain maries and use hot water heated with fuel burners.

Marcus says:

There are many different pieces of equipment, some with English names and some with French. You may hear both names in a kitchen.

Top marks!

Research how energy can be saved in a kitchen.

Chef's tip

Top energy saving tips

1 Turn on items of equipment only when needed.
2 Turn down the heat control knob down when it is not immediately needed. If the equipment is not needed for a longer time than it takes to heat up again, turn it off.
3 Cook more than one item of food on a stove or in an oven to make best use of the energy cost.
4 Replace old kitchen equipment with new, as old equipment was not built with today's energy efficiency performance.
5 Ensure fridge doors are kept closed. Open doors waste energy as the fridge tries to bring the temperature back down to its set thermostat level.

Small equipment

Scales – used to weigh ingredients in kilograms and grams and/ or pounds and ounces. Modern scales have digital displays making the weighing very accurate.

Measuring jugs – used to measure volumes of liquids and have a graduated scale on the side.

Mixers – popular labour-saving devices that come in a variety of sizes and models. They use a high-speed motor and blades to chop, purée or blend foods such as soups and sauces.

Food processor – has a high-speed cutting blade and variety of attachments to help with vegetable preparation or use as a liquidiser. It speeds up **mise en place** such as slicing or grating and produces a consistently high standard. Safety features are incorporated to ensure the operator is in no danger when the power is turned on.

Figure 5.13 a) scales, b) measuring jug, c) blender, d) mortar and pestle, e) spoons, f) skimmer, g) spatula, h) spider, i) fish or egg slice, j) ladles, k) whisk, l) tongs, m) cutlet bat

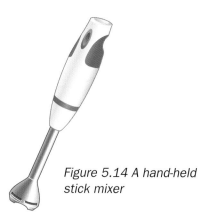

Figure 5.14 A hand-held stick mixer

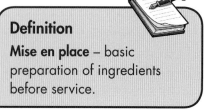

Definition

Mise en place – basic preparation of ingredients before service.

Figure 5.15 A food processor

Mortar and pestle – used to grind herbs and spices into powders and pastes.

Spoons – can be solid or perforated and have heat-resistant handles.

Skimmer – used for removing impurities on top of stocks and soups.

Rolling pin – used to roll out pastry.

Spatulas – made of high-density plastic and used in non-stick frying pans and dishes.

Spiders – used to remove items from oil and boiling water.

Slices – used for a variety of tasks including frying, turning and serving food.

Ladles – come in a variety of sizes; used to measure out liquids, skim the top of stocks and serve soups and sauces.

Tongs – used for handing and serving certain foods safely – e.g. sausages.

Whisks – come in a variety of types and sizes; used for mixing solids and liquids together or get air into a mixture, e.g. egg whites when making a meringue.

Cutlet bat – used to tenderise steaks before cooking or coating with breadcrumbs.

Figure 5.16 a) saucepans, b) sauté pan, c) griddle pan, d) wok, e) bowls, f) cooling rack, g) baking tins and trays, h) strainer, i) colander

Saucepans – come in a variety of shapes and sizes with one or two handles and lids.

Sauté pans – designed for cooking main dishes that are first fried and then a stock and sauce added before finishing in the oven.

Griddle pans – used to fry food, allowing the juices and fat to drain.

Woks – used in Chinese cooking to stir fry dishes.

Bowls – come in a variety of shapes and sizes; used for storage and mixing ingredients.

Trays – used to lay out food before cooking or storing. They come in a variety of shapes, sizes and depths.

Cooling racks – used to allow air flow around products that need to be cooled quickly, e.g. cakes and biscuits.

Baking tins and trays – come in a variety of sizes; used in baking.

Moulds – come in a variety of sizes; used in baking.

Sieves – come in a variety of sizes; used to sift any impurities or lumps out of food such as flour.

Strainers – come in a variety of sizes; used to drain liquids from food, e.g. vegetables cooked in water.

Colanders – come in a variety of sizes; used to drain liquids from food, e.g. vegetables cooked in water.

Materials used to make kitchen utensils

Small equipment and utensils are made from a variety of materials, including:

- stainless steel
- non-stick coated metal
- iron
- aluminium.

Stainless steel

This is a widely used material for many items of small equipment and heavy duty pans. The saucepans usually have an extra thick base that allows for excellent heat distribution. Stainless steel has the added advantage that it does not rust.

Non-stick coated metal

A wide variety of non-stick kitchen utensils (saucepans, frying pans, baking and roasting trays) are available and used in many types of catering operations. Care should be taken not to damage the non-stick coating. You should:

- avoid excessive heat over prolonged periods
- use plastic spatulas or other non-stick utensils to avoid scratching the surface
- use cloths or paper to clean, never use scourers.

Figure 5.17 Non-stick kitchen utensils

Iron

Black wrought iron is used for items of equipment such as frying pans and omelette pans that need to withstand extreme direct heat. Special attention needs to be taken when preparing and storing black wrought iron. The fewer times they are washed the more effective they are. Before use they should be lightly oiled. After use while they are still warm, simply wipe clean using a dry cloth.

Aluminium

Aluminium is not widely used any more in catering equipment as stainless steel is the preferred choice. Aluminium does have the advantage of strength and durability, but it is expensive. It has the disadvantage of causing some food to discolour – e.g. white sauces and cabbage.

Figure 5.18 Black wrought iron kitchen utensil

Cleaning and maintenance of kitchen equipment

Regular cleaning, disinfection and maintenance of kitchen equipment are vitally important to prevent the build up of grease and dirt that can cause food to be contaminated and food poisoning bacteria to breed. It is also a legal requirement for all food premises to keep premises and equipment clean. See Chapter 2 on Food Safety.

All catering equipment has to be manufactured to allow it to be cleaned easily. Large items of equipment need to be cleaned regularly and should be inspected by your supervisor as part of the company's hazard analysis of food safety.

Investigate!
One hazard analysis system in use is called "Safer Food Better Business". Find out what this is. What are the 4 Cs?

149

Cleaning large equipment

It is not usually possible or practical to dismantle large items of catering equipment and specialist companies will be contracted to carry out a "deep clean" on a regular basis, e.g. every 3 or 6 months. However, this is not an alternative to regular cleaning on a daily, weekly or monthly basis, depending on how much the equipment is used.

All equipment is manufactured with ease of cleaning in mind and it will be possible for trained staff to dismantle and reassemble. The procedures are determined by the management who will draw up a cleaning schedule and checklist that must be followed. Records should be kept of when the cleaning has taken place.

When cleaning any large item of catering equipment you should do the following.

1 Switch off and unplug or isolate the power supply
2 Allow equipment such as ovens and grills to cool down.
3 Remove any parts that could be cleaned in a sink, e.g. oven shelves.
4 Remove any particles of food using a cleaning cloth or brush.
5 Do not use any chemicals until you have been trained to use them. Follow the manufacturer's instructions on the cleaning solution or powder for the protective clothing you should be wearing (rubber gloves and apron at a minimum). Follow the instructions on how to use, e.g. dilution ratio. These can be found on the container or on an information poster. Thoroughly clean all parts inside and out using a suitable detergent and disinfectant such as a sanitiser.
6 Rinse thoroughly, dry and reassemble the machine.
7 Test that you have reassembled the machine correctly.
8 Store all your cleaning equipment correctly.
9 Note on the cleaning schedule what you have cleaned.
10 Inform your supervisor of any problems.

Cleaning small equipment and utensils

Small items of electrical equipment such as food processors or hand blenders should not be submerged in water. These should be unplugged before cleaning and any removable parts cleaned separately in the sink.

The majority of small equipment should be cleaned using the six
stages of cleaning method described in Chapter 2:

1 Pre-clean
2 Main clean
3 Rinse
4 Disinfect
5 Final rinse
6 Dry.

There are three ways of cleaning:
1 by hand (stages 1–6)
2 by machine (stages 2–6)
3 by hand and machine (stages 1–6).

Most kitchens will have a specific wash area, where only cleaning
is carried out. In larger kitchens there may be a specially designed
utensil washer or conveyor belt-type washer that is used. In
each case it is important that utensils are thoroughly cleaned,
disinfected and dried before use.

You may need to use special techniques for cleaning certain items,
such as avoiding the use of certain chemicals or metal scourers
that could damage coatings of non-stick pans.

Take special care when cleaning sieves, strainers and graters as
food particles can clog the holes. These can be pre-cleaned using
the force of water from the tap or with a brush.

Take care when cleaning sharp instruments such as the blades
from a food processor or a mandolin slicer. Following the rules for
knives, these should never be left unattended in a sink.

Piping bags made of plastic should be cleaned using hot water,
rinsed and allowed to dry.

Figure 5.19 A utensil washer

Safe and hygienic storage of equipment
and utensils

The storage of small items of catering equipment and utensils
needs careful planning. In a busy kitchen chefs in each section
need to have the pots and pans they use frequently close to hand.
This prevents unnecessary movement between stations, which
would cause delays and getting in each other's way.

151

Large and small items of equipment are stored on stainless steel or metal racking with a number of shelves. The storage needs to be planned for ease of use and also health and safety reasons.

○ Large, heavy equipment should be stored on lower shelves.
○ Saucepans or containers should be stored upside down to ensure the drying process is completed and to prevent physical contamination.
○ All handles of pans should be facing inwards.
○ Utensils can be hung on the sides of the racking.

Knives

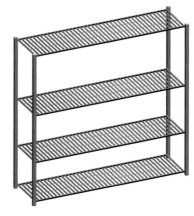

Figure 5.20 A utensil rack

Where a kitchen supplies knives for staff to use (most chefs have and look after their own) a number of options are available for safe storages. These are:
○ knife wallets
○ knife blocks
○ magnetic knife racks.

It is not safe to store knives in drawers or loose in containers as accidents may occur. Special consideration as to hygiene should be taken with knife wallets, chefs' knife boxes and wooden blocks as these can harbour dangerous bacteria.

Safe use of cleaning materials

It is essential to use cleaning materials and chemicals correctly and safely. For instruction in how to use chemicals safely, see page 102 of Chapter 3.

When cleaning areas of the kitchen or specific pieces of equipment:
○ always use the correct cleaning chemical for the job
○ use any specialist equipment and personal protective equipment (PPE) required
○ always follow the instructions provided with the cleaning chemicals used in your workplace.

Figure 5.21 is an example of safety instructions for use with cleaning chemicals.

Application

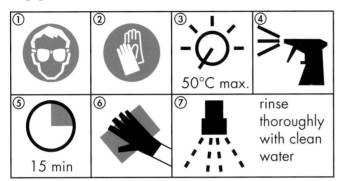

Ingredients: <5%: Non-ionic surfactants, anionic surfactants

Corrosive

Contains Sodium Hydroxide.
R35 Causes severe burns. S2 Keep out of the reach of children. S26 in case of contact with eyes, rinse immediately with plenty of water and seek medical advice. S36/37/39 Wear suitable protective clothing, gloves and eye/face protection. S45 In case of accident or if you feel unwell, seek medical advice immediately (show the label where possible).

Figure 5.21 Example of a cleaning chemical's safety instructions

Test yourself!

1 Name three large pieces of catering equipment you would use to produce a three-course meal.

2 Name six items of small equipment or utensils you would need to produce a three course meal.

3 What cleaning and protective equipment would you use to clean the kitchen at the end of the day?

Use knives and cutting equipment

In this section you will learn how to handle, maintain and care for your knives and other kitchen cutting equipment. It is important that you carefully and correctly select and use appropriate tools and equipment for each cutting task. Most professional chefs own and look after their own knives.

It is vital that you are aware of the safety rules and considerations for the use of knives. Knife skills, including selection, care, food safety and sharpening, will be assessed during your practical assessments.

Range of knives and cutting equipment

Always use the correct knife for the job. A knife that is too large will be a danger to you as you will not have control and will be more likely to have an accident.

Straight-edged knives

a Cook's knives – come in various sizes and have strong rigid blades. They are suitable for most basic jobs in the kitchen, such as cutting vegetables, chopping herbs, shredding, dicing and slicing meat or poultry.

b Paring knife – a small knife with a thin and flexible blade, making it ideal for preparing small fruits and vegetables.

c Turning knife – similar to a paring knife but with a curved cutting edge; used for shaping mushrooms or turning vegetables such as potatoes and carrots into barrels.

d Filleting knife – a knife with a thin bladed, available in various lengths; used mainly for filleting meat or fish.

e Boning knife – needs to have a strong blade that will not break easily. Available in various styles, including straight and curved blades. Used for removing bones from joints of meat and poultry.

f Carving knife – has a long blade with either a pointed or rounded end and either a serrated or straight edge; used for carving joints such as ham on the bone.

g Palette knife – has a plain or serrated edge with a flexible or rounded top; used for cake decoration or turning food during cooking.

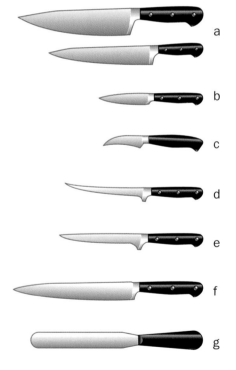

Figure 5.22 A set of straight-edged knives: a) cook's knives, b) paring knife, c) turning knife, d) filleting knife, e) boning knife, f) carving knife, g) palette knife

Serrated-edged knives

Bread knife – usually has a long, narrow blade with a serrated edge.

Saw knife – used to cut through the bones of carcasses of meat to produce a clean cut and prevent bone splinters.

Cleaning knives

Chefs who use knives should be responsible for cleaning and maintaining them. It is important that both the handle and the blade are kept clean. This will prevent any chance of your hand slipping while you use it and bacteria spreading. Wash your knives thoroughly in between tasks using detergent sanitiser. Take great care when cleaning to keep your fingers away from the sharp edge of the blade. Knives should then be rinsed using very hot water and dried thoroughly using a clean disposable paper towel.

Sharpening knives

A sharp knife will allow you to perform your cutting tasks easily and efficiently to the standard required for the recipe. Blunt knives mean you have to apply more pressure and are more likely to slip and cause an accident to yourself or others.

You must know how to maintain the sharpness of your knives using a wet stone or steel. Incorrect use can be dangerous. With really blunt knives the steel will not bring the sharpness back to the blade. It may be necessary to take them to someone such as your local butcher who will be able to use a grinding stone to sharpen the blade.

Your lecturer will also demonstrate how to perform these tasks safely.

Knives should always be thoroughly cleaned after sharpening as there may be metal filings on the blade.

Using a sharpening stone

A sharpening stone has two sides – one coarse, one fine. You will either have a wet stone or an oil stone. Depending on the type, it should be soaked in water or mineral oil – not both.

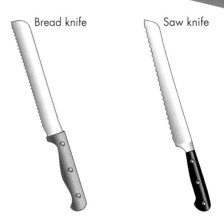

Bread knife   Saw knife

Figure 5.23 Serrated-edged knives: a) bread knife, b) saw knife

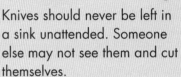

Remember!
Knives should never be left in a sink unattended. Someone else may not see them and cut themselves.

Chef's tip
A good way to test whether a knife is sharp enough is to slice a tomato.

155

1

Place the stone on a damp cloth to stabilise it.

2

Hold the knife at an angle on the stone – 20 degrees is ideal.

3

Draw the whole blade across the stone, using the other hand to apply even pressure on the blade.

4

Turn the blade over and repeat the process.
Repeat several times on each side until the blade is very sharp.

Using a steel

Wipe any excess oil off the blade, then use the steel to finish the edge.

1

Hold the steel in one hand with your fingers behind the guard.

2

Slide the knife blade from handle to point down the steel at the same angle used on the stone.

3

Repeat on each side a number of times until you are satisfied with the sharpness of the edge.

Knife safety

When cutting with a knife, it is important to ensure that you have a secure cutting surface such as a cutting board or butcher's block. The heavier the board the better, as it will be less likely to slip. However, most kitchens use colour-coded polyethylene boards that require a non-slip mat or damp cloth underneath them to prevent slipping. Always use a flat, even surface.

COLOUR CODED CUTTING BOARDS

- ■ Raw meat
- ■ Raw fish
- □ Cooked meat
- ■ Salad and fruit
- ■ Vegetables
- □ Bakery and dairy

Figure 5.24 A set of colour-coded cutting boards and chart

Take care when you are not using your knives. Place them well away from the edges of tables where they could be knocked off.

Storing knives

Always store your knives in a purpose-made knife case or wooden block. Some kitchens will have magnetic racks attached to the wall.

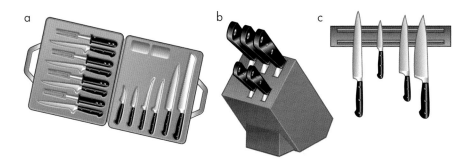

Figure 5.25 a) a knife case, b) a wooden knife block, c) a magnetic knife rack

Never store knives in a drawer or box where they cannot be seen and are more likely to be left to go blunt.

Remember!

- Do not try to catch a knife you accidentally knock off a table.
- Keep your work area clear and tidy and do not allow knives to get covered with packaging or food trimmings.
- Always carry knives around the kitchen with the point facing down and the sharp blade facing behind you. Do not carry knives on the cutting board, even if you are taking them to the wash up area.
- Never use a knife that has a greasy, damaged or broken handle. It is more likely to carry dirt and bacteria, as well as being dangerous.
- Keep your knives sharp. You are more likely to have an accident using a blunt knife as you will have to apply more pressure and may cause it to slip.
- Never put knives into a washing up sink.
- Always clean knives by wiping the edge away from the hands.

Cutting techniques

It is important that you use the correct cutting techniques with your knives. The French cuts in the list below appear in many recipes. Every chef using different types of vegetables needs to practise them to perfect their knife skills.

○ Jardinière – 4mm x 1.5cm pieces
○ Macedoine – 5mm dice (or larger)
○ Julienne – matchsticks
○ Mirepoix – roughly chopped, often quite large, of no specific shape
○ Paysanne – even, thin pieces cut in triangular, round or square shapes with a 1cm diameter
○ Brunoise – 2mm dice
○ Chiffonade – finely shredded ingredients (such as lettuce or cabbage)

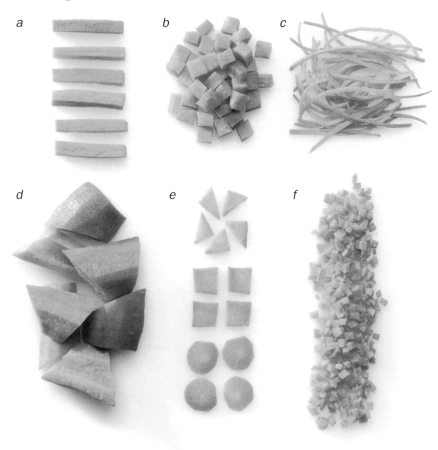

Figure 5.26 Different cuts of vegetables: a) jardinière, b) macedoine, c) julienne, d) mirepoix, e) paysanne, f) brunoise

Did you know?
You have to be over 18 to purchase knives.

Did you know?
Chiffonade means "made of rags".

Figure 5.27 A chef practising the chiffonade cut

Other cutting equipment

Food processor – see page 146 and Figure 5.15.

Box grater – used for grating, cheese, carrots, zest of citrus fruits (a).

Peeler – used for peeling fruit and vegetables.

Corer – used to remove core of fruit such as apples (b).

Cutters – can be round or fluted; used in pastry preparation (c).

Can openers – can be hand-held or table-mounted (d).

Scissors – fish scissors are used for removing some bones and fins of fish (e).

Cleaver – used to prepare meats by cutting through thick bones (f).

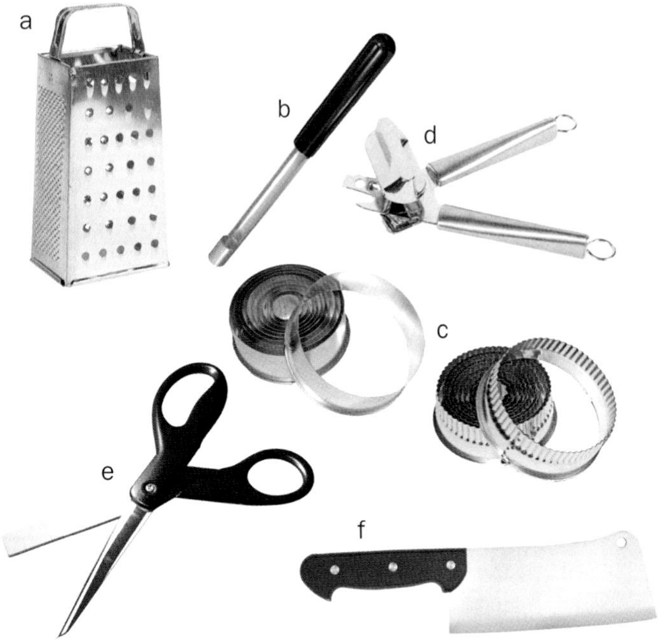

Figure 5.28 Cutting equipment:
a) box grater, b) corer, c) cutters
– round and fluted, d) hand-held can
opener, e) fish scissors, f) cleaver

Mandolins

Mandolins are used to prepare a variety of salad and vegetable ingredients, including cucumbers and potato slices. Always place mandolins on a stable surface and adjust to the required width. Use a guard to hold the vegetable item in place and then push it through the blade. Take extra care with the last few slices near the blade, as you could accidentally cut your fingers.

Gravity feed slicer

This is one of the most dangerous pieces of equipment in a professional kitchen. Gravity feed slicers can be either manually or electrically operated and are mainly used to slice cooked meats and cheeses. They contain a lot of moving parts and the width of the slices can be adjusted to suit each dish. They are ideal for portion control as the chef can ensure the correct number of slices for each joint of meat.

Specialist training is needed for any member of staff who has to use the slicer. A risk assessment may state age restrictions (usually over 18) on its use. Training should include the following:

○ To ensure no damage to the blade occurs and the guard is fitted and in place during use.

Figure 5.29 A mandolin food slicer
used for vegetable preparation

- Each section that comes into contact with food is cleaned, sanitised and carefully dried, especially between cutting different types of meat, e.g. roast beef and boiled ham.
- Blades are sharpened regularly. There is usually an in-built system or stone that will sharpen the blade.
- All moving parts need to be oiled and the oil kept well away from food contact surfaces.

Figure 5.30 A gravity feed slicer

Test yourself!

1 Identify the knives in the pictures below and suggest a suitable task or process each could easily do. Copy and complete the table.

Knife	Name of knife	Suitable task or process
a.		
b.		
c.		
d.		
e.		
f.		
g.		

2 Name two pieces of equipment that can be used to sharpen a knife.

3 Why is it important to have a safe and secure surface when using knives?

4 Name the six colours of cutting boards and what they are used for.

Further information

Further information on catering equipment can be found at the following websites. Links have been made available at www.heinemann.co.uk/hotlinks – just enter the express code 3729P.

Falcon Foodservice Equipment
Catering Equipment Suppliers Association (CESA)

Practice assignment tasks

Task 1

Write a short report identifying types of cutting equipment (not including knives) used in kitchens and what they are used for. Include a separate section for:

- manually operated cutting equipment
- electrically operated cutting equipment.

Task 2

Write a brief training booklet on choice and use of knives in the kitchen.

You should include:

- safe use of knives
- handling knives correctly
- sharpening techniques
- cleaning and storing knives.

Task 3

List the six French cuts of fresh vegetables and a suitable dish they are used in.

(**Tip:** you can use the same dish more than once.)

Practise these cuts as often as you can, as you will be assessed on them.

Task 4

Draw a diagram of a small professional kitchen, including and identifying as many pieces of large kitchen equipment as possible.

Personal workplace skills

6

This chapter covers the following outcomes from Diploma unit 106: Introduction to personal workplace skills

- Outcome 106.1 Be able to maintain personal appearance
- Outcome 106.2 Be able to demonstrate time management skills
- Outcome 106.3 Know how to work effectively in a team
- Outcome 106.4 Know how to deal effectively with customers

Working through this chapter could also provide the opportunity to practise the following Functional Skills at Level 1:

Functional ICT: Using ICT – select and use software applications to meet needs and solve straightforward problems

Finding and selecting information – search engines, queries; recognise and take account of currency, relevance, bias and copyright when selecting and using information.

In this chapter you will learn how to:

- Maintain personal appearance
- Demonstrate time management skills
- Work effectively in a team
- Deal effectively with customers

Maintain personal appearance

Working in food production is a very responsible job and a good chef is well-respected by everyone. A person who is well-presented in the kitchen creates a professional and efficient impression and has every chance to do well at their job.

There is a good deal more information about correct uniform in Chapter 2. See the illustration of the chef in Figure 2.13 on page 46.

Uniform

A chef's uniform should include:

- clean, well-pressed whites
- apron worn correctly
- well-fitting hat and hairnet if you have long hair
- clean trousers of the correct length
- clean safety shoes.

The chef's uniform is designed for both comfort and protection.

- The jacket has two layers of material across the front and long sleeves for protection against heat and burns.
- The apron should be worn to just below knee length to protect from spillages of hot liquids.
- Footwear should be of thick, strong material and cover the whole foot to protect from items being dropped.

Personal grooming

Personal grooming is very important when creating a positive first impression and professional appearance. It is also very important for hygiene reasons. Your appearance is even more important when you are working front of house, perhaps carving joints for a carvery or serving at a buffet. Personal grooming involves:

- clean, neat and tidy hairstyle and hairnet if necessary
- clean-shaven (for males)
- no make-up or jewellery
- clean, short and well-kept nails
- brushed teeth
- upright posture
- happy disposition
- genuine smile.

Did you know?

Chefs working in the pastry area of a kitchen may wear jackets with short sleeves.

Did you know?

There are a range of hats that can be worn in the kitchen.

Figure 6.1 The range of hats that can be worn in the kitchen

Top marks!

Remember that you will be graded on the standard of your appearance. Try to ensure that every time you turn up for work in the kitchen you are on time, full of energy, alert and keen. Make sure that your uniform is clean and in good condition in plenty of time before your shift starts. That way you have time to put right anything that is not of the correct standard – such as replace buttons, iron a creased apron, etc. Make sure your chef's trousers are not too long and drag on the floor – you could trip over them!

Professional behaviour

It is important to create a good impression by showing a professional and mature attitude in the kitchen. This is particularly important as a high standard of hygiene, health and safety is required in a catering kitchen.

Figure 6.2 Should these chefs be at work?

You can maintain a professional attitude by:

○ always being well groomed
○ behaving in a mature, responsible manner
○ taking pride in your appearance and your work
○ making sure that you are on time for work every day
○ working efficiently and productively, using good time management
○ communicating politely with other staff and customers at all times
○ being consistent when carrying out your tasks
○ taking the first step to help yourself and others
○ working at a good speed
○ working accurately and producing good-quality work
○ being organised and methodical in your work area – e.g. tidying as you go along
○ good mise en place to allow you to work more quickly during service.

Try this!

Make a collage showing an appropriately dressed member of a kitchen brigade. There are a range of jacket and trouser styles available. Don't forget to find appropriate shoes, hat and necktie!

Did you know?

Neckties are worn to catch the sweat that can trickle down the face and neck of a chef when working over a hot stove.

Different colours of necktie can be worn to show the level of chef – e.g. trainee or section leader.

Poor hygiene and practices

It is very important that you work in a hygienic manner at all times. You must never do the following in the kitchen:

○ **Smoke** – this can contaminate food with bacteria from your mouth.

○ **Eat or drink** – except when tasting items you are preparing. This must be done using a clean spoon for each tasting. Never put a spoon you have used for tasting back into any food or drink without washing it thoroughly first. You may be provided with disposable spoons for tasting purposes which are only used once.

○ **Wear your uniform outside the premises** as it can get dirty and contaminate food if you then wear the same clothing inside the kitchen without changing first (see page 47).

○ **Not wash your hands thoroughly** at the appropriate times (see page 50).

> **Did you know?**
>
> A chef's apron should have long strings so that the apron can be tied up at the front. This means it can be undone quickly in the event of an accident – such as a hot liquid being spilled.

Test yourself!

1 Why should a chef wear a long-sleeved jacket when working at the stove?
   a To protect their arms from burns.
   b To keep their arms clean.
   c To keep their arms cool.
   d To stop hair and skin falling in the food.

2 What is the most important reason for good personal appearance in the kitchen?
   a To look smart
   b To be comfortable
   c To be hygienic
   d To impress the Head Chef

3 Which type of shoes should be worn in the kitchen?

4 State three bad habits that are not allowed in the kitchen.

Time management skills

Time management is all about being well organised. It involves being able to work well without rushing or getting stressed and tired. It means that you can get a large amount of work completed without working through your break or having to stay later at work.

Why are time management skills important?

It is very important to make sure you are on time to start your shift at work. If you do not appear in the kitchen when you should, changed and ready to work, someone else may have to start your jobs for you. They may have to do your work as well as their own and not be happy about having to work so hard. You also need to return from your break promptly.

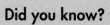

Did you know?

Time management is about making the best use of the time available to complete tasks. One of the best ways of doing this is to organise the order of your work before you start. This helps to avoid wasting time or having to repeat jobs.

Case study

Lesley worked in a restaurant kitchen. During service times she was often very busy and the other staff in the kitchen came to help her. When she took her break she liked to chat to her friends. Often she didn't notice the time and was over ten minutes late getting back to work. The other staff in the kitchen became very fed up with Lesley, as they had to stop their own tasks and cover her work when she didn't come back on time. In the end the other staff stopped helping her out during her busy times.

○ **Why do you think the other staff stopped helping Lesley?**

○ **What could she do to change the situation?**

Figure 6.3 Don't let your breaks run on too long

If you cannot come to work you need to let your employer know as soon as you can. This is so that arrangements can be made to cover the work you would normally do that day. If you do not let your employer know, they will not be able to arrange for someone else to come and work in your place. This means that the other people in the kitchen will have your work to do as well as their own. If someone else does not turn up for work one day without letting the employer know, you could have to work longer hours or have to try and do part of their job as well as your own in the same time. The quality of the work and the standard of the food produced might suffer as a result.

Did you know?

When you start work you will be given a contract of employment. This will state what you have to do in your job and the hours you have to work. It will also tell you what to do if you are unable to get to work for any reason. If you do not follow these instructions you could lose your job.

167

Getting organised

To be able to work well you need to be organised. Part of being organised means planning ahead to make sure you have everything you need for a job before you start. You also need to position the items you are going to use sensibly on your work area. Remember the following guidelines.

○ Leave yourself enough space to carry out the task.
○ Do not have any equipment in your work space that you are not going to use.
○ Use the shelves that are above or below your work area. Do not overload shelves or position anything on them that might fall off easily.
○ Include waste bowls or trays on your list of equipment. They should be big enough to hold trimmings and peelings without overflowing. But they should not take up too much space on the worktop and cramp the work area.
○ If working with high risk foods, avoid any risk of contaminating any of the items.
○ Make sure you can work in a safe manner so you do not endanger either yourself or others.
○ Keep food covered and refrigerated between tasks.

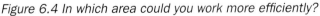

Figure 6.4 In which area could you work more efficiently?

Using your work time effectively

When working in a kitchen you must have very precise time management. Every chef in a kitchen may have up to three deadlines every day – breakfast, lunch and dinner – and some establishments serve food all day. Customers will not accept an excuse if their food is not ready – they will go elsewhere to eat, and probably not come back to your outlet again.

To be able to manage your time well you must:

○ plan your time to schedule the order of your work
○ assemble all the equipment you will need before you start the job
○ fill in "gap" times when items are cooking or resting, with other tasks
○ clear and clean as you go – include time for this on your work plan
○ include a break in your plan at a suitable time.

Try this!
How organised are you?

While you carry out one of your routine preparation jobs, make a note of how many times you have to leave your workplace to fetch items you have forgotten. Time yourself from when you start to get ready until when the task is finished.

The next time you have the same job to do, take a few minutes in advance to write out all the supplies and equipment you will need, then get them ready. Time yourself from the start of assembling the equipment to the end of the job and see if you have saved any time — you should have!

Try this!
Write an order of work for a simple task you have done several times before — e.g. making a sandwich. Set yourself a realistic amount of time to complete the task. Include time for gathering the items you need at the beginning and make sure you put aside time to clean equipment at the end.

When you have finished answer these questions:

○ *Did your plan work?*
○ *Did you find that it helped you to be more organised?*
○ *Did you find that you completed the task in less time because you took the trouble to plan it out first?*

Time	Job/Activity	Equipment needed

Figure 6.5 A time planning sheet

Try this!

Now develop your skill of time management by planning a task that needs more than one person to complete it.

An example is making 100 sandwiches in a limited period of time. You will need to organise the work area and gather together the equipment and supplies. Then decide how many people you need to help you.

You might need: one to butter the bread, one to spread the filling, one to put the top on the sandwich and cut it and another to wrap the sandwich.

Now try to do this with another task that involves several people.

Figure 6.6 Organising a task that needs several people

Skills that help with time management

○ Working in a clean, organised manner with no mess around
○ Planning the order of tasks and getting the equipment needed in advance
○ Helping other members of the team if they are struggling
○ Wasting as little as possible of any ingredients
○ Getting faster and more skilled in the jobs that you do.
○ Cleaning as you go in your work area so that it can be kept tidy, safe and hygienic.

Test yourself!

1 What is time management?

2 State three reasons why it is important to be on time to start work.

3 What should you do if you are unable to get to work when you are expected?

4 Give three reasons why it helps to be organised in your workplace.

Working effectively in a team

Being able to work with others is vital in the hospitality industry. A good standard of service and production cannot be provided by people working on their own. There are several areas of the hospitality industry where people have to work together in teams. These include:

- reception
- bar service
- food service
- kitchen
- housekeeping.

You will need to be able to co-operate with all of these different teams.

A successful meal service depends on all the staff in the kitchen and restaurant working together to ensure:

- correct timing
- smooth service
- the correct dish is served
- good quality of food
- food served at the correct temperature.

Some work teams are very large. A conference and banqueting centre serving over 1000 meals a day may need a team of over 30 chefs. A small restaurant serving around 20 customers may only have one chef with an assistant to wash up.

A good team will consist of members who:

- want to get the job done
- work to the same standards
- are well-organised
- communicate well with each other
- support and help each other.

The benefits of good team work for the establishment are:

- more work can be carried out for less effort
- people are usually happier working in a group
- responsibility for work and decisions is shared
- team members are loyal to each other
- work is done on time and customers are happy.

Did you know?

If a team at work gets on well together, their work is usually of a very good standard and is produced very quickly at service time. Many groups of chefs working together also enjoy socialising together. This is known as developing a good "team spirit".

Remember!

Never:
- be rude or swear at anyone
- be nasty or spiteful
- take people for granted
- let your standards slip.

Always:
- show respect for others
- be enthusiastic
- be helpful
- listen carefully to others.

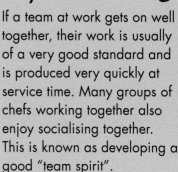

Head chef (Team leader)

|

Second/Assistant chef

|

Kitchen porter

Figure 6.7 A small team in the kitchen of a 40-seater restaurant

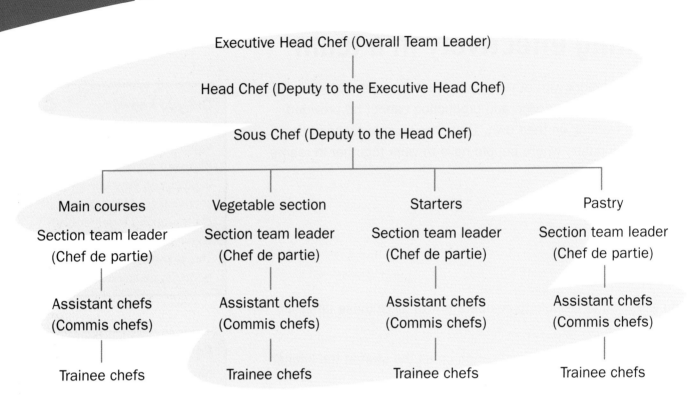

Executive Head Chef (Overall Team Leader)

Head Chef (Deputy to the Executive Head Chef)

Sous Chef (Deputy to the Head Chef)

Main courses	Vegetable section	Starters	Pastry
Section team leader (Chef de partie)	Section team leader (Chef de partie)	Section team leader (Chef de partie)	Section team leader (Chef de partie)
Assistant chefs (Commis chefs)	Assistant chefs (Commis chefs)	Assistant chefs (Commis chefs)	Assistant chefs (Commis chefs)
Trainee chefs	Trainee chefs	Trainee chefs	Trainee chefs

Figure 6.8 A large team in the kitchen of a conference centre

The benefits of good team work for the individual are:
- feeling more valued at work
- being able to learn from others
- being able to show others what you can do
- greater job satisfaction
- having the support of others.

Investigate!
Look on the internet or in the catering press for jobs available in catering kitchens. Try to find advertisements for a range of different positions. How many of them say that they are looking for someone who works well in a team?

Remember!
A good team member will:
- always be reliable and on time for work
- be organised, work cleanly and methodically
- complete all tasks required within a reasonable time
- help other people to complete their work if necessary
- share information and learn from other team members
- communicate clearly with others.

Effective teamwork

To be able to work well with others, you need to develop a variety of skills:

- co-operate with other team members
- communicate effectively with other team members
- watch and anticipate the needs of others (customers as well as staff)
- deal with problems and complaints (from customers as well as staff).

All teams must have a good leader. The success of a team depends very much on this person. The leader of a team should:

- set a good example
- be respected by all the team members
- be consistent in decisions made
- encourage and support team members.

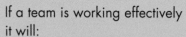

Remember!

If a team is working effectively it will:

- complete the required work on time and to a good standard
- be able to learn new skills and techniques easily
- have good communication between team members
- motivate the team members to work harder and be successful
- work to and achieve a common aim.

The working day is much less tiring and stressful for everyone if teams work together well.

Figure 6.9 Staff complaining

Figure 6.10 Staff working well as a team

Case study

Sheila had worked in the kitchen for nearly five years. She was proud of the section she ran and had a team of four staff to help her. At the start of every shift she gathered her staff together to brief them on the tasks that had to be completed that day. She made sure that they all understood what they had to do. If she saw any of them struggle with their workload she would make sure they had help so they could finish their tasks on time. If a member of her team had a problem she would always notice they were not happy and find out why. Sometimes she asked one of her staff to help out one of the other sections in the kitchen if they were short of staff.

○ Sheila seemed to run her team well. Which of the teamwork skills listed above did she use to achieve this?

Try this!
Think of your team leader at work. Do they do a good job? Can you identify what they do to make the team work well together?

When to ask for help

Sometimes, particularly when starting a new job, you may not be sure what to do. Being uncertain about a task can result from:

○ not being shown how to do it

○ being unsure of the standard expected

○ forgetting how to carry out a task

○ being uncertain if you have enough time to carry out a task properly

○ not knowing how to operate equipment.

You need to ask for help whenever necessary, particularly at the start of a new job. If you do not, you could:

○ waste materials and time carrying out the task incorrectly

○ injure yourself or someone else

○ produce a sub-standard item

○ annoy other members of your team who then have to put your mistake right.

Remember!
If you keep asking for help all the time your team members and your supervisor may get fed up with you. Pay attention to help that you are given. Make notes so you are sure what to do and have them to hand for next time. Ask questions when the person is helping you, not after they have gone back to their own work. The more you carry out a task, the more confident and skilful you will become.

You have looked for something and cannot find it

You are asked to use equipment you haven't been trained to use

You are asked to do something you have not done before

You are still uncertain about a task

You have not understood instructions

Figure 6.11 When to ask for help

Communication skills in a team

Being able to work well as a team is only possible if you communicate well. This does not just mean talking to each other. Different forms of communication include:

○ verbal:
 – talking face to face
 – speaking on the phone
○ written:
 – sending an email
 – sending a text message
 – writing a message or letter
○ non-verbal:
 – body language
 – facial expressions.

Most communication in the kitchen is done by speaking and body language. However, sometimes there is a need to write things down – e.g. food orders, stock requisitions, messages for other members of staff.

Talking face to face

This is the most effective method of communication, as both people can see the expressions on each other's faces as well as hear what they are saying. This helps them understand better.

Many people do not listen carefully to what is being said to them. This is where many problems occur. The best way to find out if someone has understood what you have said is to ask them a question about it. Alternatively, you could ask them to repeat back what you have said to them. If you have been telling them how to do something, you could ask them to do it while you watch.

The catering and hospitality industry is international. You may have to communicate with someone who does not speak the same language as yourself or who speaks English as an additional language. To ensure they understand what you are trying to say to them you may need to:

○ show them what you mean
○ draw a picture to help you explain
○ get someone who speaks both languages to help you.

Try this!

Design an information poster for staff in the kitchen who do not speak English as their first language. The poster should show how to carry out a task — e.g. how to arrange a work area tidily, how to wash and care for knives or how to present a set of dishes.

You will need to use few words and lots of pictures to present the information.

Kitchens can be noisy, particularly at service time. There is the background noise of extraction fans, equipment such as blenders, oven doors opening and closing and the banging of pans on the stove. Sometimes there is the crashing of dishes being dropped on the floor!

It is important when speaking in the kitchen to make sure you are heard. You need to be able to:

○ talk loudly without shouting

○ speak clearly so that others can tell what you are saying

○ hear what someone speaking to you is saying, so that you know you have been heard and understood.

Did you know?

In a busy kitchen there is always a chef standing at the hot plate. This person is sometimes called the "aboyeur" or "barker". They call out the orders to all the staff working in the different sections in the kitchen. The staff need to show that they have heard and understood the dishes they need to be cooking and serving next. They shout out "yes chef" to each order for their section.

Figure 6.12 The aboyeur

Talking on the phone

Speaking on the phone is something that we are all used to at home and on our mobiles. At work, telephone communication must be more precise and very accurate. The phone is used at work in order to receive an instant response to a question from someone who is not in the same area.

When speaking on the phone you must remember:
○ to speak clearly
○ not to speak too quickly
○ to give your name and your job title when you answer
○ to smile as you speak (it does make a difference!)
○ to write down any important information you are given
○ to repeat back to the caller any important information to ensure it is accurate. This is particularly important with telephone numbers and prices of commodities, for example.

When you answer the phone, you may need to take a message for someone else. Always keep a record of:
○ the name of the caller
○ the time of the call
○ the date of the call
○ the contact number to return the call
○ the name of the person the message is for
○ when the call has to be returned.

Body language

Body language is the way people communicate with each other without using words. Instead they use gestures and facial expressions. We often do not notice what body language we are using. You need to be aware of the effect body language can have. If you are trying to hide your feelings from someone, be very careful – body language never lies!

In a busy kitchen you can usually tell who enjoys their work and who does not simply from the way they move about their work area. You can also tell who is under pressure and has too much work to do and who is having an easy time with a light work load. By looking at people in this way you will be able to tell who may need help to get their job done and who would be a good person to ask for help if you are struggling.

Figure 6.13 When talking on the phone, listen carefully and be precise

Try this!
Design a telephone message pad to use to record the details of important information that must be passed on to someone else. Make sure that all the essential details cannot be forgotten. How can you ensure that the message reaches the correct person in time?

Did you know?
Out of what we communicate to each other:
70% is transmitted by body language
20% by tone of voice
10% the words that we use!

Try this!

Look at Figure 6.14 and decide what feeling or mood each face is showing. The only features that change are the eyebrows and mouth – this shows just how expressive they are!

Figure 6.14 A person's facial expression tells us a lot about their mood

Look out for examples of different body language. Can you work out what they mean?

For example:

o *Folded arms – could mean the person doesn't feel safe.*

o *Glancing away – could mean the person is bored.*

o *Moving around a lot – could mean the person is nervous or stressed.*

o *Slouching – could mean the person is not interested in what is being said.*

Test yourself!

1 Give an example of why working in a team can be better than working on your own.

2 Name three reasons why good teamwork helps you do your job better.

3 List three situations when you should ask for help.

4 What are the rules for speaking on the phone?

5 How would you describe body language?

6 What are the most important ways of communicating in the kitchen?

Dealing with customers

There are two types of customers in any hospitality or catering establishment. These are:
○ internal customers
○ external customers.

Internal customers are your work colleagues, including:
○ front of house staff – who have contact with the customers (e.g. waiting staff)
○ back of house staff – e.g. kitchen staff.

External customers are the guests who come to eat in your establishment. This section covers dealing with external customers.

Working in a kitchen, you may think that you won't have to communicate directly with customers. You may not often speak to them, but in fact you are communicating with them all the time through the standard of the work that you produce. A customer can be impressed by the work of the staff in the kitchen by:
○ the quality of the food produced
○ the size of the portion
○ the taste and seasoning of the items
○ the attractive presentation of the food
○ the temperature of the dish.

Sometimes a member of the kitchen team may have to speak directly to a customer. You may need to explain the ingredients in a dish or a customer may not be happy with a dish and ask to speak to the chef responsible. You even may find yourself helping out in the restaurant if this area is short of staff.

Speaking to customers

When speaking to customers, remember:
○ always acknowledge the customer, even if you are busy doing something else – a glance, a smile or a nod in their direction will let them know you have noticed them
○ try to put yourself in their position (this is called empathy)
○ explain as clearly as you can – customers may not understand words you use in the kitchen such as "prep" and "service"

- if the customer is not happy with the food produced, apologise on behalf of all the kitchen staff
- ask the customer what they would like done to put the matter right – this may mean re-serving a dish, providing a different item or preparing a dish individually
- make sure that the customer gets what they asked for!

When dealing with customers it is very important to know:
- the ingredients of dishes
- any ingredients that may cause allergies
- dishes that are suitable for different diets, e.g. vegetarian, religious
- the methods of cookery involved
- the way the dishes are served
- the customer service policy of your employer.

It is very important to be able to communicate effectively with customers. If a customer is happy they will return to the same place again. You have to listen to customers carefully so that you fully understand their requests. One way of making sure that you have understood what is required is to repeat the information back to them.

Remember!

If a customer is not happy then they will go elsewhere to eat. They will also tell their friends about their bad experience at your establishment.

Did you know?

When dealing with a customer request or complaint, remember to use LEARN:
- o Listen
- o Empathise
- o Act
- o Revisit to check customer happy
- o Never be rude!

Case study

Susie was taking a breakfast order from a customer in a restaurant. The customer ordered two eggs "sunny side up". Susie did not understand what he wanted. She didn't want to ask him because she didn't want to look as though she did not know her job properly. Susie decided that this was probably how the eggs were normally cooked, so she put her order through in the usual way. The customer was not happy when the eggs arrived, sent them back to the kitchen and asked to speak to the manager.

- o What could Susie have done to avoid this situation happening?
- o Why was the customer not happy?

Eggs sunny side up please.

Figure 6.15 What should Susie have done?

Communication skills

Speaking

Be careful when speaking to customers, if:

- you are speaking in a foreign language (if English is not your first language)
- you are speaking to someone for whom English is a foreign language
- you speak English with a strong regional accent
- you have to project your voice across a noisy kitchen
- you are having to speak in a hurry
- if you are speaking to someone who has a hearing problem.

Listening

Listening carefully is a skill that needs work. Many people, particularly if they are in a hurry, do not listen carefully. They hear what they think the person should be saying rather than what they actually say. To check you have understood what the customer is saying, repeat back what you have heard.

Writing

Many people working in a kitchen do not like writing very much. Some of them are not very good at it and find it difficult. If you have to write something down for someone else to read they must be able to read your writing.

When writing information for others – such as food orders or lists of jobs, make sure:

- your writing is clear (write in capital letters if necessary)
- your spelling is correct (ask others for help if you are unsure)
- the layout of the writing on the page is easy to read and understand – e.g. a list has one item directly below the other.

Reading

You will need to read customer orders and other instructions. Your establishment may have customer comment cards that you will need to read. People often read something quickly and miss a word or two out which can change the meaning completely. How often have you heard people saying "I must have missed that bit"? Missing out part of a food order can cause all sorts of problems so make sure you read them carefully. If you cannot read very well, ask for help.

Body language

Positive, friendly body language is very important when dealing with customers. It will help create a good impression of your establishment.

To help with good communication with customers, make sure that you:

o face the person you are talking with

o keep eye contact

o maintain a good posture

o keep your arms unfolded

o have a friendly facial expression.

Body language can also tell you if a customer has any problems which may make communication difficult, such as:

o being drunk or under the influence of drugs

o being stressed

o suffering from personal problems

o acting aggressively or rudely.

If necessary when dealing with difficult customers or colleagues, get help from your supervisor.

Figure 6.16 Good body language will help you communicate with a customer

Test yourself!

1 Why is it so important to deal with customers correctly?

2 How can you acknowledge a customer?

3 What is the best way to deal with a customer request?

4 When are reading and writing skills important to a chef?

Practice assignment tasks

Task 1

This unit is all about developing good standards of appearance and behaviour in the workplace. You need to get into the habit of making sure you are correctly dressed and on time for work every day. To try and get into this routine keep a diary for three weeks. Every day record the following information:

○ the time you set off for work
○ the time you arrived at work
○ if your uniform was put on clean that day (if not, how many shifts have you already worn it?)
○ if you have cleaned your shoes before putting them on that day
○ if you have had a shower; washed your hair; scrubbed your nails before coming to work.

Try to improve your performance each week until you have a perfect result!

Task 2

Imagine you have to organise a team of three people to prepare a set meal for a party of 12 customers.

1 Decide on the menu. Then draw up a table with five columns to plan your preparation.
2 Use the first three columns to do a time plan for the preparation of the food and allocate tasks to each of the three people you have in your team.
3 In the fourth column write down what could go wrong with each procedure – e.g. a team member might not know how to make a certain dish; customers might arrive late or bring along more people than they booked for.
4 In the last column write down the best type of communication for this part of the plan.

For example: the start of your plan could look something like this:

Time to service	Task	Member of staff	Possible problems	Best communication method
4 hours	Check all ingredients	Julie	Some ingredients missing	Phone stores

Task 3

Read the following scenario and answer the questions.

Sadie is a kitchen assistant in a café serving all day breakfast. She has to help with general food preparation, making the hot and cold beverages and keeping the service area clean and well stocked with equipment. The café is very busy in the morning with customers coming in for breakfast before they go to work. Sadie has to start work very early.

One evening Sadie forgot to set her alarm to get up for work. She arrived nearly an hour late for work and pulled on her dirty uniform in the changing room. She had forgotten to bring her work shoes and had to wear her trainers instead.

Sadie found a long queue of customers at the counter wanting drinks and toast. Her work colleague, John, was doing his best but the toaster was broken. Several customers were tired of waiting and walked out of the café.

1 List three problems that could have occurred because Sadie was late.
2 What should Sadie have done when she knew she was going to be late for work?
3 What problems may occur with the uniform Sadie was wearing that day?
4 What could Sadie or John do about the broken toaster?
5 State three things that make for good team work.

Boiling, poaching and steaming

7

This chapter covers the following outcomes from Diploma unit 107: Prepare and cook food by boiling, poaching and steaming

- Outcome 107.1 Be able to prepare and cook food by boiling
- Outcome 107.2 Be able to prepare and cook food by poaching
- Outcome 107.3 Be able to prepare and cook food by steaming

Working through this chapter could also provide the opportunity to practise the following Functional Skills at Level 1:

Functional Maths: Analysing – solve problems requiring calculation, with common measures, including money, time, length, weight, capacity and temperature.

In this chapter you will learn how to:

- Check that food items and cooking liquids for boiling, poaching and steaming are of the correct type, quantity and quality
- Select the right equipment for preparing and cooking boiled, poached and steamed foods
- Prepare and cook food items according to dish specifications, monitoring quality at all stages
- Demonstrate control of time and temperature throughout preparation, cooking and serving
- Finish and present the product in line with dish and customer requirements
- Work in a safe and hygienic manner.

Prepare and cook food by boiling

In this section you will learn how to prepare and cook the following range of food using the boiling method:

- vegetables
- eggs
- pasta
- pulses and grains
- fish
- meat.

What is boiling?

Boiling is a wet method of cooking foods. The food is cooked in a liquid at boiling point (100°C) over a direct heat source. The liquids used for boiling can include water, **stock**, milk, wine or **infused liquids**.

The purpose of boiling food is to tenderise it, making it easy to digest, pleasant and safe to eat. How the food is boiled will depend on its type. Overcooking will make food unsuitable for service and more nutrients will be lost.

The process of boiling

When boiling, food can be either placed into a boiling liquid or placed in a cold liquid and brought to the boil.

Method 1: Adding food to boiling liquid

If food is added to a boiling liquid, the flavour and nutritional value and colour of the food is sealed in. It can also reduce the cooking time. Once the liquid is boiling the heat is reduced and the food is allowed to simmer.

Method 2: Adding food to cold liquid

If food is added to a cold liquid and brought to the boil, the natural flavours and goodness are extracted into the liquid. This method is often used to make **nutritious**, well-flavoured stocks that are the basis of good soups and sauces.

Although boiling may seem to be an easy method of cooking, you need to take care to prepare, time and finish the dishes properly.

Definitions

Stock – a broth used as a braising liquid (see Chapter 8), a sauce base or liquid for soup. It can be made from chicken, beef, veal, game, fish or vegetables. Ready-made stocks are used in some establishments for speed and convenience.

Infused liquids – liquids used in the cooking process that have herbs and spices added to provide a particular flavour – e.g. saffron in Spanish paella or a studded onion in a white sauce.

Nutritious – containing nutrients required for a healthy diet.

Healthy eating

Use margarine or olive oil instead of butter, and semi-skimmed or skimmed milk.

Chef's tip

Soft water extracts the juices from meat more easily than hard water. Hard water is best for boiling meat or vegetables. If only soft water is available, add salt in order to preserve vegetables during cooking.

Simmering

Simmering is used for food such as cheaper cuts of meat and root vegetables that need longer cooking times, e.g. mutton, carrots or swede. Simmering breaks down the fibres, tenderises and extracts the goodness and natural flavours.

When simmering, it is important to stick to the recipe time and temperature to prevent under- or overcooking. Soups and sauces should always be simmered rather than boiled.

Always use the correct amount of liquid to cook rice and pasta and it should be cooked until slightly firm (al dente). Meat and poultry should be well cooked and tender; vegetables should not be over cooked.

Equipment

You will need the following equipment for boiling food:
- a pan such as a saucepan or stock pot that is large enough to hold the food and liquid
- spiders, perforated spoons or colanders to remove the food from the liquid
- cloths to protect you from heat.

Figure 7.1 Equipment needed for boiling

Definitions

Simmer – to gently heat food just below boiling point.

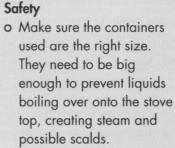

Remember!

Safety
- Make sure the containers used are the right size. They need to be big enough to prevent liquids boiling over onto the stove top, creating steam and possible scalds.
- Make sure the pan handles do not become hot from other heat sources or stick out from the stove top.
- Take extra care when moving pans of hot liquids and always use a clean, dry oven cloth.

Did you know?

Ordinary water has some gases and air dissolved in it. When the water is boiled, all of the air and gases are driven off. For this reason boiled water has a flat taste. Water that has boiled and been left to stand for some time should not be used for cooking or drinking.

Eggs

Most eggs we use come from chickens. Eggs can be boiled using either method of boiling:

○ placed in boiling water and simmered

○ or brought to the boil and simmered.

Eggs from the fridge should not be plunged into boiling water as they are likely to crack. Every chef has a personal preference as to which method they use. Always use a saucepan that is big enough so the eggs are fully covered, but not so big that the eggs bounce around in the water and may break.

Hard-boiled eggs take 8 to 10 minutes to cook. They can be served hot in their shells or cooled rapidly in cold running water, shelled and used in salads, sandwiches and garnishes. Eggs that have been boiled for too long or not cooled quickly will be spoiled as the yolk will go black and the white flesh will be rubbery.

Quails' eggs are small and are noted for their flavour and colour. They only take five minutes to hard boil.

Chef's tip

Always use a kitchen timer when boiling eggs.

Investigate!

What other types of eggs are used in the catering industry?

Did you know?

It takes longer to boil liquids at high altitude due to the atmospheric pressure. A hard-boiled egg (usually 8–10 minutes) takes twice as long to cook at 10,000 metres!

Vegetables

Vegetables suitable for boiling include:

○ potatoes
○ carrots
○ runner beans
○ fresh peas
○ broccoli
○ cauliflower
○ beetroot
○ brussels sprouts
○ cabbage
○ parsnips
○ turnip
○ swede.

Figure 7.2 A selection of vegetables suitable for boiling

Vegetables grown above the ground take a short time to cook. They should be placed in hot water and brought to the boil quickly. Vegetables grown in the ground need a longer time to cook. They should be put into cold water and then brought to the boil. The exception to this is very new potatoes which can be placed into boiling water.

When you are preparing vegetables for cooking, it is important to cut them to the same size. This will ensure that they are all cooked evenly and at the same time. If vegetables are to be served directly onto the plate, they need to be cut into even, bite-sized pieces.

Top marks!

Say which vegetables from the list above should be cooked by method 1 and which by method 2.

Cauliflower

1 Trim the stem and remove the outer leaves.
2 Hollow out the stem using a peeler or remove the florets and wash in cold water.
3 Cook in lightly salted water or steam. Cook for 10–15 minutes for the whole cauliflower or 3–5 five minutes for the florets. Take care not to overcook.
4 Drain well and serve with melted butter and chopped parsley.

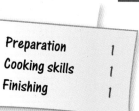

Preparation   1
Cooking skills   1
Finishing   1

Variations

• Cover with a Mornay or cheese sauce, sprinkle with cheese and brown under the grill.
• Serve with a hollandaise or butter sauce
• Lightly brown some fresh breadcrumbs and mix with chopped parsley and a sieved boiled egg. Sprinkle over the cooked cauliflower and serve. This mixture is called "polonaise".

Blanching

Vegetables can be **blanched** in boiling water to prevent them from deteriorating or to remove their skins, e.g. a tomato when preparing a tomato salad or sauce. After blanching, vegetables need to be **refreshed**, then drained and stored in a refrigerator or freezer. Be careful not to blanch for too long, or the flesh will become too soft and mushy and unsuitable to use.

Blanching is a useful technique to speed up service when cooking vegetables for large numbers of people. The vegetables are nearly cooked ahead of time, and are then cooled and refreshed. When required for service the vegetables can be reheated quickly either in boiling water, a steamer or stir fried.

Blanching is a term used for other methods of preparation as well. For example, chips can be blanched – they are cooked without colour, then crisped and coloured later.

Definitions

Blanching – fruit and vegetables are immersed in boiling water for between ten seconds and two minutes depending on size and type.
Refreshing – cooling food after blanching or boiling by plunging into cold water or running under cold water.

Video presentation
Watch *How to blanch tomatoes.*

Pasta

Pasta is a versatile product and comes in various shapes and sizes. It is available either fresh or dried. Pasta should be plunged into boiling salted water. Cooking times vary depending on the type: 3–8 minutes for fresh pasta and 8–15 minutes for dried pasta. It is important not to overcook pasta as it becomes stodgy, swells and breaks apart.

Pasta may be combined with other ingredients and baked, e.g. lasagne, or stuffed with a variety of fillings, e.g. ravioli, cannelloni.

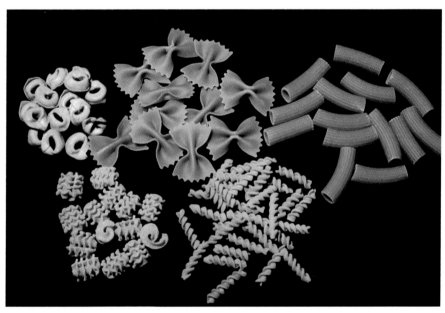

Figure 7.3 Assorted dry pasta

Rice

There are over 250 varieties of rice which are broken down into three main categories:

- long grain rice – ideal for plain boiled rice or savoury dishes
- short grain rice – ideal for risotto and paella dishes
- round grain rice – ideal for sweet puddings.

Rice is full of carbohydrates. It is cooked by boiling or steaming and is popular served with Indian and Chinese dishes.

Boiling rice is the easiest cooking method. The most commonly used type of rice is long grain. After washing, it is plunged into boiling salted water for 15–20 minutes. The rice is cooked when it is light, white and fluffy with a little bite.

The rice is then drained, refreshed in a colander and any remaining starch washed off before it needs to be reheated for service. Failure to remove the starch will make the rice become sticky and unsuitable for food service. Rice can also be cooked by steaming, stewing, braising and baking. See Chapter 8.

Cooked rice is mainly eaten hot, so it needs to be reheated to a core temperature of 75°C. This can be done by heating small batches carefully in a microwave oven, a steamer, or by stir frying. Cooked rice is a high risk food and should be kept covered in a fridge for a maximum of three days and only reheated once. Once reheated the temperature must be kept above 63°C.

Did you know?

For a main dish, the ideal portion of uncooked rice is 65g. This will provide 20g of carbohydrate.

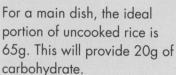

Chef's tip

Cooking rice in stock with herbs and spices, e.g. saffron, will add flavour and enhance the dish.

Remember!

Food safety

Cooked rice is classed as a high risk food and special care needs to be taken during the cooking, storage and reheating to prevent the growth of food poisoning bacteria.

Investigate!

Find out about other types of rice.

Where in the world are risotto and paella dishes from?

Pulses

Pulses are the dried edible seeds of plants. They are a good source of protein, carbohydrate, B vitamins, iron and some are high in fibre.

There are three main types:

1 beans – e.g. black, black-eyed, broad, borlotti, butter, haricot, red kidney, soya
2 peas – e.g. chick, split green, yellow
3 lentils – e.g. orange, green, yellow, puy.

Investigate!
What kind of beans are used in baked beans?

Storage and food safety

Dried pulses should be stored in clean airtight containers and should be checked for physical contamination such as food pests before use. Pulses can be stored fresh, frozen or tinned and should be stored away from any raw foods.

Cooking pulses

Some pulses should be soaked in cold water to allow them to rehydrate and absorb the liquid prior to boiling. The time will vary according to the variety and can be a few hours to overnight. During the soaking process, pulses should be stored below 5°C. Some pulses do not require soaking and only require around 30 minutes to cook, e.g. puy lentils.

Did you know?
Dhal is the Hindi word for dried peas and beans.

Top marks!
Pulses are very popular with vegetarians. Find a main course vegetarian dish that uses boiled, poached or steamed pulses.

Healthy eating
Pulses contain no saturated fats and are a healthy alternative to meat.

Did you know?
Adding salt to pulses during the soaking or cooking process will cause them to toughen. Salt and other seasoning can be added at the end if required.

Purée of lentil soup

Lentils, red	250g
Pork or bacon rind	30–40g
Onion, diced	30–40g
Carrot, diced	30–40g
Water	1.25 litres
Bouquet garni	1
Salt	to season
Butter, clarified	40g
Milk, boiling	150–200ml
Bread for croûtons	100g
Cooking time	1 hour
Serves	6

Method

1. Wash the lentils well and soak for half an hour.
2. Lightly sauté the diced bacon or pork rind in 25g butter, using a thick-bottomed pan.
3. Add the diced carrot and onion, lightly colour.
4. Add the strained lentils and stir. Cook gently for 10–15 minutes.
5. Add water and bouquet garni. Cover with a lid and simmer until the lentils are tender and fully cooked. Add salt in the last ten minutes.
6. Remove bouquet garni. Pass the soup through a sieve.
7. Reboil, pass through a fine chinois.
8. Reboil, taste for seasoning. Check the thickness, adding a little boiling milk if necessary. The consistency of the soup should be like thick double cream.
9. Add the clarified butter (15g) to complete the soup. Check the seasoning and add salt, if necessary.
10. Serve croûtons separately.

Healthy eating

Purée soups are healthier than cream of velouté soups.
Avoid the use of fresh cream, butter or cream and egg yolk liaison to finish the soups.
Avoid over-seasoning the soups.
Serve toasted croûtons instead of croûtons shallow-fried in butter.

Chef's tip

Omit the pork or bacon rind for a vegetarian option.

Figure 7.4 Dried pulses: a) chickpeas,
b) lentils, c) split yellow peas and split
green peas

Marcus says:
Ensure you use the correct method of boiling for each ingredient. Some require boiling from cold and some need to be put in to boiling water. Don't forget to season the water, unless you are cooking pulses, which will go hard in salty water.

Other ingredients suitable for boiling

Fruit is usually boiled to make jam or other preserves, e.g. strawberries, raspberries, plums.

Poultry can be boiled and this method is used to cook older and tougher birds (capons or broilers). Young poultry is usually poached.

Meats – cheaper cuts of beef such as silverside can be boiled or simmered after soaking in water overnight. Allow 25 minutes per ½ kg. It can be served with vegetables and dumplings.

Shellfish – boiling is the most common method of cooking shellfish. Fish are not usually boiled but poached.

Sous vide

Sous vide is a modern method of cooking. Either raw or cooked food is placed in an air-tight, sealed plastic pouch. The food is refrigerated and stored and then cooked or reheated in boiling water when required. This method of cooking has the advantage that texture, nutrients and flavour are retained that would be destroyed through conventional reheating methods.

Remember!
Food safety
Great care is required when turning simmering meat. Do not use a fork to turn the meat as its juices will escape into the liquid and it will lose flavour.

Did you know?
Sous vide was invented by Michelin star chef George Pralus in 1974 to drastically reduce the amount of foie gras lost during traditional cooking methods.

Prepare and cook food by poaching

In this section you will learn how to prepare and cook the following range of food using the poaching method:

○ chicken
○ eggs
○ fish
○ fruit.

What is poaching?

Poaching is a wet method of cooking food slowly and gently in a simmering liquid. The amount of liquid depends on the dish being cooked.

The liquid is generally boiled first and then kept just below boiling point at approximately 80–90°C. For some delicate dishes, such as poached salmon, the temperature can be lower. The poaching liquid may affect the food being cooked, as it may add flavour. Poaching liquids can include stock, milk, wine and water.

Foods suitable for poaching

Fish, eggs and vegetables are examples of food that is suitable for poaching Poaching helps tenderise the fibres in the food and makes the raw food edible.

Methods and equipment

The two methods of poaching are shallow and deep.

Deep poaching

This is usually carried out on top of the oven and the food is fully covered by the cooking liquid.

Shallow poaching

The food is partially covered by the cooking liquid and the process is started on top of the oven and completed in the oven. As the food is partially covered it is usually covered with a **cartouche** and/ or a lid.

Various types of equipment can be used for poaching, including: saucepans, fish kettles, round or oval pans. A palette knife, fish slice or perforated spoon can be used to drain the food from the poaching liquid.

Foods such as cuts of fish and chicken are cooked in a minimum of liquid and should never be allowed to boil. This can be achieved by finishing the dish in a moderately hot oven.

Whole fish or cuts of fish, e.g. salmon, can be deep poached in a **court bouillon** and chicken in a white stock.

Eggs should be deep poached in gently simmering water with a little vinegar added. The acid in the vinegar helps to set the protein in the egg.

Deep poaching	Shallow poaching
Fruit – usually poached in syrup	Fish
Eggs	Poultry
Poultry	Eggs

Figure 7.5 Foods suitable for deep and shallow poaching

> **Definitions**
>
> **Cartouche** – a greased greaseproof paper that is placed over shallow poached food to prevent the food drying out.
>
> **Court bouillon** – a flavoured liquor for cooking fish, made by adding vinegar, parsley, thyme and peppercorns to water.

> **Marcus says:**
>
> If you are poaching eggs, make sure the eggs are fresh, so that the white clings to the yolk, and of course for the best colour.

Eggs

Poached eggs can be used as an accompaniment or eaten on their own as a breakfast meal or as or in a starter dish to a main meal.

How to poach an egg

1 Put some water, a splash of vinegar and a pinch of salt into a pan.

2 Bring the water to the boil, then allow it to simmer just below boiling point.

3 Gently crack an egg into a dish and then place it into the water. Leave it to poach for 3–5 minutes depending on size.

4 Use a perforated spoon to gently remove the cooked egg.

5 Trim and drain.

Poached eggs can be drained, refreshed in iced water to stop the cooking process and stored in the refrigerator for later use. To reheat a poached egg, put it into very hot (but not boiling) salted water. When the egg starts to float, turn it once and leave it for one minute. Then remove it from the water using a perforated spoon. Drain, then serve.

Investigate!

Look on the internet for video demonstrations of how to poach an egg. Compare the methods with how you have been taught. Practise at home to ensure you pass the practical assessment.

Eggs florentine

Butter	25g
Spinach	75g
Salt and freshly ground black pepper	to taste
Free-range eggs	2
Double cream	100ml
Oven temperature	200°C
Cooking time	10 minutes
Serves	1

Preparation	1
Cooking skills	2
Finishing	1

Method

1 Preheat the oven to 200°C.
2 Melt the butter in a frying pan over a medium heat. Add the spinach and sauté for three minutes, or until wilted.
3 Place the spinach into a small ovenproof dish and season well with salt and freshly ground black pepper.
4 Crack the eggs into the dish and pour over the cream, then place into the oven and bake for 10 minutes, until golden and bubbling.
5 Serve in the ovenproof dish.

Tossed green salad with lardons

Cos lettuce	1
Little gem lettuce	1
Cucumber	½
Green pepper	1
Celery	1–2 sticks
Bacon lardons	100g
Olive oil	15ml
Seasoning	to taste
Bread cubes	50g
Garlic	1–2 cloves
Serves	2

Preparation	2
Cooking skills	2
Finishing	2

Method

1. Roughly chop all the ingredients and toss in the olive oil.
2. Crush the garlic cloves into a paste. Add with a little olive oil into a frying pan. Heat.
3. Add the bread cubes and fry till golden brown all over.
4. Remove bread cubes and drain .
5. Add the bacon lardons to the hot oil and fry until golden brown and crisp.
6. Remove the bacon lardons and drain off excess oil.
7. Add the fried bread and lardons to the tossed salad and serve.

Chicken

White stock is usually used to poach chicken breasts off the bone. This takes approximately 20 minutes. If you add a **bouquet garni** and other vegetables, you can use the stock to make the accompanying sauce, e.g. mushroom sauce.

Chef's tip

To check that the chicken is cooked, insert a temperature probe. A core temperature of 75° should be reached and any juices should run clear.

Boiled or poached chicken

Preparation	2
Cooking skills	2
Finishing	3

1 Place the chicken in cold water. Bring to the boil and skim.
2 Add peeled, whole vegetables (onion, carrot, celery), bouquet garni, peppercorns and salt.
3 Simmer until cooked. Test using a skewer and ensure the juices are clear.
4 Make a velouté sauce in a separate saucepan using the cooking liquor – see recipe below.
5 Season with salt and pepper.
6 Strain into a clean saucepan and bring back to the boil.
7 Coat the chicken pieces with the sauce and serve with poached rice.

Velouté sauce

Butter, margarine or oil	75g
Flour	75g
Stock	1 litre

(use the cooking liquor from poaching the chicken)

1 Melt the butter or margarine or warm the oil.
2 Add the flour to make a **roux**.
3 Gradually incorporate the cooking liquor to a smooth consistency. Bring to the boil and simmer to allow the ingredients to cook and the sauce to thicken
4 Season with salt and pepper.
5 Pass through a fine strainer. Reheat, stirring all the time.
6 Finish by adding cream just before serving. Do not reboil.

Variations

- For chicken à la king, add button mushrooms, pimentos and sherry to the velouté sauce.
- Serve in a vol au vent.
- For coronation chicken, mix cold diced boiled chicken with mayonnaise, pineapple, finely diced onion and curry paste. Use as a sandwich filling.

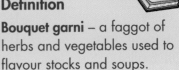

Definition

Bouquet garni – a faggot of herbs and vegetables used to flavour stocks and soups.

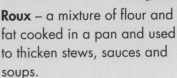

Definition

Roux – a mixture of flour and fat cooked in a pan and used to thicken stews, sauces and soups.

Healthy eating

Use yoghurt instead of mayonnaise.

Fish

Fish can be poached in stock, wine or a court bouillon.

Poached fillet of fish

Preparation	3
Cooking skills	3
Finishing	3

Fillets of white fish	600–800g
Finely chopped sweated onion	15g
Fish stock	90ml (120ml if not using wine)
White wine (optional)	30ml
Lemon, squeezed	½
Serves	6

Method

1. Fillet and skin the fish (if using whole), trim and wash.
2. Butter and season an earthenware dish.
3. Sprinkle with the sweated onion.
4. Place the fish on top.
5. Season, add the fish stock, wine (optional) and lemon juice.
6. Cover with buttered greaseproof (cartouche).
7. Poach in the oven at a moderate temperature of 150–200°C for 5–10 minutes.
8. Drain well, keeping the cooking liquid. Place on a clean and warmed serving or earthenware dish.
9. Use the cooking liquor to add to the sauce of your choice.

Sauces

- White wine sauce: Use the cooking liquor to make a velouté, add some butter and cream and coat the fillets. Serve.
- Bonne-femme: Add sliced white mushrooms before cooking, and add chopped parsley and an egg yolk to the velouté sauce before covering the fish and browning under the grill.
- Mornay: Use the reduced cooking liquor to make a cheese sauce. Correct the seasoning and strain. Add butter and cream, coat the fish and sprinkle with grated cheese and place under the grill to brown.

Folding flat fish

When poaching flat fish such as plaice or sole, it can be folded or rolled. This is done for ease, space saving and presentation purposes.

Other poached fish dishes

Smoked haddock is a popular breakfast dish. Simmer the smoked haddock on top of the stove in milk and water. Drain well and serve with a poached egg.

To poach a whole salmon: immerse the fish in a court bouillon, ideally in a fish kettle.

To poach cuts of fish, such as salmon darnes or fillets, place the fish into simmering liquid to seal in the flavours.

> **Chef's tip**
>
> The fish cooking liquor can be strained and butter added. Whipped double cream is added if the sauce is to be **glazed**.

> **Definition**
>
> **Glazed** – browned in the oven or under a grill.

Figure 7.6 A fish kettle is the perfect tool for deep poaching a whole fish

Fruit

Most varieties of fruit can be poached, although hard fruit such as apples, pears and peaches are most commonly cooked in this way. Fruit can be poached in sweetened red or white wine or in a stock syrup.

Poaching fruit in stock syrup

Preparation	1
Cooking skills	1
Finishing	2

Sugar	115g
Water or sweet red or white wine	285ml

Approximately 450g of fruit, e.g.:
- 2–3 whole pears depending on size
- 4–6 peach halves
- 12 apricots

Method

1 Put sugar and water or wine into a saucepan.
2 Boil them and skim off any impurities.

At this stage you can add flavours such as cinnamon sticks, lemons, oranges and coriander seed.

Preparing the fruit

Apples and pears are usually peeled and can be cut into even-sized pieces before poaching. They can also be poached whole. Peaches need only be halved and the stone removed as the skin will come off more easily after the fruit has been poached.

Poaching the fruit

1 Add the fruit to the poaching liquid, ensuring it is simmering and not boiling.
2 Cover with a lid or greaseproof paper to ensure the fruit stays submerged as it cooks.
3 Simmer as gently as possible until the fruit is cooked but still firm. Use a knife to test – the fruit should offer no resistance but not be mushy.
4 Carefully remove with a slotted spoon.
5 If using whole apples or pears, use a knife or spoon to remove the core.
6 Gently remove the skin on peaches.

Prepare and cook food by steaming

In this section you will learn how to prepare and cook the following range of food using the steaming method:

○ chicken

○ vegetables

○ fish

○ sweet and savoury puddings.

What is steaming?

Steaming is cooking food using moist heat from steam generated by boiling water. Steaming can be done either at atmospheric pressure or at high pressure, using special pressurised equipment.

Steaming is an easy and popular method of cooking as it preserves the nutrients within food far better than other cooking methods.

Steaming methods

Atmospheric or low-pressure steaming

This can be either direct or indirect.

○ Direct steaming involves placing the food directly into the steam – e.g. vegetables placed in a steamer pan above a saucepan of boiling water.

○ Indirect steaming means that the food is sealed in a container such as a basin before being placed in the steam – e.g. a steamed pudding.

High-pressure steaming

This involves purpose-built equipment that does not allow the steam to escape. In a commercial kitchen the steamer is an important piece of equipment. The pressure is allowed to build up and this reduces the cooking time.

When steaming food, the texture will vary according to the type of food, type of steamer used and the degree of heat, pressure and time taken – e.g. steamed sponges will be light in texture.

Marcus says:

It is important to keep an eye on the pan, especially if cooking something for a long time, such as a pudding. The water will evaporate and not only affect the cooking process, but ruin your pan too!

Using a commercial steamer

Check there is enough water in the steamer before turning it on. Be careful! Steam can be extremely dangerous. It can cause severe scalds so take care when you open the steamer door and do not touch the hot equipment surfaces.

Allow the pressure to release before opening the door or removing the lid. Use the door as a shield on commercial steamers.

Follow the manufacturer's instructions to clean and operate the steamer.

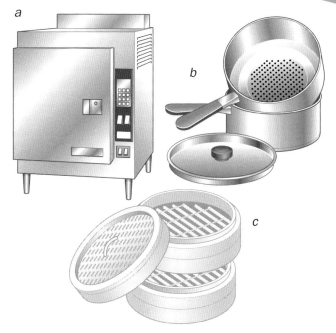

Figure 7.7 Different types of steamer: a) an industrial steamer, b) a simple two-part steamer with lid, c) a covered bamboo steamer used in Oriental cookery

Foods suitable for steaming and cooking techniques

Chicken

A combination steamer oven (see page 143) can be used to steam chicken. The chicken is steamed first to retain nutritional value and flavour and to prevent the chicken from drying out. The oven can be programmed to go onto a normal convection programme to add colour to the skin.

Vegetables

Many vegetables are suitable for steaming, including: potatoes, carrots, cauliflower, broccoli, swede, turnip, Brussels sprouts, beans and peas. Some vegetables will retain their acids and will turn an unappetising dark colour as a result of steaming.

Care should be taken when steaming delicate vegetables such as mangetout or broccoli.

Did you know?
Steaming food is widely used in Oriental and Asian cookery, using wicker baskets over woks.

Healthy eating
By steaming vegetables and pulses the goodness or nutritional value is preserved, unlike any other method of cooking.

Meat

Meats are not usually steamed, but can be combined with other ingredients to produce steamed dishes such as steak and kidney puddings.

Fish

Any fish or cut of fish that can be poached or boiled can also be steamed. In a commercial kitchen catering for large numbers, steaming has the advantage of cooking the fish to a consistent standard, retaining its nutritional value and keeping its flavour and colour.

Did you know?

The Chinese often steam fish and recipes may also include vegetables, herbs and spices to enhance the dish.

Investigate!

Find a Chinese steamed fish recipe on the internet.

Rice

Steamed rice is popular in Chinese-style cookery. There are many types of rice – all can be boiled and most can be steamed. The two main methods of steaming rice are as follows.

○ Method 1: Wash the rice in cold water and put it into a steamer pan over boiling water for 20–40 minutes.
○ Method 2: Boil–steam the rice by covering the rice with 1.5 times as much cold water in a saucepan. When the water boils, put on a tight-fitting lid and turn down the heat until all the water is absorbed or evaporated.

Rice pudding

Short grain rice	75g
Caster sugar	75g
Milk	750ml
Butter or margarine	15g
Vanilla essence	3–4 drops
Grated nutmeg	

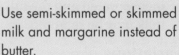

Preparation   1
Cooking skills   1
Finishing   –

Method

1. Wash the rice and place in an ovenproof dish.
2. Add the sugar and milk and mix.
3. Put in the butter and vanilla essence and sprinkle the nutmeg on top.
4. Place on a baking sheet and place in the oven to bake at 180–200°C until the milk starts simmering.
5. Reduce the heat and allow the pudding to cook slowly for 1½–2 hours.

Healthy eating

Use semi-skimmed or skimmed milk and margarine instead of butter.

Sweet and savoury puddings

Sponge puddings of various flavours can be cooked in **sleeves**, **dariole** moulds or pudding basins in a steamer. They can be served with a variety of toppings and sauces.

When making steamed puddings, grease the basins, then fill them and cover with greased greaseproof paper or foil. This is done to prevent moisture penetration which will result in a soggy pudding. The paper or foil is folded into pleats before placing over the basin. This is to allow the mixture sufficient space to expand. You will not need to butter or oil the greaseproof paper, as the sponge will not stick to it.

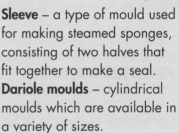

Definitions

Sleeve – a type of mould used for making steamed sponges, consisting of two halves that fit together to make a seal.
Dariole moulds – cylindrical moulds which are available in a variety of sizes.

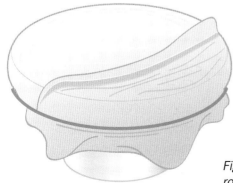

Figure 7.8 Folding paper allows room for the pudding to expand

Basic sponge pudding

Soft flour	250g
Baking powder	5g
Butter	250g
Caster sugar	250g
Medium eggs	4

Preparation	2
Cooking skills	1
Finishing	2

1 Sift flour and baking powder together into a bowl.
2 Flour and butter 10 individual dariole moulds.
3 Cream together the butter and sugar until light and fluffy.
4 Beat in the egg a little at a time.
5 Add the sifted flour and baking powder. Lightly mix until incorporated and the mixture falls easily from a spoon. Some milk may be required.

Variations

- Syrup pudding: Put 25g of syrup per portion into the bottom of a dariole mould before filling with sponge mix.
- Lemon sponge pudding: Add the grated zest of one lemon and a couple of drops of lemon essence to the mixture. Serve with a lemon or vanilla sauce.
- Fruit pudding: Add 100g of dried fruit (sultanas, raisins or currants) to the basic recipe. Serve with custard sauce.

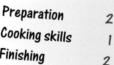

Investigate!

Find recipes for at least five varieties of steamed puddings other than those listed in the recipe below.

Remember!

Food safety

Make sure the insides of commercial steamers are clean before use, as they are ideal breeding grounds for bacteria.

Orange sauce

Oranges	2
Caster sugar	50g
Water	50ml
Cornflour	10g
Lemon juice	few drops

Preparation	1
Cooking skills	1
Finishing	1

Method

1 Wash, zest and juice the oranges.
2 Dilute the cornflour with the water.
3 Boil the orange juice with the sugar.
4 Add the diluted cornflour, whisking continuously.
5 Reboil until clear. Strain.
6 Add orange zest and a few drops of lemon juice.

Try this!

Write down three advantages and three disadvantages of steaming foods.

Chef's tip

Add 20ml of brandy, Grand Marnier or Cointreau to enhance the flavour.

Test yourself!

1 Identify which categories of food can be boiled, poached or steamed. Complete the table.

	Boiled	Poached	Steamed
Vegetables			
Eggs			
Pasta			
Pulses and Grains			
Chicken			
Fish			
Fruit			
Sweet Puddings			
Savoury Puddings			

2 Name four liquids used to poach food.

3 What are the two different methods used to boil food? When is each method used?

4 Why is vinegar added to the water to poach an egg?

5 List three safety points when handling hot or boiling liquids.

6 Name at least three steamed vegetables that can be used in a panache (or selection) for an accompaniment to a main course.

7 Give two examples of varieties of steamed puddings and two accompanying sauces.

8 State the quality points to look for in a hard-boiled egg.

Practice assignment tasks

Task 1

Write a report on the basic principles of cooking vegetables. Include the following.

○ Produce a table listing examples of vegetables suitable for different cooking methods.
○ Explain why it is best to cook each type of vegetable using the particular method chosen.
○ Work out a time plan to cook a selection (panache) of six vegetables using at least two cooking methods.

Task 2

Write a report on how to poach an egg.

○ List all the equipment required to make the dish.
○ Identify the key preparation and cookery skills used to make the dish.
○ State how you would finish the dish.
○ Identify three dishes for which a poached egg could be used as an accompaniment.

Task 3

Write a report on steamed puddings.

○ Name two types of puddings and give an example of each.
○ Explain why safety is very important when using a high-pressure steamer.
○ Identify the key preparation and cooking skills required to make a steamed sponge pudding.
○ Give two reasons why folded greaseproof is tied to the top of the pudding basin.

Stewing and braising

8

This chapter covers the following outcomes from Diploma unit 108: Prepare and cook food by stewing and braising

- Outcome 108.1 Be able to prepare and cook food by stewing
- Outcome 108.2 Be able to prepare and cook food by braising

Working through this chapter could also provide the opportunity to practise the following Functional Skills at Level 1:

Functional Maths: Analysing – solve problems requiring calculation, with common measures, including money, time, length, weight, capacity and temperature; convert units of measure in the same system.

In this chapter you will learn about:

- Food items which can be stewed and braised
- Purpose and use of these cooking methods
- Liquids used to stew and braise
- Methods and ways to stew and braise
- Equipment used when cooking this way
- Associated techniques when stewing and braising
- Quality points to look for when preparing, cooking and finishing dishes when braising and stewing

Introduction

Stewing and braising are so similar that they are almost identical. Both involve cooking food over low heat, in liquid in a covered container for a long period of time. Both methods produce dishes which are easily prepared, relatively low in cost and full of flavour. They are great ways of preparing food ahead. They taste better the next day and freeze reasonably well.

The difference between the two is that braising calls for less liquid than stewing and the meat is either left whole or in large pieces. Stews are usually made of small pieces of meat totally covered with liquid, most often water. The meat may or may not be browned first, and the cooking liquid becomes the sauce, which can be thickened with flour. Some definitions suggest that braising is carried out in the oven and stewing on the top but this isn't always the case.

Stews and braises offer the caterer creative opportunity. Strong vegetables such as onions, carrots and parsnips are suitable to be cooked for a long period of time. More delicate types of vegetable, like mushrooms, potatoes, peas, and green beans, will lose their colour and shape when overcooked. This type of vegetable should be added during the final 20 or 30 minutes of cooking. If the dish is made ahead, these vegetables can go into the pot at the reheating stage.

Try this!

Before reading on, think of five dishes that are stewed and five dishes that you think are braised and then compare your answers with a colleague.

History

This ancient method of cooking a meat or vegetable – with liquid in a covered dish using low heat – has been around for at least 300,000 years, ever since human beings first learned to prepare food on this planet.

Half a million years ago, before they tamed fire, early humans ate raw fruits, tubers and the occasional wild game. This involved constant foraging and lots of chewing. A caveman's feast on the carcass of a wild animal would have involved hours of chewing to break down the fibres in the meat.

Once humans learned to cook, everything changed. The heat in cooking breaks down the fibres in meat and plants. This makes chewing easier and allows us to consume many more calories in far less time.

Figure 8.1 The front legs of the animal do more work because they have to support the head. So the meat is tougher and more suitable for slow wet cooking methods such as stewing and braising.

What happens when you stew or braise meat?

The meat that we eat is made up of muscle fibres and connective tissue. The muscle fibres are the long red strands we usually think of as meat. The connective tissue is the thin, translucent film that helps hold the bundles of muscle fibre together. Connective tissue is made up of mostly **collagen**.

Braising or stewing meat involves breaking down tough connective tissue and changing it into collagen. Moist heat is applied for a period of time depending on what you are cooking. If cooked at a temperature of about 60°C for long enough, the collagen breaks down and dissolves into gelatine.

At the same time as the connective tissue is breaking down, the muscle fibres start to contract, coil and expel moisture. In effect, the heat is drying out the meat, like squeezing a sponge. As the process continues and the meat breaks down, it becomes more tender but very dry.

Eventually the muscle fibres begin to relax. When this happens they begin to absorb back some of the melted fat, cooking liquid and gelatine, giving the meat a wonderful texture and flavour. This is why braised or stewed meat tastes so incredibly good when cooked properly.

Definition

Collagen – a very strong protein found in meat that breaks down if enough heat is applied to it.

Healthy eating

Use more heart-healthy proteins such as fish, poultry, beans and low-fat or non-fat dairy products. Use less red meat, which contains high levels of saturated fat.

213

Preparing and cooking food by stewing

What is stewing?

A stew is a combination of solid food ingredients that have been cooked in water or another water-based liquid. Stews are normally simmered at low temperatures. They are served without draining the cooking liquid.

The ingredients in a stew can include any combination of vegetables (e.g potatoes and beans), fruits (e.g. peppers, tomatoes, apricots or prunes), meat, poultry and seafood. Water is the most commonly used stewing liquid, but these days wine, stock, cider and beer are also used.

Stewing is suitable for the least tender cuts of meat. They become tender and juicy with the slow moist heat method. Stews are often thickened by the addition of flour – the pieces of meat are coated with flour before seasoning. For more on thickening methods see page 218.

Advantages of stewing

The advantages of stewing are that:
- the meat juices are retained as part of the stew
- nutrients are conserved with this cooking process
- tougher meats cuts are tenderised during the cooking
- the correct slow cooking results in very little evaporation
- it is more economical in labour because stew can be bulk cooked.

Typical stewed recipes include: beef bourguignonne, beef goulash, navarin of lamb and fricassée of veal.

Marcus says:

A great way to use cheaper cuts of meat - you can leave the bones on for flavour and either serve them such as lamb shanks or remove prior to serving. Remember to stagger the cooking time for your ingredients, meat first and then vegetables. The cooking time is affected by the size of the chunks and the texture of each vegetable.

Equipment used for stewing

For stewing you will need:

- heavy gauge pan with lid and handles
- chopping board
- kitchen fork
- preparation and serving platters
- spoon and tongs
- digital thermometer
- good-quality knife.

Heavy gauge pan with lid and handles

This is very important. A heavy gauge pan will help ensure that the stew does not burn during cooking. A tightly fitting lid will prevent the liquid evaporating during the cooking process.

Chopping boards

Most catering establishments now have plastic colour-coded chopping boards. The colour coding is to avoid possible cross-contamination. One board should be used for raw meat and different boards for cooked foods, vegetables and other foods.

For cutting ingredients such as raw meats, a larger board may be more comfortable as it gives you more room to work. However, you must be able to wash the cutting board easily in the sink.

Kitchen knives

Knives come in all sizes and shapes, and each has a different function. The most commonly used is the chef's knife. This is normally about 17 to 25 cm long. You may use two or three different knives during the preparation of food for a stew. You must know which knife to use for which purpose.

Good control of the knife is the essential to cutting all ingredients. You must hold the knife firmly and your cutting action should be light but definite. Use a sawlike action, allowing the knife to roll slightly forwards and backwards. Good control is often the means of preventing injury.

For more information on choosing and using knives, see Chapter 5 on pages 154–157.

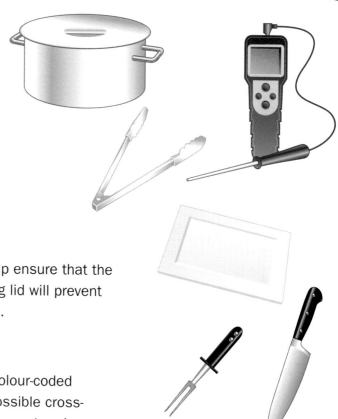

Figure 8.2 Equipment used for stewing

Chef's tip

Cleaning and handling knives and chopping boards

To safely clean knives, it is best to place the blade on a flat surface and wipe one side with a wet cloth, then turn and wipe the other side. Always use hot, soapy water to clean a knife that has been used to cut poultry, meat or fish.

To help prevent contamination, wash chopping boards with hot, soapy water immediately after use. Let the board stand for a short time, then wipe it with a clean cloth.

Methods and processes
Meat and vegetable stew

beef	500g
oil	25ml
onions	100g
carrots	150g
celery	150g
potatoes	125g
flour	15g
stock	500ml
bouquet garni	1 small
parsley (chopped)	
salt and pepper	to taste
Serves	4

Preparation	3
Cooking skills	2
Finishing	1

1 Cut all the ingredients into roughly the same-sized pieces so that they cook evenly. Stews are usually made up of smaller pieces of meat and vegetables so that the pieces are bite size and their flavours can mingle.

2 Heat a large saucepan or stockpot over medium-high heat and add the oil – enough so that the meat won't stick.

3 Season the meat with salt and pepper and add it to the pan. The pan should be hot enough for the meat to sizzle. Brown the meat thoroughly, but don't cook it all the way through.

4 Remove the meat when it is browned and add all the vegetables except the potatoes. Most stews use a mixture of onions, celery and carrots. Cook these for a few minutes, stirring them around.

5 Add about 15g of flour for each 500ml of cooking liquid you will use in step 7. This will thicken the stew as it cooks. Stir the flour into the vegetables and cook for a few minutes before placing the meat back in the pan.

Add a bouquet garni.

Cover the stew with liquid: water, stock, wine or a combination of these. Homemade stock is best, but low-sodium canned stock will do. Any dry wine will work – different wines give your stew different tastes.

Bring the mixture to a boil, lower the heat to a simmer and cook until the meat is done (see Figure 8.3 for approximate cooking times). Add the potatoes for the last 30 minutes of cooking. Sprinkle on freshly chopped parsley or another herb that will complement the flavours of the stew.

Main ingredients	Cooking time	Points to note
Vegetables only – no meat	20–25 minutes	Needs constant checking to ensure it does not overcook.
Poultry	60 minutes	Timings may vary depending on the size of the pieces of meat. To check if the meat is cooked, remove a piece and taste it – it should be tender but not mushy.
Lamb and veal	90 minutes	
Beef	up to 3 hours	

Figure 8.3 Cooking times for stews

Quality points

Tougher cuts make the best stew meat, because the slow cooking tenderises the meat. Long stewing actually makes tender cuts tougher. Look for "stewing meat" in the supermarket or butcher's. It's usually the cheapest. If using beef, cubed chuck makes the best stew.

Potatoes are indispensable in most stews. The trick is to add them after the stew has simmered for a while so that they don't overcook and fall apart. Add potatoes cut in quarters or large cubes when there is about 30 minutes of cooking time left.

Healthy eating

With all recipes, decrease the meat content and increase the vegetables to make the dish healthier.
Use low-salt products instead of normal cooking salt.

Associated techniques

Some of the associated techniques that you could use during or after the cooking process of stews include the following.

Skimming

You might need to skim a stew if there is too much oil in the cooking container. The oil will float to the top of the cooking liquid and can be skimmed off using a perforated spoon.

Straining

You can use a sieve or colander to separate the desired elements of the stew from unwanted material. You might do this to separate the cooking liquid from the solid food items.

Thickening methods

Roux – a cooked mixture of flour and fat used to thicken stews, sauces and soups. Heat 2 tbsp oil and 4 tbsp flour together, stirring constantly until the mixture turns light brown. Whisk this into the stew just before the end of the cooking time and simmer for about 15 minutes. Repeat if necessary to increase the thickness further.

Beurre manié – a dough, consisting of equal parts of soft butter and flour, used to thicken soups, stews and sauces. The flour and butter are kneaded together, then the beurre manié is whisked into a hot or warm liquid. The butter melts, releasing the flour particles without creating lumps. Beurre manié is similar to roux but the flour and butter are not cooked first.

Liaison – a mixture of egg yolk and cream, used as a thickener in stews, sauces and soups. To prevent curdling, the liaison should be added off the heat and just before serving. Egg yolks must be mixed with a little hot liquid before adding to the stew in order to prevent curdling.

Reduction – a way of thickening a liquid mixture, like a soup, stew or sauce, by boiling rapidly to evaporate some of the liquid until the desired thickness is reached. Reduction can also intensify the flavour.

Healthy eating
Instead of using white flour to make the roux use a whole-grain version.

Healthy eating
In recipes calling for milk or cream, use the reduced fat type instead of full fat.

Stewed dishes

Coq au vin (Chicken cooked in wine)

Chicken	2 × 1.2kg
Bacon	100g
Brandy	25ml
Bouquet garni	1 small
Garlic	1 clove
Button onions	24
Button mushrooms	100g
Red wine	250ml
Chicken stock	125ml
Beurre manié	100g
Heart shaped croutons	8
Oil	
Parsley (chopped)	
Salt and pepper	
Serves	10

Method

1 Cut the chicken for sauté – see pages 220 to 222. Peel and crush the garlic.
2 Cut the bacon into lardons, blanch and refresh them. Peel the onions.
3 Season the chicken pieces, fry in the hot oil to a golden brown. Pour in brandy and set the brandy alight.
4 Remove the chicken from the pan and place in a casserole dish with a bouquet garni and the garlic.
5 Peel the onions and sauté with the mushrooms and lardons in the chicken juices until lightly coloured, then put them aside. Swill out the sauté pan with the red wine and chicken stock, add seasoning and pour over the chicken.
6 Cover with a tight fitting lid and cook in an oven at 200°C until the chicken is tender.
7 Transfer the chicken pieces into a warm serving dish and garnish with the onions, mushrooms and lardons. Keep hot.
8 Reduce the cooking liquor by a third and lightly thicken with the beurre manié.
9 Adjust the seasoning, then strain the sauce over the chicken. Reheat and serve garnished with the parsley and croutons.

Cutting a chicken for sauté

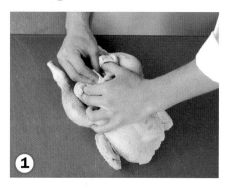

1

Make sure all the giblets have been removed. Clean the cavity – if necessary wash it out under cold running water and wipe it with a kitchen towel.

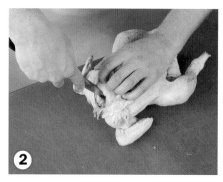

2

To remove the wishbone, pull the skin back around the neck area. Use an 8–10-inch chef's knife to rub the flesh on each side to expose the wishbone. You can see where the wishbone is joined to the shoulder blade.

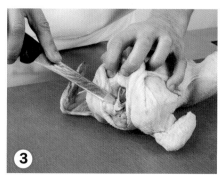

3

Using the point of the knife cut through the bone on each side.

4

Run your finger along each side of the bone to the top. At the top there is an oval-shaped piece of bone attaching the wishbone to the breast. Pinch this and pull to remove the wishbone.

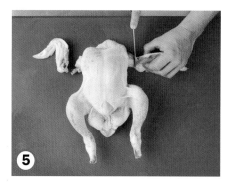

5

Cut above the wing joint. Scrape flesh back to expose a clean bone.

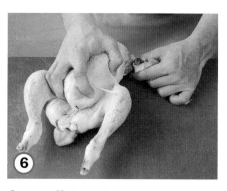

6

Snap off the wing at the joint. Repeat on the other side.

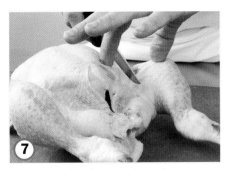

⑦ Pull out the leg and make a small cut through the skin to expose the flesh.

⑧ Push the thigh backwards to expose the bone. Hold the leg and pop the bone from the socket.

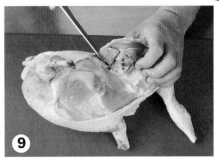

⑨ Work around the small piece of flesh on the back. This is the "oyster".

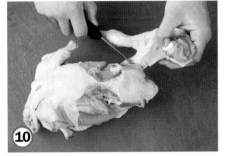

⑩ Remove the leg. Repeat to remove the second leg (2 pieces).

⑪ Cut the flesh at the bottom of the drumstick and scrape it back to the joint.

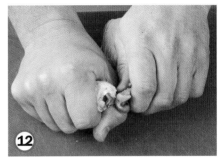

⑫ Snap the joint, leaving a small piece of clean bone exposed.

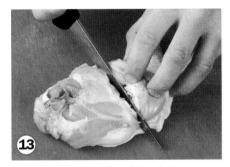

⑬ Smooth the skin. Put the meat skin side down. There should be a visible line of fat. Using this as your guide, cut through between the drumstick and thigh. Repeat on the other side (4 pieces).

⑭ Remove the ball joint from each drumstick. Press down with the heel of the knife to cut off the bone. Repeat with the other leg.

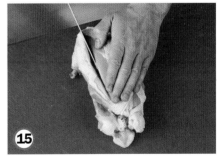

⑮ Have the cavity end towards you. Follow the feather lines along the breast, cutting through the shoulder.

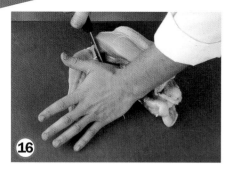

16 Put your hand over the front of the knife to steady it. Push the knife down to cut right through the bones. Remove the wing with part of the breast. Repeat on the other side (6 pieces).

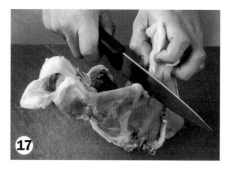

17 Turn the chicken onto its side. Cut the remaining carcass from the breast.

18 Cut across the breast bone. You will need to press on the heel of the knife to cut through the bone.

19 Reassemble the 8 portions on a tray, tidying the skin as you do this.

Finished dishes

Always finish each stewed dish by serving the contents in a clean serving platter or serving casserole dish. Be careful when transferring the contents from the cooking container, which will be very hot.

Accompaniments vary according to individual taste and the dish being served. A suggestion could be stewed red cabbage with apple and freshly boiled new potatoes. Some dishes are traditionally always served with a particular accompaniment. For example, Hungarian goulash is served with flavoured rice.

Hungarian goulash

Silverside/thick flank	1kg
Olive oil	50ml
Onions	200g
Garlic	1 clove
Flour	25g
Paprika	25g
Tomato purée	25ml
Beef stock	200ml
Red wine	50ml
Fresh tomatoes	200g
Parsley (chopped)	
Potatoes	10
Serves	10

Preparation	3
Cooking skills	2
Finishing	3

Method

1 Cut the meat into 20mm dice. Peel and dice the onions. Crush the garlic.
2 Blanch and skin the tomatoes, remove the seeds and cut the flesh into quarters.
3 Trim the potatoes into barrel shapes.
4 Season the meat and shallow fry it in hot olive oil, then add the onions and garlic and cook for 4 minutes.
5 Add the flour, paprika and seasoning and cook for a further 4 minutes.
6 Add the tomato purée, tomato quarters and the stock. Bring to the boil, skim and simmer, either on top of the stove or in the oven for about 90 minutes at 180°C.
7 Add the potatoes and continue to simmer until they are cooked and the meat is tender.
8 Skim and adjust the consistency. Transfer to a warm serving dish and serve garnished with chopped parsley.

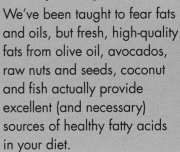

Healthy eating

We've been taught to fear fats and oils, but fresh, high-quality fats from olive oil, avocados, raw nuts and seeds, coconut and fish actually provide excellent (and necessary) sources of healthy fatty acids in your diet.

Test yourself!

1 Name a stew dish in which a liaison is added to the sauce.

2 List three different liquids that could be used for stock with stewing.

3 List two safety considerations when stewing.

Preparing and cooking food by braising

What is braising?

The process of braising means cooking food slowly with moist heat, typically in a covered pot with an amount of liquid. It is an ideal way to cook tougher cuts of meat because the moisture and slow cooking breaks down tough tissues in the meat.

There are two methods of braising – brown and white.
- In brown, joints or cuts of meats are sealed by browning on all sides in a hot pan on the stove. Sealing the meat helps to retain the flavour and the nutritive value and gives a good brown colour. The meat is then placed in a braising container with the liquid and other flavourings and cooked slowly in an oven.
- In white, vegetables and **sweetbreads** are first blanched and refreshed. Then they are cooked on a bed of root vegetables with a white stock in a covered container in the oven.

Definition

Sweetbreads – a dish made of the pancreas glands of a young animal, usually a lamb or calf.

Advantages of braising

The advantages of braising are that:
- older and tougher or even cheaper cuts of meat can be used
- maximum flavour and nutritive value is retained
- because braised dishes can be bulk cooked.

Typical braised dishes include beef olives, braised duck and pheasant.

Equipment for braising

The equipment is similar to that used for stewing – see page 215.

Methods and processes

Most braises follow the same basic steps. The meat or poultry is first seared in order to brown its surface and enhance its flavour. A cooking liquid that includes an acidic element – such as tomatoes, beer or wine – is added to the pot, often with stock. The dish is cooked covered at a very low simmer until the meat is fork tender. Often the cooking liquid is finished to create a sauce or gravy.

Braising meat and vegetables

1

Make sure that whatever cuts of meat or vegetables you are using are roughly the same size so they cook evenly. (See Quality points on page 226 for which cuts work best for braising and why.)

2

Heat a heavy frying pan, then add a little oil and heat it.

3

Season the meat or vegetables on both sides with salt and pepper or whatever seasonings your recipe requires.

4

When the oil is nice and hot, add the meat or vegetables and sauté at high heat to quickly brown the outside. This adds colour and flavour. Without browning, meat would look grey and lifeless and vegetables would be limp at the end of the cooking time.

5

When nicely browned, add enough liquid to the pan to come about halfway up the sides of the meat or vegetables. Liquid used for braising is usually water, stock, wine or a combination.

6

At this point you can either:
○ lower the heat and simmer the recipe slowly until everything is tender
○ or place the whole pan (provided it is ovenproof) in the oven and bake it.
It's up to you which you do.

What is more important is that the meat or vegetables cook slowly in the liquid and that the liquid never evaporates. See the section on Basting (page 227) to help you decide whether to cover the dish.

Be aware that braising is a slow cooking method. Most braised dishes take from 45 minutes (for smaller cuts of meat and poultry) to 6 hours for really tough shanks, ribs or even whole joints.

Braising joints

A really good braised joint can only be cooked in a well-sealed dish in the oven at moderate heat: 180°C, so that the outside heat can penetrate from all sides. Each joint should not weigh more than 2.4–4.3kg. If necessary, larger pieces can be carefully browned in a larger pan and then braised with the necessary liquid and ingredients. It must be possible to close the lid on the pan tightly.

Braising and Stewing Guide for Meat		
Cut of meat	**Thickness/Weight**	**Approx. total cooking time**
Poultry, Bone-in Breast, Leg Quarters	1.8–2.7kg	1¼–1½ hours
Lamb Shank	0.9–1.8kg	2–2½ hours
Veal Shank	3.5cm thick, 0.9–1.8kg	1½–2 hours
Beef Shank	3.5cm thick, 0.9–1.8kg	2–2½ hours
Stew Cut Meat	2.6cm cubes, 0.9–1.8kg	1¼–1½ hours
Ribs, Spare	1.6–2.7kg	1½–2½ hours
Short Ribs of Beef	3.5cm by 9cm thick, 1.8–2.7kg	2–2½ hours

Figure 8.4 Use this chart as a general guide for braising and stewing times

Quality points

Braising is good for any tough or semi-tough cut of meat, such as oxtail or beef ribs and shanks, whole joints, chuck roasts, poultry legs and thighs. It also works well with vegetables such as cabbages, onion, fennel, carrots, beetroots or artichokes and even fruit such as pineapples and apples.

Although braising vegetables and fruit is similar to braising meat, it takes much less time – only 30 minutes or less. It's easiest to cut the vegetable or fruit in half and brown it on the flat cut side.

When braised dishes are cooked correctly with the proper liquids (stocks or wine) and the right root vegetables and herbs, they have more flavour than boiled or stewed dishes. Braising doesn't dry out or burn food the way roasting can.

Braising never drowns the food. Instead, there is just enough liquid to help break down the toughness of the food, to penetrate and season it with juices and to help produce a well-flavoured sauce.

Healthy eating

When selecting vegetables to include in dishes and for garnishes, go for vegetables with bright colours, as these contain more vitamins, minerals and antioxidants. Dark green and orange vegetables, from broccoli, kale and mustard greens to butternut squash and sweet potatoes, are all excellent choices.

Associated techniques

The techniques used in braising are very similar to those used in stewing: skimming, straining and reduction. Basting can also be used.

Basting

If you want to use the braising liquid as a sauce, you can leave the pan uncovered so moisture can evaporate, thus concentrating the flavours. In this case you may need to baste the meat by pouring the sauce over it from time to time to prevent it drying out.

Often other ingredients, such as vegetables or herbs and spices, are added to flavour the liquid. But make sure the liquid level doesn't get too low, or you'll be baking and not braising, and the result will be totally different. Also, only do this with cuts that take less than 90 minutes or so to cook. Otherwise, just cover the pan.

Preparation	1
Cooking skills	2
Finishing	2

Rice pilaff

Butter	50g
Onion, chopped	100g
Long grain rice	400g
White chicken stock	800ml
Salt and pepper	to taste
Parsley, chopped	
Oven temperature	230°C–250°C
Cooking time	15 minutes
Serves	4

Method

1 Place 25g of the butter in a small sauteuse. Add the onions.
2 Cook gently without colour for 2–3 minutes. Add the rice.
3 Cook gently without colouring for a further 2–3 minutes.
4 Add twice the amount of stock to rice.
5 Season, cover with a buttered cartouche (buttered paper) and bring to the boil.
6 Place in a hot oven (230°C–250°C) for approximately 15 minutes until cooked.
7 Remove immediately to a cool sauteuse.
8 Carefully mix in the remaining butter with a two pronged fork.
9 Correct the seasoning and serve sprinkled with chopped parsley.

Braised dishes

Navarin of lamb

Lamb (boneless)	1kg
Onions	50g
Carrots	50g
Oil	25ml
Flour	50g
Tomato puree	25ml
Brown stock	1 litre
Salt and pepper	
Parsley (chopped)	10g
Glazed turnips	200g
Boiled potatoes	450g
Glazed button onions	200g
Glazed carrots	200g
Peas	50g
Bouquet garni	1 small
Serves	10

Preparation	3
Cooking skills	3
Finishing	2

Method

1 Cut the lamb into 25mm dice.
2 Heat the oil in a saucepan and fry the meat quickly to seal. Drain off any excess fat.
3 Peel and roughly dice the carrots and onions and fry them to a golden brown with the meat.
4 Sprinkle the flour over and cook in a hot oven at 200°C for 10 minutes. Remove from the oven.
5 Cover with the stock, add the tomato purée, seasoning and bouquet garni. Bring to the boil and skim.
6 Cover with a lid and simmer in the oven at 180°C for 1½ hours.
7 Transfer the meat to a serving dish. Strain the sauce and remove any surplus fat.
8 Warm the cooked vegetable garnish with a little of the sauce and add it to the meat, then pour the remaining sauce over. Garnish with parsley and serve.

Definition

Navarin – a French lamb stew, usually cooked with root vegetables. If possible use new season spring lamb which has the very best flavour.

Braised steak

Braising steak, cubed	500g
Onions	50g
Carrots	50g
Tomato purée	25g
Bouquet garni	1 small
Brown stock	375ml
Brown sauce	1.75 litre
Glazed button onions	200g
Glazed button turnips	100g
Glazed baton carrots	100g
Parsley (chopped)	
Salt and pepper	
Serves	10

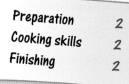

Preparation 2
Cooking skills 2
Finishing 2

Method

1 Season the steak, shallow fry it in hot oil and place it in a pan.
2 Peel and roughly dice the onions and carrots, place them with the meat. Add the brown stock, brown sauce, tomato purée and bouquet garni.
3 Bring to the boil, cover with a lid and cook at 180°C for 2 hours until tender.
4 Cook the glazed vegetable garnish (button onions, turnips and baton carrots).
5 Place the steak on a warm serving dish and garnish with the glazed vegetables.
6 Strain the sauce, remove any surplus fat, adjust the seasoning and correct consistency and pour over the steak.
7 Garnish with the parsley before serving.

Test yourself!

1 What is the difference between a beef stew and braised steaks?

2 List three other main ingredients that could be braised apart from meats.

3 Think of three different liquids that could be used for stock with braising.

Practice assignment tasks

Task 1

State the differences between stewing and braising.

List three liquids that can be used as stock.

List all the equipment required to produce a stewed meat dish.

Describe five quality points to consider when making a basic lamb stew.

Task 2

Write a report on the advantages of stewing and braising.

Name three thickening methods and describe each method.

What is the idea of skimming the sauce of a stew or braised dish?

Task 3

Write a report on the safety points when working with hot equipment in a kitchen environment.

Baking, roasting and grilling

9

This chapter covers the following outcomes from Diploma unit 109: Prepare and cook food by baking, roasting and grilling

- o Outcome 109.1 Be able to prepare and cook food by baking
- o Outcome 109.2 Be able to prepare and cook food by roasting
- o Outcome 109.3 Be able to prepare and cook food by grilling

Working through this chapter could also provide the opportunity to practise the following Functional Skills at Level 1:

Functional Maths: Representing – understand the equivalences between common fractions, decimals and percentages

In this chapter you will learn how to:

- o Check that food items are of the correct type, quantity and quality
- o Select the correct equipment for the preparation and cooking of food
- o Prepare, cook and present food to the requirements of the dish
- o Demonstrate control of time and temperature
- o Finish and present the dishes in line with dish/ customer requirements
- o Work in a safe and hygienic manner

Prepare and cook food by baking

What is baking?

Baking means cooking food by surrounding it with heat. This is done by placing the food item in a preheated oven. No additional food is needed to aid the cooking process (unlike, for example, roasting which needs the addition of fat). The heat converts the water content of the food into steam which cooks the food.

Methods

There are three different methods used when baking food:

- **dry heat** – used for e.g. baked potatoes, cakes and pastry products
- **combination oven** – allows steam to be introduced to increase the humidity – used for e.g. bread and pre-prepared products
- **bain marie** – used to slow down the cooking process and to ensure the heat is distributed evenly – used for e.g. egg custard-based products.

Rules when baking

- Preheat the oven to the correct temperature before baking the food, otherwise the food may spoil – particularly bakery and pastry products.
- Prepare the moulds or trays correctly for the type of dish you are cooking, otherwise the food may stick.
- Use a dry, thick oven cloth when taking things out of the oven to prevent burns. Heat will cause a wet cloth to steam which can cause serious burns.
- The position of the food in the oven is also important. The top of the oven is the hottest in a normal oven. In a fan-assisted oven the temperature is constant throughout the oven
- In a normal gas or electric oven the food should be positioned in the oven so that the bulk of the food is parallel to the heat source.
- To ensure products cook at the same time bake evenly sized items together.

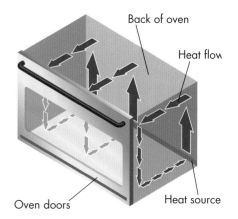

Figure 9.1 Side view of a gas oven, showing the flow of heat inside. The top is the hottest part.

Definition

Bain marie – a shallow dish of warm water that helps prevent food cooking too fast.

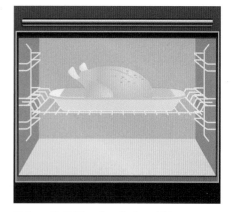

Figure 9.2 The food should be parallel to the heat source in the oven

Foods suitable for baking

Foods suitable for baking include:

- flour-based foods (both sweet and savoury) – e.g. biscuits, pastry, bread
- milk and egg-based foods – e.g. rice pudding, bread and butter pudding, quiche
- fruit – e.g. apples, pears
- vegetables – e.g. potatoes, sweet potatoes
- pre-prepared products – e.g. half-baked bread.

Marcus says:

The time and temperature of cooking is dependent on your oven type. A fan oven generally cooks faster and more evenly than a convection oven, but each individual oven is different and you need to get to know yours!

Purpose of baking

Baking helps to:

- tenderise food
- make food digestible
- make food palatable
- add texture
- develop existing flavours within the food
- retain nutritional value
- make food safe to eat.

Investigate!

Obtain a menu from a local restaurant and list the best method of cooking each dish.

Flour–based foods

Breads

Bread has been eaten by people for thousands of years. In every culture in all parts of the world bread is included in the diet. Throughout the world the fundamental ingredients of flour, yeast, salt and water do not change, even if different flavours and production methods are used – e.g. flat bread (such as pitta) or stripy tiger bread (a rice paste is applied, which cracks and dries during baking, making the stripes).

Basic bread – unsweetened yeast dough can be used to make loaves, bread rolls, and many other types of bread and bread products. Flavoured breads can be made by adding other ingredients to the basic bread dough – e.g. olives, tomatoes or nuts.

Soda bread – made using bicarbonate of soda as the raising agent instead of yeast. The liquid added to the bread dough causes a chemical reaction with the bicarbonate of soda. This means that the bread does not need time to **prove** before cooking. Soda bread is popular in Ireland.

Naan bread – an Indian flat, **leavened** bread cooked in a tandoor oven. Traditionally the tandoor oven is made from clay and heated by charcoal. Naan bread is only proved once before cooking, unlike traditional bread.

Pizza dough – an unsweetened yeast dough flavoured with olive oil, originally from Italy.

Pitta bread – a leavened dough that is proved only once and cooked on the top shelf of an oven.

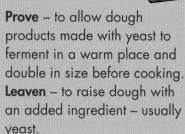

Definitions

Prove – to allow dough products made with yeast to ferment in a warm place and double in size before cooking.
Leaven – to raise dough with an added ingredient – usually yeast.

Basic bread dough

(Makes 16 rolls)

Preparation	2
Cooking skills	1
Finishing	–

Strong flour	500g
Butter	50g
Salt	10g
Sugar	5g
Fresh yeast	15g
Tepid water	approx 300ml

Method

1 Sieve the flour and salt into a large mixing bowl.
2 In a separate bowl or jug, dissolve the sugar and yeast in half of the tepid water.
3 Add the butter to the flour and rub in.
4 Make a well in the centre and add all the yeast mixture and half the remaining water.
5 Mix and draw the flour from the edge of the bowl. Make it into soft and pliable dough, adding more water as required. The dough should come away from the edge of the bowl cleanly.
6 Place the dough onto a lightly floured work surface and **knead** until it is smooth.
7 Place the dough back in the bowl, cover and allow to prove.

Chef's tip

Salt is important not only for flavour but also to stabilise the protein in the flour – which is called **gluten**. This helps the colour to develop during baking. Bread dough made without salt trends to be softer and stickier than dough made with salt.

Definitions

Gluten – the protein found in flour which gives it its strength. The strength of the gluten depends on the type of wheat and when and where it was grown.
Kneading – pressing and stretching the dough with the heel of the hand. This assists the development of the gluten and helps to make sure that the yeast is distributed throughout the dough.

Note: *The amount of liquid given is approximate. The actual amount of water needed will vary depending on the quality of the flour.*

Proving the dough

Cover the dough with a clean damp cloth or lightly oiled plastic to prevent **skinning**. Keep the dough in a warm place at a temperature of between 24°C and 29°C. Leave to prove until it has doubled in size. This should take approximately 30–40 minutes depending on the temperature. A **proving cabinet** can also be used if available.

Testing the dough

At this stage the dough should feel soft and smooth – a bit like an inflated balloon. If the dough feels tight and dry, the yeast will not be able to make the dough rise. Dough that has not had enough liquid added will produce bread that has a tight and heavy texture. It will be dry with a very hard exterior.

> **Chef's tip**
>
> The water should be body temperature (37°C) so you can test by placing your finger in the water – if your finger does not feel either hot or cold in the water, the temperature is correct. If the temperature is too high (above 49°C) it will kill the yeast.

> **Chef's tip**
>
> Do not use too much flour on the work surface when kneading, as this will be absorbed by the dough and change the balance of the recipe.

> **Definitions**
>
> **Skinning** – this is when dough is left uncovered and the surface of the dough starts to dry out. If this skin is mixed back into the dough, it will create dry pieces in the finished product.
> **Proving cabinet** – a steam-heated cabinet used to ensure even proving.
> **Knocking back** – removing the air produced during proving. It is done by kneading the dough again.
> **Scaling** – cutting and weighing the dough to the required size pieces.

Bread rolls

Preparation	1
Cooking skills	–
Finishing	2

1 While the dough is proving, prepare the trays to bake the rolls on. Lightly oil the tray and dust the surface with flour, ground rice or semolina.
2 Once the dough has doubled in size remove the cover and **knock back** by kneading the dough again. This provides an even texture during baking.
3 **Scale** the dough into 50g pieces. Keep the pieces covered to prevent skinning.
4 Mould the pieces into the desired shape.
5 Transfer each roll to the baking tray and repeat the process with the other pieces of dough.
6 Once all the rolls are moulded, cover with oiled plastic and allow to prove until double their size.

Hand moulding

Round rolls – This is the first shape to master and will assist in making other shapes correctly. Take a scaled piece of dough and knead the dough to remove any air. Then press the dough onto the work surface with the palm of your hand. Start to slowly rotate your hand whilst pressing down quite hard. As the ball forms slowly cup your hand until a nice smooth ball is achieved. The surface of the dough must be smooth with no cracks, otherwise the roll will crack during proving and cooking.

Fingers – Once you have mastered round shapes, the next shape to master is easier. Complete the moulding as for rounds. Once the smooth ball has been achieved, roll the piece backwards and forwards until a finger shape has been made. Transfer onto the baking tray as for rounds and allow the roll to prove.

Once the moulding of rounds and fingers are mastered then there are many different shapes that can be achieved. These include: knots, double knots, three-strand plaits, five-strand plaits, twists, ropes and brioche shapes.

Glazing and finishing

Once the rolls have doubled in size they are ready to be baked. To give them a more pleasing look they can be glazed and either left plain or finished with seeds – e.g. sesame, poppy, cumin or oats.

Use either an egg wash or a milk glaze:

- **egg wash** – well-beaten eggs either as they are or thinned with a small amount of milk
- **milk glaze** – full fat or semi-skimmed milk – this will produce a less shiny surface than the egg wash once cooked.

With a soft pastry brush, brush the egg wash or milk glaze all over the surface of the rolls, ensuring an even coat. Be careful not to knock the air out of the rolls and cause them to collapse.

Rolls and bread do not always have to be glazed – they can just be dusted with flour. The flour browns as the rolls bake and also helps prevent the surface of the bread becoming too hard.

To achieve a different effect, make small cuts into the surface of the rolls with a small, very sharp paring knife. If you make the cuts before proving, they will expand and give the rolls an attractive finish.

Baking

Once glazed, the rolls are ready for baking. Place into an oven at a temperature of 225°C for 20–25 minutes.

To test if the rolls are cooked, lift one of the rolls off the tray (using a cloth) and tap on the bottom. If it sounds hollow then the roll is cooked. The rolls should be glossy and golden brown in colour.

> **Chef's tip**
> Do not allow the rolls to over prove or they will collapse (no more than double their size).

Figure 9.3 Bread rolls can be made in many attractive styles

Remove from the oven and allow to cool for a few minutes before transferring them onto a **cooling wire**. If left on the baking tray the steam from the rolls will cause the base of the rolls to go soggy as they cool.

Plain scones

Plain flour	500g
Baking powder	30g
Salt	good pinch
Butter	100g
Caster sugar	100g
Egg	1 medium
Milk	230ml
Oven temperature	225°C
Baking time	15–20 minutes
Makes	16 scones using a 5–6cm pastry cutter

Preparation 2
Cooking skills 1
Finishing 1

Method

1 Sift the flour, salt and baking powder together into a bowl.
2 Rub in the butter.
3 Make a well. Add the sugar to the well.
4 Break egg into a jug. Add the milk.
5 Add the egg and milk mixture to the well and dissolve the sugar.
6 Draw in the flour and butter and continue mixing until a soft dough is achieved. Do not over-mix at this stage, but gently knead to smooth off the dough.
7 Pin out on a lightly dusted floured surface to a thickness of approximately 2cm.
8 Cut out using a scone cutter. Transfer onto lightly greased trays.
9 Knead the trimmings into a ball, pin it out and cut out as before.
10 Egg wash the tops and allow the items to relax for 15 minutes.
11 Put into the oven. To test if they are cooked, tap the bottom of the scone – it should sound hollow.
12 Allow to rest for ten minutes and transfer onto cooling wires.

Use these suggestions to make different types of scones:

Sultana scones: add 125g washed and dried sultanas. Add them at the same time as the flour, before the liquid.
Cheese scones: use 125g of grated cheddar cheese instead of sugar. Add a teaspoon of English mustard powder and a teaspoon of cayenne pepper. The spices bring out the flavour of the cheese.
Treacle scones: replace 50g of the sugar with 50g of black treacle. Add the treacle with the milk.
Wholemeal scones: replace 375g of flour with 375g of wholemeal flour. A little more milk may be required.
Potato scones: replace up to 50 per cent of the flour with cold mashed potato and omit the sugar. Pin out to a thickness of 0.5cm and cook on a lightly oiled griddle.

Biscuits

Shortbread (Makes 12–15 biscuits)

Caster sugar	100g
Butter	200g
Soft plain flour	300g

Preparation	2
Cooking skills	2
Finishing	1

Method:

1. Cream together the butter and caster sugar.
2. Sift and add the flour.
3. Mix until a soft pliable paste is formed.
4. Wrap in cling film and store in the fridge for 20 minutes to rest.
5. **Pin out** the dough to 5mm thick
6. Cut into the desired shapes and transfer to a lightly greased baking tray.
7. **Dock** the surface of each biscuit lightly.
8. Sprinkle the surface of each biscuit with caster sugar.
9. Bake in the oven at 200°C for 20 minutes or until a light golden brown.
10. Sprinkle again with caster sugar while still hot.
11. Cool slightly before transferring to a cooling wire.

Once cool, store in an airtight container until ready for service.

Variations

- Replace 25g of flour with 25g of rice flour to lighten the texture.
- For a nutty flavour add 25g of poppy seeds with the flour.
- For a citrus flavour add 25g of lemon zest with the sugar and butter.
- For a crumbly texture replace 50g of flour with either polenta (corn meal), semolina or ground almonds.

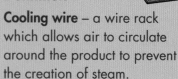

Definition

Cooling wire – a wire rack which allows air to circulate around the product to prevent the creation of steam.

Chef's tip

When making biscuits, it is best to use very soft flour, known as biscuit or cake flour. If only is strong flour available, you can replace up to 50% of the flour with cornflour. This will reduce the gluten content in the flour

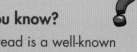

Definitions

Pin out – roll out using a rolling pin.

Dock – make holes in the surface with a tool called a docker or a fork. This allows steam to escape during cooking and prevents the item rising.

Did you know?

Shortbread is a well-known Scottish biscuit which was traditionally pressed into decorative wooden moulds prior to baking.

Figure 9.4 A shortbread mould

Savoury flour-based products

These include ready-made frozen products such as sausage rolls and pasties. All ready-made products must be cooked in accordance with the manufacturer's instructions. Recipes for some freshly made products are included below.

Short pastry

Commonly called **short paste**, this is used in many savoury recipes.

Preparation	–
Cooking skills	3
Finishing	–

Soft plain flour	500g
Salt	5g
Cornflour	25g
Butter	125g
Lard	125g
Cold water	200ml

Notes

- Here the proportion of fat to flour is 1:2. Different recipes have higher fat ratios. The pastry being made will have different qualities and requires different methods of preparation.
- Adding cornflour to the recipe softens the flour and assists in producing a better quality pastry.

Method

1. Sift the flour and salt together into a bowl.
2. Rub the butter into the flour.
3. Make a well. Add 80% of the water and mix to form a soft dough. Add more water if required. Mix gently to combine but do not overmix.
4. Wrap in cling film and allow to rest in the fridge for at least 30 minutes.

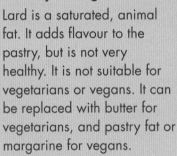

Healthy eating

Lard is a saturated, animal fat. It adds flavour to the pastry, but is not very healthy. It is not suitable for vegetarians or vegans. It can be replaced with butter for vegetarians, and pastry fat or margarine for vegans.

Chef's tip

If you overmix short paste it will become tough and dry because of the development of gluten. This type of paste will be difficult to handle and more likely to shrink and harden during cooking.

Chef's tip

All the ingredients for short paste should be cold, especially the water. This helps to prevent the development of gluten and makes the pastry crisper when cooked.

Savoury flans

Savoury plans and quiches have a short paste case, which is **blind baked** and filled with savoury ingredients, then an egg custard mix and baked until set.

Basic flan

Short paste	180g
Milk	225ml
Double cream	225ml
Medium eggs	4
Salt and pepper	to taste
Serves	8

Preparation	2
Cooking skills	2
Finishing	2

Method

1 Line a 20cm flan ring with the pastry. Place the flan into the fridge to rest for 20 minutes.
2 Fill the base with beans and blind bake the base for 15 minutes to prevent the base being uncooked and soggy
3 Remove the blind baking beans and fill with your chosen ingredients (see Variations below).
4 Whisk together the eggs, milk and double cream. Season to taste.
5 Pour this mixture trough a conical strainer (to remove the stringy part of the eggs). Then pour into the flan base.
6 Bake at a temperature of 200°C for approx 25 minutes.

To test: The flan should be golden brown on the top and the egg custard mix should be firm to the touch. Do not overcook or the egg mix will curdle (this means that the ingredients separate) and a clear liquid will appear on the surface of the flan.

7. Allow to cool slightly before removing the flan ring.

Variations

- Quiche Lorraine – add cheese, sweated onion and ham.
- Prawn and broccoli – add prawns, blanched broccoli florets and cheese.
- Mushroom – add cheese, sweated onions and mushrooms.
- Courgette and tomato – add sautéd courgettes, cheese and tomatoes.

Definitions

Blind baking – cooking a flan case without the filling in it. The flan is lined with greaseproof paper (cartouche) and filled with baking beans. The beans help to keep the shape during cooking.

Cartouche – a greased greaseproof paper that is placed over food while it is cooking to prevent the food drying out.

Video presentation

Watch the video presentation *Line a flan ring.*

Sweet baked products

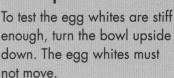

Preparation	2
Cooking skills	2
Finishing	–

Meringues

Egg whites	10 medium	Lemon juice	3–4 drops
Caster sugar	500g	Serves	10

Method

1 Add lemon juice to the egg whites and whisk until firm.
2 Gradually add half the sugar and continue whisking.
3 Once the egg white is stiff, gently fold in the remaining sugar.
4 Pipe out meringues in suitable shapes onto **baking parchment**.
5 Bake in a cool oven preheated to approx 110°C for about 4 hours or until dry but still white.

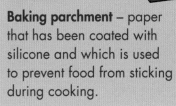

Chef's tip

To test the egg whites are stiff enough, turn the bowl upside down. The egg whites must not move.

Definition

Baking parchment – paper that has been coated with silicone and which is used to prevent food from sticking during cooking.

Preparation	2
Cooking skills	2
Finishing	–

Baked egg custard

Eggs	6	Vanilla pod	1
Granulated sugar	150g	Nutmeg (grated)	2g
Milk	565ml		

Method

1 Place eggs and sugar into a bowl. Whisk to mix but do not incorporate air as this will affect the final product.
2 Split the vanilla pod and put the seeds into the milk. Warm the milk to **infuse** the flavour. Do not boil.
3 Pour the hot milk onto the egg and sugar mix. Whisk to mix but do not make frothy.
4 Strain through a conical strainer to remove the stringy bit of the egg and the vanilla pod.
5 Transfer to a buttered dish and grate nutmeg onto the surface.
6 Cook in a bain marie in the oven for 30–35 minutes at 200°C until set.

Once cooked allow to cool. Store in the fridge until required for service.

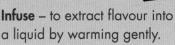

Definition

Infuse – to extract flavour into a liquid by warming gently.

Variations

- Cook the egg custard inside a blind baked sweet pastry case.
- Crème caramel – the egg custard is baked in small moulds with a caramel sauce.
- Queen of puddings – an egg custard dish with raspberry jam added. Once cooked it is finished with meringues and apricot and raspberry jam. The egg custard mix can also be flavoured with lemon zest.

Lemon tart

For the sweet pastry:

Soft flour	125g
Cold butter	75g
Caster sugar	35g
Egg (beat one whole egg and then use half)	½
Oven temperature	180°C
Cooking time	15 minutes

For the filling:

Eggs	3
Caster sugar	140g
Lemon, grated zest	1
Lemon juice	70ml
Double cream	90ml
Oven temperature	120°C
Cooking time	30 minutes
Serves	4

Preparation	3
Cooking skills	3
Finishing	2

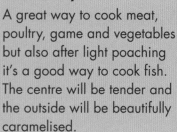

Marcus says:

A great way to cook meat, poultry, game and vegetables but also after light poaching it's a good way to cook fish. The centre will be tender and the outside will be beautifully caramelised.

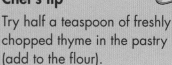

Chef's tip

Try half a teaspoon of freshly chopped thyme in the pastry (add to the flour).

Method

For the pastry flan case:

1. Mix together the egg and the sugar.
2. Sieve the flour.
3. Cut the butter into small pieces and rub into the flour until it resembles fine crumbs.
4. Add the egg/sugar mixture and stir together using a wooden spoon or hands.
5. Ensure that all ingredients are combined well but do not overwork the pastry.
6. Wrap in cling film and refrigerate for at least 30 minutes.
7. When cool, line a 15cm flan case with the pastry and blind bake at 180°C.
8. Seal the base (not the sides) with egg white and finish baking the pastry case.

For the filling:

1. Whisk the eggs with the caster sugar and strain.
2. Add lemon zest, lemon juice, and the cream. Continue to whisk until all the ingredients are thoroughly combined. Skim any froth from the top.
3. Pour the filling into the prepared tart case and bake at 120°C° for about 30 minutes or until fully set.
4. Chill for at least 1 hour before serving.

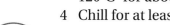

Baked fruit and vegetables

Firm fruit is best for baking, for example, apples and peaches. Soft fruit and berries do not withstand the baking process and end up turning to pulp.

Vegetables suitable for baking should be firm. Take care to adjust the baking time depending on the type of vegetable – for example, potatoes can take up to 2 hours to bake, whereas aubergine may only take 20 minutes.

Baked potatoes

Potatoes	10 (even sized)
Salt	
Serves	10

Preparation   1
Cooking skills   1
Finishing   –

Method

1 Scrub the potatoes well.
2 Prick with the point of a small knife.
3 Place onto a baking tray that has a layer of salt on it.
4 Bake in the oven for 1–1½ hours at 230°C. Halfway through cooking turn the potatoes over

Note: The salt helps season the potatoes as they absorb some of the salt during cooking.

To serve

Once the potato is cooked, cut a cross into the potato and squeeze to open the potato.
The potatoes can be served unfilled or filled with different hot and cold fillings.

Healthy eating

Instead of using salt, wrap the potatoes in foil or place them directly onto the wire oven racks.
To cook a large number of potatoes in one go it is better to put them onto a tray covered in baking parchment.

Baked pumpkin or squash

Pumpkins and other squashes can be baked in a preheated oven at 200°C until tender. Top the squash and remove the seeds and fibrous material. Season the inside with salt and black pepper. Replace top and bake until the flesh is tender.

Once cooked, remove the flesh. The flesh can be eaten as it is or used in different dishes.

Baked aubergine

Aubergines can be baked in a preheated oven at 200°C for approximately 15–20 mins or until tender. Select even-sized aubergines, wash and dry them and place onto baking trays. Put into the centre of the oven.

Once cooked cut in half and remove the flesh. This flesh can be used in different dishes

Pre-prepared products

Frozen food – must be baked in accordance with the manufacturer's instructions. Always cook in a preheated oven.

Part-baked bread – can be baked in a combination or dry oven. Alternatively, place a bain marie in the bottom of the oven to add steam during baking. The steam assists in crisping the surface of the bread and forms a crust with a high gloss.

Chef's tip
Dough products cooked with the addition of steam do not need glazing prior to baking.

Prepare and cook food by roasting

What is roasting?

Roasting is cooking food in a preheated oven. Unlike baking it requires the addition of either oil or fat. The fat or oil assists in giving the food products colour and prevents the surface of the food drying out.

Meat being roasted must be **basted** with oil during cooking to help retain the moisture in the food and to help the colour develop.

Definition
Baste – to moisten during cooking by spooning a liquid over the food.

Equipment

A sturdy roasting tray must be used that has a suitable lip to retain the oil/juices that come from meats. Flimsy trays are likely to bend when being removed for the oven and cause serious burns so should not be used for roasting.

Figure 9.5 A roasting tray

Methods

Oven roasting

Meat can be roasted in the oven on a bed of root vegetables – this is called a **trivet** of vegetables. This helps make the roast gravy and prevents the meat from sticking to the roasting tray.

Definition
Trivet – a bed of vegetables that lifts meat off the roasting tray. Also, a roasting tray which holds the meat still during carving.

Spit roasting

This involves cooking food over a heat source while the meat turns to prevent the food burning and drying out. The turning also ensures the fat in or on the product continuously bastes the product during cooking. This helps prevent the food from drying out and the surface from becoming hard.

Investigate!
Find a supermarket that has a spit roasting system and list the food products they offer for sale.

Pot roasting

This means roasting food which is sealed in a cooking vessel and cooked in the oven. This method of roasting helps retain all the flavours.

Rules and purpose of roasting

The same rules as for baking should be followed when roasting (see page 232). The reasons for roasting food are also the same (see page 233).

Foods suitable for roasting

Food products suitable for roasting include meat, poultry, game and vegetables.

Meat

Beef – only good-quality joints of beef should be used for roasting. The following cuts of meat are suitable (see Figure 9.6): fore rib (or chine rib), topside, rump, sirloin.

Silverside is often sold in supermarkets as a roasting joint. This cut is not a prime roasting joint but can be used, though it will not be as tender as topside.

Lamb – cuts of lamb suitable for roasting are: shoulder, leg, best end and loin.

> **Marcus says:**
>
> Roasting is a great way to cook meat, poultry, game and vegetables, but also, after light poaching, it's a good way to cook fish. The centre will be tender and the outside will be beautifully caramelised.

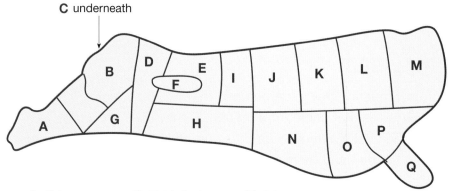

C underneath

A Shin	**G** Thick flank	**M** Sticking piece
B Topside	**H** Thin flank	**N** Plate
C Silverside	**I** Wing ribs	**O** Brisket
D Rump	**J** Fore rib	**P** Leg of mutton cut
E Sirloin	**K** Middle rib	**Q** Shank
F Fillet (whole)	**L** Chuck rib	

Figure 9.6 Cuts of beef

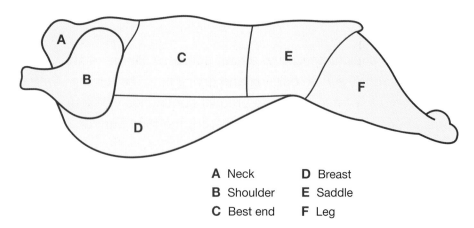

A Neck	**D** Breast
B Shoulder	**E** Saddle
C Best end	**F** Leg

Figure 9.7 Cuts of lamb

Pork – cuts of pork suitable for roasting are: shoulder, leg and loin.

Recently belly pork has been used for roasting – this is slow roasted to **render** the fat content, but it is not a traditional roasting joint.

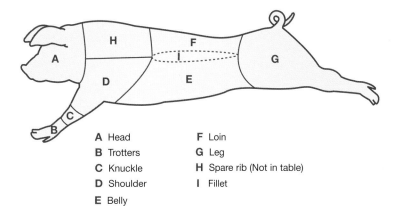

A	Head	F	Loin
B	Trotters	G	Leg
C	Knuckle	H	Spare rib (Not in table)
D	Shoulder	I	Fillet
E	Belly		

Figure 9.8 Cuts of pork

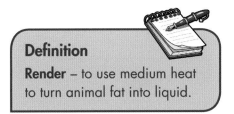

Definition

Render – to use medium heat to turn animal fat into liquid.

Veal – cuts of veal suitable for roasting are: topside, silverside, rump and loin.

Meat	Approximate cooking time	Probe check internal temperature at thickest part	
Beef	20 minutes per 450g + 20 minutes extra	Rare	55–60°C
Lamb	20 minutes per 450g + 20 minutes extra	Medium	66–71°C
Pork	25 minutes per 450g + 25 minutes extra	Cooked	78–80°C
Veal	20 minutes per 450g + 20 minutes extra		

Figure 9.9 Cooking guidelines for roasting meat

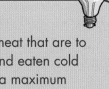

Figure 9.10 Roast beef with traditional accompaniments

After roasting, the meat should be left to rest for approximately 15–20 minutes. This will enable the meat to relax and the juices to be distributed evenly.

Meat	Accompaniments
Roast beef	Roast gravy, horseradish sauce and Yorkshire pudding
Roast lamb	Roast gravy and mint sauce
Roast pork	Roast gravy, sage and onion stuffing and apple sauce
Roast veal	Same as beef

Figure 9.11 Traditional accompaniments for roast meats

Remember!

All joints of meat that are to be roasted and eaten cold should have a maximum weight of 2.25kg and should be less than 25mm thick. This is so that the meat can cool sufficiently before refrigeration. The internal temperature of 75°C should be achieved to ensure the food is safe to eat.

Poultry

Chicken – roasting chickens are usually three months old. A baby chicken (known as a poussin) is a six-week-old chicken that can also be roasted. A poussin serves one portion.

Turkey – younger turkeys are normally used for roast and they weigh 2–14kg each. Some establishments use the crown – which is only the beast meat kept on the bone – as the breast meat is more popular and easier to carve. Roasting the breast meat separate from the legs also helps prevent the breast meat from drying out.

Figure 9.12 Roast turkey with traditional accompaniments

> **Investigate!**
>
> Research which turkeys are used in the food industry. Which one is recommended for roasting? Find out the reasons why.

> **Chef's tip**
>
> Use the roasting tray to make the roast gravy (known as jus rôti) to enable all the meat juices to be used for the gravy.
>
> **Method**
>
> Remove all the fat from the meat juices. Place the roasting pan onto the stove and bring the juice to the boil. Add stock and bring to the boil. With a plastic spoon stir the baked-on juices into the stock. Reduce the stock to thicken slightly, season to taste and strain to remove the vegetables. Serve hot.

Quality points

Poultry for roasting should have:

- pliable breast bone
- unbroken white skin
- firm flesh
- fresh smell
- no feathers on the legs
- be completely drawn (insides removed).

Poultry	Cooking times	Oven temperatures
Chicken	20 minute per 450g + 20 minutes extra	200°C–230°C Start at 230°C and reduce to 200°C after 20 minutes
Turkey	15 minutes per 450g + 1 5 minutes extra	180°C–200°C Start at 200°C and reduce to 180°C after 30 minutes

Figure 9.13 Cooking guidelines for roasting poultry

Poultry	Accompaniments
Roast chicken	Roast gravy, bread sauce, **game chips**
Roast turkey	Roast gravy, cranberry sauce

Figure 9.14 Traditional accompaniments for roast poultry

> **Definition**
>
> **Game chips** – thin slices of potato deep fried, very similar to crisps.

Roast chicken, turkey or duck

Preparation	2
Cooking skills	1
Finishing	3

Turkey, chicken or duck	one whole bird
Oil	25–35ml
Salt and pepper	to season
Bed of root	1
Oven temperature	200–230°C for 20 minutes, reducing to 190°C for the remaining time
Cooking time	See page 248 for roasting times
Serves	4 if chicken or duck 6–12 if a turkey

Method

1. Wash the poultry and remove any excess fat.
2. Coat the bird in oil, season and put it on a bed of root on its side.
3. Roast for 20 minutes. Reduce the heat. Turn the bird onto its other side. Continue to turn at intervals of 20 minutes to obtain good even colour all over the bird.
4. Finish cooking breast side up.
5. Check internal temperature to ensure bird is cooked correctly.
6. Serve roast chicken with gravy, bread sauce, game chips and watercress. Serve roast turkey with cranberry sauce. For a duck, a fruit-based sauce such as orange or plum is a lovely accompaniment.

Video presentation
Watch *Prepare a whole chicken for roasting* before following this recipe.

Definition
Bed of root: chopped root vegetables which act as a base to put the bird on to prevent sticking and burning on the tray.

Gravy to accompany roast chicken

Preparation	1
Cooking skills	1
Finishing	1

Roasting tray containing the juices and sediment from the roasted chicken brown stock	300ml
Serves	4

1. Put the roasting tray on the stove and heat gently.
2. When the juices and sediment have settled and coloured slightly, drain off the fat.
3. Add the brown stock and allow the mixture to simmer for a few minutes.
4. Season to taste and pass through a fine strainer.
5. Skim any excess fat from the surface.
6. Serve hot.

The better the quality of stock used, the better flavour the gravy. Bay leaf and rosemary could be added at stage 3 to provide a more aromatic result.

Roasting vegetables

Carrots, parsnips, swede, shallots, peppers, butternut squash, courgettes, aubergines and even leeks are all suitable for roasting.

Vegetables must be cut to an even size to ensure they roast evenly. They do not require blanching before roasting, but they can be if you wish to reduce the cooking time. If you do this, the roast flavour will not be fully developed.

To assist roasting, oil or fat is used – plain vegetable oil, olive oil or a flavoured oil can be used.

Figure 9.15 Vegetabes suitable for roasting

Method

1 Cut prepared vegetables into even sized pieces.
2 Coat the vegetables in cooking oil and season.
3 Place into a roasting tray. Roast in a preheated oven at approximately 200°C until golden brown and tender.
4 Turn the vegetables over during cooking to allow more of the surface of the vegetables to obtain the roast flavour.

Chef's tip

o Whole garlic bulbs can be added to the vegetables to add flavour. Once soft, the garlic flesh can be squeezed out and added to the roast vegetables.
o Fresh herbs can also be added for additional flavour.

Prepare and cook food by grilling

What is grilling?

Grilling means cooking food by placing it either over heat, under heat or between heat sources. Barbecuing is also a form of grilling in which the food is cooked over charcoal or wood.

Equipment for grilling

The different types of grill are:

○ **Over heat**: grills

Figure 9.16 A grill and other equipment needed for grilling

○ **Under heat**: salamanders

Figure 9.17 A salamander

○ **Between heat**: contact grills

Figure 9.18 A contact grill

○ **Barbecue**

Figure 9.19 A barbecue

Other equipment needed for grilling includes:

- **tongs** – used to turn over items
- **trays** – used to hold food before or after cooking, or for food items that need additional cooking in the oven
- **griddle** – a heavy cast-iron plate that is used to create a pattern on the food and to provide a distinctive flavour.

Grilling methods

Over heat

Cooking food over heat gives it a distinctive flavour. It is also used to decorate the surface of the food with a pattern. This can be done by turning the food during cooking, which leaves a crisscross, or by leaving in one position, which leaves single cooking marks on the surface.

The cooking surface of the grill is normally bars over a heat source. These bars need oiling prior to use to prevent the food sticking to them during cooking.

Generally the food is started on the hottest part of the grill and then moved to a cooler area to ensure it is fully cooked.

Marcus says:

Grilling gives food a great smokey flavour but beware, the grill should be ultra hot otherwise the food will stew rather than grill. Cooking is very fast and food can easily burn if forgotten.

Investigate!

Research your local area and list the restaurants that use this method of cooking.

List the reasons why you think they have chosen to use this cooking method.

Under heat

Most kitchens have a salamander, which is often mistakenly called a grill. Some salamanders also have the ability to lower or raise the heat source as required.

Between heat

With this type of grill, foods are cooked between electrically heated contact plates. This method is often used for small cuts of meat and vegetables.

Barbecue

Barbecuing means cooking food over preheated charcoal, wood or gas. Barbecuing gives the food products a distinctive flavour. If using solid fuel, the flames must die down before the cooking starts or they will burn the surface of the food.

Barbecuing is a very popular way of cooking food in the summer because of its speed and the ease of cooking.

Foods suitable for grilling

Foods suitable for grilling include:

- Sausages – no additional fat required, do not pierce with a fork
- Chicken breasts, legs and whole chickens
- Bacon – no additional fat required
- Tomatoes – cut in half, brush with melted butter and season
- Steaks – season during cooking
- Corn on the cob – can be blanched first
- Mushrooms – large field mushrooms are best
- Pork steaks – season during cooking
- Burgers – no additional fat required, make sure you cook them right through
- Bananas – grill in their skins
- Kebabs – the metal skewer assists in cooking the centre
- Fish – may need brushing with fat before cooking unless you use oily fish
- Turkey – no additional fat required
- Asparagus – can be blanched before grilling
- Pork spare ribs – baste in barbecue sauce during cooking
- Kidneys – additional fat is required to start the cooking process.

Investigate!

Find two recipes for each of the foods listed that use grilling as the cookery method.

Quality points

Only the best-quality food should be used, as the speed of cooking ensures that the food keeps a maximum of nutrients and flavour.

Purpose of grilling

Grilling can be a very healthy method of cookery. Grilling food helps to:

○ tenderise it
○ make it digestible
○ make it palatable
○ add texture to the food
○ develop flavour
○ retain the nutritional value
○ make the food safe to eat.

Advantages of grilling

The advantages of grilling include:

○ speed of cooking
○ distinctive flavour
○ greater control of cooking
○ healthy as little or no fat needs to be added
○ a large variety of foods can be cooked using this method.

Rules of grilling

○ Do not overfill trays.
○ Use trays with a lip to prevent spillage.
○ Seal food over the hottest part of the grill and finish cooking over a cooler area.
○ Use tongs for turning meat. Do not pierce with a fork.
○ Use fish slices for moving and turning larger items or soft food.
○ Oil the bars or the grill before cooking.
○ Preheat the appliance before cooking starts.
○ Food should be of an even thickness.
○ Some foods can be **marinated** before cooking.
○ If grilling a whole chicken, flatten it first – e.g. a spatch cock has the back bone removed and is then flattened.

> **Definition**
>
> **Marinate** – to immerse meat or fish in a flavoured liquid, allowing the flavours to be absorbed by the meat or fish.

Figure 9.20 A grilled whole chicken

Grilled recipes

Grilled salmon

Salmon fillets	6 × 170g
Melted butter	75g
Lemon juice	50g
Salt and pepper	to taste
Serves	6

Preparation	1
Cooking skills	2
Finishing	1

Method

1 Place the fillets onto a baking tray, service side face up.
2 Season both sides with freshly ground black pepper.
3 Brush with melted butter.
4 Place under a preheated grill for approximately 10 minutes on each side, depending on the thickness of the fish.
5 Serve immediately, with a lemon wedge and garnished with picked parsley or dill.

Notes

- You can coat the salmon in seasoned flour before cooking to protect the fish and prevent it from drying out.
- If grilling on a grill that is heated from underneath, place the presentation side down first.

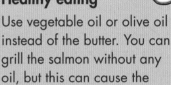

Healthy eating
Use vegetable oil or olive oil instead of the butter. You can grill the salmon without any oil, but this can cause the salmon to dry out.

Grilled peppers

Red peppers	3
Yellow peppers	3
Green peppers	3
Olive oil	100ml
Salt and pepper	to taste
Serves	10

Preparation	1
Cooking skills	1
Finishing	–

Method

1 Cut the top off each pepper and remove the seeds and any white pith.
2 Cut each pepper in four.
3 Season with salt and pepper
4 Coat each piece with olive oil (the oil can be plain or flavoured).
5 Place onto a preheated griddle for approximately 3–5 minutes per side.
6 Serve immediately.

Test yourself!

1 List two baked dishes using the following ingredients. Copy and complete the table.

Item	Dish 1	Dish 2
Apples		
Potatoes		
Aubergine		
Pumpkin		

2 List the heat source for the following types of grill. The first has been done as an example.

Cookery equipment	Heat source
Griddle plate	Below
Salamander	
Contact grill	
Griddle	
BBQ	

3 What is meant by baking using a bain marie?

4 List two rules that should be followed during baking.

5 What is a cartouche? And what is it used for?

6 Why is meat left to rest after roasting?

7 What oils/fats can be used when roasting vegetables?

8 List three bread products that are glazed before being baked.

9 Which statement is true about roasting meat and poultry?
   a The oven should be cold before cooking the meat.
   b The oven should not be preheated.
   c The oven temperature should be reduced after the meat has been in the oven for a certain amount of time.
   d The oven temperature should be increased after the meat has been in the oven for a certain amount of time.

Practice assignment tasks

Task 1

Write a report on baking. You should:

- Describe the difference between baking and roasting.
- Include and describe at least one product from the following: savoury dough product, sweet dough product, fruit, potato dish, a sweet pastry dish and a dessert.
- Highlight the items that can be glazed before baking and their glazing mediums.

Task 2

Write a report on roasting including:

- what basting is and what it is used for
- the different roast vegetable dishes
- how roast gravy is made
- the accompaniments for roast meats, to include chicken, beef, turkey, pork and lamb.

Task 3

Write a report on grilling including:

- the preparation of all grilling equipment prior to cooking
- the type of equipment that should be used when grilling
- where the food should be placed during the cooking process
- a list of different foods that are suitable for grilling, to include: meat, poultry and vegetables.

Deep and shallow frying

10

This chapter covers the following outcomes from Diploma unit 110: Prepare and cook food by deep frying and shallow frying

- Outcome 110.1 Be able to prepare and cook food by deep frying
- Outcome 110.2 Be able to prepare and cook food by shallow frying

Working through this chapter could also provide the opportunity to practise the following Functional Skills at Level 1:

Functional English: Writing – Use correct grammar, including correct and consistent use of tense; ensure written work includes generally accurate punctuation and spelling and that meaning is clear.

In this chapter you will learn about:

- The process of cooking food items by deep and shallow frying
- The purpose of deep and shallow frying
- The food items which may be deep and shallow fried
- The frying mediums which may be used when deep and shallow frying
- The importance of using associated techniques to achieve the finished dish requirements
- Associated products for deep and shallow frying
- The points to consider when deep and shallow frying
- The methods used when deep and shallow frying
- Suitable equipment to deep and shallow fry
- The quality points to look for during selection of food items, preparation, cooking and finishing of dishes

Deep frying

What is deep frying?

Deep frying is cooking food immersed in hot oil or fat. This method of cooking gives an even colour and crisp surface. Deep frying food helps to vary the menu and makes the food appetising, palatable and safe to eat.

Mediums for deep frying

Food is fried in some kind of oil or fat, including:

○ vegetable oil

○ sunflower oil

○ olive oil – expensive and tends to burn before reaching the required temperature for deep frying

○ lard – not commonly used nowadays due to healthy eating and waste removal problems

○ other animal fats – not commonly used nowaways due to healthy eating and waste removal problems.

All waste oils and fats must be disposed off via a contractor and not poured down the sink or in normal waste, due to the environmental impact they can have. Some major food suppliers provide this service free of charge.

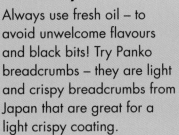

Marcus says:

Always use fresh oil – to avoid unwelcome flavours and black bits! Try Panko breadcrumbs – they are light and crispy breadcrumbs from Japan that are great for a light crispy coating.

Foods suitable for deep frying

Foods suitable for deep frying include:

○ meat and poultry

○ vegetables

○ fish

○ fruit

○ flour-based foods

○ ready-made foods.

Types of deep fryer

Pressure fryers

This type of deep fryer is mainly used in industrial kitchens. It allows the food to be cooked at a high temperature for a short time. This means the surface of the food is crispy while inside is moist and cooked. Some chicken fast food outlets use this style of cooking. Always follow the manufacturer's instructions when using a pressure fryer.

Friture

This is a deep pan used for deep frying on top of the stove. It normally has a wire basket inside. Only small amounts of food can be cooked with this method. Do not leave unattended when in use. This type of deep fat fryer is a common cause of house fires.

Thermostatically controlled fryers

This is the type generally used in the catering industry. They are heated by either gas or electricity and the heat is regulated by a thermostat. The thermostat makes it easier to control the correct temperature for deep frying different foods.

They are available in different sizes, ranging from table top for small catering establishments or home use to free-standing large deep fat fryers that are used in fish and chip shops.

Some have timers which indicate when the food is cooked.

Rules for deep frying

○ Do not over or under fill fryers with oil. There will be a minimum and maximum level indicator on the fryer.
○ Do not mix clean and old oils as this reduces the **flashpoint** and makes the oil more likely to catch fire.
○ Ensure foods are dry before cooking.
○ Cook foods at the correct temperatures. Too hot and the food will brown but will be raw inside. Too cool and the food will absorb the oil.
○ Do not leave the fryer unattended, even if the appliance is thermostat controlled. The thermostat may be faulty.

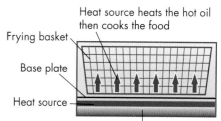

Heat source heats the hot oil then cooks the food

Frying basket

Base plate

Heat source

Cool zone – particles fall into this well during cooking. As the oil is colder than above the heat source, it does not burn during cooking. Oil must be removed on a regular basis.

Figure 10.1 How a deep fat fryer works

Definition
Flashpoint – the temperature at which oil ignites.

- Always check that the drainage plug is closed before filling with oil.
- Cook the food as close to service time as possible or the food will become soggy.
- Use a spider to remove cooked food if not using the basket.
- Allow the oil to cool before emptying and cleaning the fryer.
- Do not leave the fryer on full when not in use, as this burns the oil and can taint the food.
- Allow the oil to reach the correct temperature after cooking before adding more food.

Advantages and disadvantages of cooking food by deep frying

Advantages

- Large amounts of food can be cooked quickly.
- Certain foods can be blanched in advance and cooked fully closer to service time.
- Certain foods can be coated and deep fried which offers different textures.

Disadvantages

- Deep frying foods increases the fat content of the food.
- Only certain foods are suitable for deep frying.
- The oil can taint other foods if it is not kept clean.

Additional equipment for deep frying

As well as a deep fryer, you will need:

- spider – a wire scoop used to lift food items out of hot oil
- frying basket – a wire basket the same shape as the fryer – used to lower and lift food items into and out of the hot oil
- colander –used to allow the oil to drain off cooked items
- tray – used under a colander to collect excess oil
- tongs – used to lift individual food items from the frying basket to prevent damage to the cooked food.

Figure 10.2 Additional equipment for deep frying

Methods of cooking

The correct cooking temperature varies depending on the food being cooked. As a general rule:

- the thicker the item, the lower the heat required, but a longer cooking time
- the thinner the item, the higher the heat required, but less cooking time.

Deep-fried food is normally cooked at 175–195°C.

When deep frying, some foods are coated to protect them during cooking and to provide texture. Some suitable coatings are:

- **pané**
- batter
- flour
- cornflour
- **tempura batter**
- Japanese-style breadcrumbs
- desiccated coconut
- almonds.

Each coating will affect the flavour and provide different textures to the food and vary the menu.

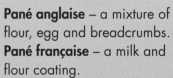

Definition

Pané anglaise – a mixture of flour, egg and breadcrumbs.
Pané française – a milk and flour coating.
Tempura batter – a light batter made of very cold water and flour. Beaten egg white is then folded in to give a light crisp texture when deep fried.

Meat and poultry

Meat and poultry are normally deep fried with a coating to protect the meat from the hot oil. This is because there is already fat in the meat and because of the mess uncoated meat makes of the oil. A popular coating is pané.

Pané for deep frying

1 Season flour with salt and pepper.
2 Whisk eggs together. (They can be loosened with milk, cream or water.)
3 Have breadcrumbs ready.

4 Dip the item to be cooked into the flour and coat fully.

5 Tap off any excess flour.

6 Place the item into the egg and coat with egg.

7 Place the item into the breadcrumbs and coat by patting the breadcrumbs onto the item.

8 Shake off any excess breadcrumbs and place onto a tray ready to cook.

Chicken goujons

Chicken goujons are strips of chicken breast coated in breadcrumbs (pané), then deep fried in hot oil until cooked and golden brown.

Preparation	2
Cooking skills	2
Finishing	1

Chicken breasts	4
Seasoned flour	50g
Eggs	2
White breadcrumbs	100g
Oil for deep frying	
Serves	6 as a starter or 4 as main course

Method

1 Cut the chicken breast into strips approximately ½cm thick by 3cm long.
2 Prepare the flour, eggs and breadcrumbs for paning (see above).
3 Pané the strips (see above) and roll between the palms of your hands to make cigar shapes.
4 Keep in the fridge until required.
5 Heat the oil to approximately 180°C.
6 Place some of the breadcrumbed strips into a frying basket and gently lower into the hot oil.
7 Once lowered completely, shake the basket to ensure the strips are not stuck to each other, otherwise the goujons will not colour evenly.
8 Continue cooking until golden brown, then lift the basket out of the oil. Tap off the excess oil.
9 Empty the strips into a colander to drain off excess oil (kitchen paper can be used).
10 Cut one goujon in half to check that the chicken is cooked through.
11 Serve immediately with garlic mayonnaise and a side salad.

Variation

• Whole chicken pieces can be deep fried in the same way, but will require further cooking in a preheated oven to ensure they are cooked through.

Vegetables

The vegetable that is most commonly deep fried is the potato – to make chips. In many establishments the chips are partially cooked and then held until an order is received. This is called **blanching**. The chips are then returned to the fryer to be finished.

Most fish and chip shops blanch their chips before service. They normally have two fryers in operation, one for blanching and one for the final cook.

Blanching chips

Preparation	1
Cooking skills	2
Finishing	–

1 Place the prepared chips in cold water to prevent them turning black.
2 Dry the chips thoroughly.
3 Heat the oil in the deep fryer to approximately 165°C.
4 Remove the frying basket from the deep fat fryer.
5 Transfer a batch of dried prepared chips into the frying basket.
6 Lower gently into the fryer. Take care that the fat does not boil over.
7 Continue lowering until the basket sits in the fryer.
8 Shake the basket to prevent the chips sticking to each other or to the basket.
9 Continue cooking until tender but with no colour. To test, lift the basket out of the fryer, push the tip of a pointed small knife into the thickest part of a chip. There should be a little resistance.
10 If ready, lift the basket out of the oil and allow the excess oil to drain back into the fryer.
11 Transfer the chips into a drainer and allow to cool.
12 Continue until all the chips are blanched. Allow the temperature of the oil to come back to the blanching temperature before adding more chips
13 Reserve the chips until required for service.

Definition

Blanching – in this instance means frying without allowing the food to colour. It is done to partially cook the food before finishing off as required.

Figure 10.3 Deep fat fryers in a chip shop

Figure 10.4 Blanched chips and cooked chips

Cooking the blanched chips

Preparation –
Cooking skills 2
Finishing –

1 Reheat the oil to a temperature of 185°C.
2 Place a batch of the blanched chips into the frying basket.
3 Lower into the fryer as before.
4 Shake to ensure an even colour.
5 Cook until light golden brown in colour.
6 Drain well.
7 Season with salt and serve.

Healthy eating

Do not add salt prior to serving and allow the customer to add their own salt.

French fried onion rings

Preparation 1
Cooking skills 1
Finishing 1

1 Cut the onions in rings 3mm thick.
2 Dip the rings in milk and pass through seasoned flour (pané français).
3 Deep fry in oil heated to approximately 185°C. Do not use a frying basket or the rings will sink and stick to the base of the basket.
4 Use a spider to remove the cooked rings from the hot oil.
5 Drain well and serve.

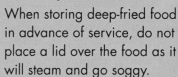

Chef's tip

When storing deep-fried food in advance of service, do not place a lid over the food as it will steam and go soggy.

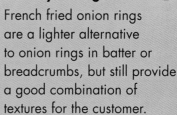

Healthy eating

French fried onion rings are a lighter alternative to onion rings in batter or breadcrumbs, but still provide a good combination of textures for the customer.

Duchess potato mix

Preparation 2
Cooking skills –
Finishing –

Prepared potatoes	1kg
Butter	50g
Egg yolks	3
Salt and pepper	to taste
Ground nutmeg	to taste
Serves	5

Method

1 Boil the potatoes, drain and dry.
2 Push through a sieve or potato ricer.
3 Add the butter and seasoning.
4 Mix well.
5 Add the egg yolks and mix.

This mixture can then be used for different potato dishes: duchess, marquise and croquette (page 268).

Croquette potatoes

Preparation	1
Cooking skills	2
Finishing	–

Croquette potatoes are duchess mix potatoes coated in flour, egg and breadcrumbs. They are shaped and then deep fried.

Method

1 Shape the duchess potato mix into cylinders approximately 5 × 2cm.
2 Pass through seasoned flour, beaten egg and white breadcrumbs.
3 Reshape with the aid of a palette knife – this will also help the breadcrumbs stick to the potato and help protect it from the oil.
4 Heat the frying oil to approximately 185°C.
5 Place some of the croquette potatoes into a frying basket and lower into the hot oil.
6 Drain and serve.

Note: Ensure the potatoes are well coated with breadcrumbs and that there are no cracks in the surface of the potato. Otherwise the hot oil can get inside the potato, causing it to split and dissolve in the oil.

Fish

Fish in batter

The fish used for fish in batter is normally white fish. Both round and flat fish can be used. The prepared fish is passed through seasoned flour and then dipped in batter. It is deep fried at a temperature of approximately 170°C until golden brown and crispy.

You can use a tempura batter, a yeast batter or a baking powder batter – see Figure 10.5. The batter protects the flesh of the fish and gives a crispy coating. The difference in texture between the fish and the crispy batter is one reason why fish in batter is so popular.

Did you know?
Fish batter has a yellow tint. This helps the batter turn golden brown during cooking.

Tempura batter		Yeast batter		Baking powder batter	
Flour	200g	Flour	200g	Flour	200g
Salt	pinch	Salt	pinch	Salt	pinch
Iced water	250ml	Yeast	10g	Water	200ml
Stiffly beaten egg white	2	Water	250ml	Vinegar	50ml
				Baking powder	10g
				Yellow colouring	2 drops

Method

Tempura batter
1 Beat the flour, salt and water together until smooth.
2 Fold the egg white into the batter just before use.
3 Use immediately.

Yeast batter
1 Dissolve the yeast in some of the water.
2 Beat the flour, salt and remaining water together until smooth
3 Add the yeast and mix well. Allow to rest for at least an hour before using.

Baking powder batter
1 Beat the flour, salt, water, vinegar and yellow colouring together until smooth.
2 Add the baking powder just before using the batter.

Figure 10.5 Batters used for battered fish

Fish in batter

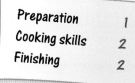

Preparation   1
Cooking skills   2
Finishing   2

Method

1 Pass the prepared fish through seasoned flour and then dip into the chosen batter – see Figure 10.5 above.
2 Remove the frying basket from the fryer. (If you used a basket, the fish would sink and stick to the basket.)
3 Gently lower the battered fish into the hot oil. Lower the fish away from the body and do not drop into the oil – splashes will cause serious burns.
4 Turn the fish during cooking to achieve an even colour.
5 Once the fish is a golden brown, remove from the oil and drain well.
6 Serve with lemon wedges and tomato sauce.

Chef's tip

A lot of people prefer tartare sauce to tomato sauce. However, tartare sauce is classically served with breadcrumbed fish dishes.

Fruit

Fruit fritters are equal-sized pieces of firm fruits dipped in seasoned flour and then into batter. They are deep fried in hot oil at a temperature of approximately 185°C until golden brown. They can then be dipped in spiced sugar (e.g. spiced with cinnamon) or they can be left plain and served with a sauce such as maple syrup. Classically, fruit fritters are served with apricot sauce.

Fruits suitable for fruit fritters are: apples, bananas and pineapples.

○ Apples should be peeled and cored.
○ Bananas should be cut into even-sized pieces.
○ Pineapples should be peeled, cored and sliced.

Healthy eating

Leave the skins on the apples to retain nutrients and fibre.

Flour-based products

Flour-based foods include dough products (such as ring doughnuts, jam doughnuts and finger doughnuts) and choux pastry.

Cooking doughnuts

Make the dough for doughnuts. Doughnuts need to be proved before frying (see page 235). Do not use a proving cabinet for this, as the moisture will make the hot oil spit. Doughnuts should be cooked at 180°C.

Once the oil has reached the required temperature and the doughnuts are fully proved, they are ready for frying.

1 Gently lower the doughnuts into the hot oil.
2 When golden brown, gently press on side of the doughnut with a spider. If it is cooked it will turn over.
3 When turned, allow to cook until the doughnuts are an even golden colour on both sides.
4 Remove the doughnuts from the hot oil, drain and coat in cinnamon sugar.

To make dough for doughnuts, see www.heinemann.co.uk/hotlinks – just enter the express code 3729P.

Figure 10.6 Dough products: ring doughnuts, jam doughnuts and finger doughnuts

Choux pastry

Choux pastry is a cooked mixture of fat, flour and water with a little sugar and salt. Eggs are then beaten into the mixture. Deep-fried choux pastries are known as "beignets soufflés" and are usually served with apricot sauce. Choux pastry is also used to make éclairs and profiteroles. You can find a recipe at www.heinemann.co.uk/hotlinks – just enter the express code 3729P.

Ready-made products

Ready-made products suitable for deep frying include:

- fish fingers
- chicken nuggets
- frozen chips
- croquette potatoes
- onion rings
- breaded mushrooms.

Cook ready-made products in accordance with the manufacturer's instructions.

Frozen chips

These must be cooked from frozen, in very hot oil at a temperature of 190°C. Take care not to overfill the fryer. Place the chips in the frying basket and gently lower into the hot oil. Cook until golden brown.

Prawn crackers

Prawn crackers can be cooked by deep frying at a temperature of approximately 200°C. During cooking they expand to at least twice their original size, so do not overfill the frying basket.

Take some of the dry crackers and place directly into the fryer or you can use the frying basket. It only takes approximately 10 seconds for the crackers to puff up. Once fully cooked transfer to a colander to drain.

Chef's tip

Finished deep-fried dough products should:

- be an even shape and size
- have an even golden brown colour
- be well-rounded and risen
- not have a greasy or crispy surface
- be evenly coated with sugar
- be cooked throughout, with no dry dough pieces.

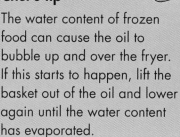

Chef's tip

The water content of frozen food can cause the oil to bubble up and over the fryer. If this starts to happen, lift the basket out of the oil and lower again until the water content has evaporated.

Shallow frying

What is shallow frying?

Shallow frying is cooking food in a small amount of fat or oil. It is also known as **sauté**. Shallow frying can be carried out using a sauté pan, a frying pan or a wok. Whichever pan you use it must be large enough to hold the food being cooked.

> **Definition**
>
> **Sauté** – to cook quickly in a shallow pan with a minimum of fat.

Mediums used for shallow frying:

Food is fried in some kind of oil or fat, including:

○ olive oil
○ sunflower oil
○ other vegetable oil
○ clarified butter (also known as ghee in Indian cookery)
○ stir fry oil
○ butter and oil mix.

The minimum amount of oil should be used. Butter can easily burn and taint the taste of the food. Adding oil to the butter allows you to increase the cooking temperature without it burning.

Clarified butter has a higher cooking temperature because all the buttermilk and impurities have been removed. This means it will not burn at higher temperatures.

Purpose of shallow frying

The purpose of shallow frying food is to:

○ make food palatable
○ make food digestible
○ make food safe to eat
○ give food colour and flavour
○ give variety to the menu.

Foods suitable for shallow frying

Foods suitable for shallow frying include:

○ meat and poultry
○ vegetables
○ fish
○ eggs
○ fruit
○ flour-based products
○ ready-made products.

Equipment for shallow frying

The different pans used for shallow frying are shown in Figure 10.7.
Always use the correct pan for the dish you are cooking.

Figure 10.7 a) bratt pan, b) shallow frying pan, c) sauté pan, d) omelette pan,
e) wok, f) pancake pan, g) blini pan

Rules for shallow frying

- Use the correct size of pan.
- Make sure the oil is hot before placing the food into the pan or the food will absorb the oil.
- Place the service side into the pan first.
- Do not keep turning the food product over as it could break.
- Use two fish slices or palette knives to turn the food.
- Clean out the old oil between cooking, as any leftover food items could burn onto the surface of the food.
- Use dry oven cloths to hold pan handles – wet cloths allow the heat to pass through the cloth and turn into steam, which can cause serious burns.
- Allow food such as steaks to rest before service.
- Heat the pan first and then add the oil – this helps prevent the food from sticking to the pan.

Meat and poultry

Fried steak

Only good-quality meat should be used for shallow frying because of the speed of cooking. Sirloin, rump and fillet steak are all suitable. After cooking, each steak should be allowed to rest for a few minutes to allow the meat to relax, complete the cooking process and to allow the meat juices to disperse evenly.

Veal escalope

Veal **escalope** can either be coated in breadcrumbs or left plain before shallow frying. Breadcrumbs protect the meat and add texture to the dish.

Figure 10.8 A veal escalope

Chicken

Chicken pieces can be shallow fried with a coating, with or without the skin left on. The skin will provide additional colour, which can be used to enhance the presentation. Chicken dishes that will be cooked in a sauce after sauté usually have the skin left on, e.g. chicken chasseur.

Chicken chasseur – chicken fillets are shallow fried and then braised in a mushroom and tarragon sauce. Tomato **concasse** is added just before service.

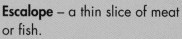

Definitions

Escalope – a thin slice of meat or fish.

Concasse – coarsely chopped tomatoes.

Different coatings can be used to provide additional flavour and texture or to protect a filling inside the chicken, e.g. chicken kiev.

Chicken kiev – a Russian dish of breadcrumbed chicken fillets filled with garlic butter, shallow fried and finished in a hot oven.

Chicken kiev

Preparation	2
Cooking skills	3
Finishing	–

Chicken breasts (skin removed)	4
Garlic cloves (crushed)	3
Chopped parsley	10g
Unsalted butter	200g
Fresh white breadcrumbs	150g
Beaten egg	2 medium
Seasoned flour	35g
Olive oil for frying	
Serves	4

Method

1. Make garlic butter by mixing the garlic and parsley into the softened butter.
2. Remove the fillet from the chicken breast and remove the **sinew** (see Chef's tip).
3. Cut a pocket into the chicken breast and fill with the garlic butter.
4. Replace the fillet to hold the butter in place. Chill the chicken until the butter is firm.
5. Pané the chicken breasts with the breadcrumbs, egg and flour (see page 264).
6. Shallow fry the chicken breasts in a small amount of oil, until golden brown.
7. Turn over the breasts and brown on the other side.
8. Once browned, transfer to a baking tray and complete the cooking in a moderate oven for approximately 10 minutes.
9. Serve immediately.

Chef's tip

Remove the sinew from the chicken breast fillet or the breast will curl during cooking.

1. Remove the fillet from the breast by gentle pulling it away from the back of the breast.
2. With a small knife lift up the sinew from the thickest end of the fillet.
3. Turn fillet over and angle the knife at 45 degrees.
4. Pull the sinew towards you keeping the knife still.
5. Discard the sinew.
6. You can then replace the fillet to prevent the filling from leaking from the breast.

Definition

Sinew – tough cord joining muscle to bone.

Stir fry pork

Pork fillet or steak	400g
Oil	15ml
Garlic, crushed	1 clove
Ginger, grated	5g
Red and green peppers	1 of each
French beans	50g
Celery	50g
Carrot	50g
Mushrooms	100g
Bean sprouts	100g
Soy sauce	60ml
Chinese five spice	1 pinch
Shallots, finely diced	1
Honey (optional)	2 tsp
Serves	4

Preparation	2
Cooking skills	2
Finishing	1

Method

1 Cut the pork into strips. Marinade in a little soy sauce and the Chinese five spice. Keep until required.
2 Wash the bean sprouts, wash and slice the mushrooms. Peel the carrots and cut into thin strips (julienne).
3 Trim the celery and cut into thin strips.
4 Top and tail the beans, cut in halves.
5 Wash and thinly slice the peppers.
6 Finely dice the shallots.
7 The green vegetables can be blanched and refreshed to retain colour.
8 Heat the oil in a wok, add the pork strips and cook quickly till coloured and sealed. Remove and keep hot.
9 Gently fry the vegetables, stirring continuously for a few minutes.
10 Add the grated ginger, garlic and five spice. Cook for a minute.
11 Add the cooked pork strips and mix in well, stirring continuously.
12 Add the soy sauce and the honey. Stir well.
13 Correct the seasoning and serve.

Fish

Fillet of fish **meunière** is a classic French dish. The fish is either served whole or a fillet is dusted in seasoned flour, shallow fried and served with **beurre noisette** flavoured with lemon juice.

Definitions

Meunière – to shallow fry.
Beurre noisette – butter that has been melted until it turns golden brown.

Fish in breadcrumbs

Preparation	2
Cooking skills	2
Finishing	–

This is a very popular dish made with white fish, such as plaice, haddock, cod or sole. The cooking time depends on the thickness of the fish. If the oil is too hot, the breadcrumbs will burn and the fish will be raw. Too cold and the breadcrumbs will absorb the oil and be greasy.

Method

1 Heat the oil in a frying pan. To test the oil, add a small cube of white bread. If the oil is hot enough, the bread will be golden brown within 30 seconds.
2 Pané the fish fillets and shallow fry in the hot oil. Place the presentation side down in the pan first.
3 Once golden brown, turn the fillets and cook on the other side.
4 Once cooked, transfer to serving dish and garnish with sprigs of parsley and a wedge of lemon.
5 Serve with tartare sauce.

Variation

Add herbs or spices to the breadcrumbs to add flavour to the dish.

Chef's tip

If you are cooking a lot of breadcrumbed items, remove the old oil and breadcrumbs and wipe the pan regularly or the oil and breadcrumbs will burn and taint the other food.

Vegetables

Stir frying vegetables is a simple way to cook them and is a healthy option, as only a small amount of oil is used. Any vegetables can be stir fried, but they must be cut into even pieces first. Some harder vegetables should be blanched before stir frying.

Some vegetables that are suitable for stir frying without blanching are:

- onions
- peppers
- mushrooms
- mangetout
- bean sprouts
- broccoli
- green beans
- baby sweetcorn
- carrots
- celery.

A wok is the best pan to use for stir frying, but a frying pan can be used instead. The vegetables can be flavoured with soy sauce, ginger, garlic and chilli sauce.

Potatoes and other vegetables

Lyonnaise potatoes – these are pre-cooked potatoes that are sliced and shallow fried with fried shredded onions. Use four times as much potato as onions. The sliced onions take longer to cook so cook these in first and then remove from the pan. Cut the pre-cooked potatoes into approximately 3mm slices. Fry the potato slices until golden brown on both sides. Add the fried onions, season and serve garnished with chopped parsley.

Sauté potatoes – these are cooked in the same way as Lyonnaise potatoes, but without the fried onions

Sauté courgettes – these are evenly sliced courgettes shallow fried in either olive oil or clarified butter. The oil or butter must be hot or the courgettes with absorb the fat and become greasy. Only cook enough courgettes for the immediate service period or they will absorb the oil/butter and they will steam and go soft.

Definition

Lyonnaise – the addition of sauté onions to a dish.

Fruit

Most fruits can be shallow fried.

Soft fruits

These can be coated in caster sugar then shallow fried in clarified butter. This turns the sugar into a sticky fruit sauce and warms the soft fruits. This can then be poured onto different desserts.

Harder fruits

These can be shallow fried and served with a sauce, e.g. pineapples or bananas in toffee sauce.

Cut the fruit into even-sized pieces. Shallow fry them in clarified butter. Once golden brown, you can **flambé** them with a spirit such as rum or brandy. Then add soft brown sugar and warm through, and double cream to make a sauce. Remove the fruit to prevent overcooking and simmer the cream and sugar mix until the correct consistency is achieved. Spoon the sauce over the fruit and serve.

Definition

Flambé – to flame food that has a spirit added – e.g. brandy. This burns off the alcohol content but the flavour remains.

Eggs

Fried eggs – these are extremely popular, either as a snack or for breakfasts. Eggs should be shallow fried in oil that is not too hot or the egg will cook too quickly and go brown and crispy around the edges and underneath.

Did you know?

Eggs can also be deep fried but this is not a common practice nowadays.

Fried egg

Preparation	–
Cooking skills	2
Finishing	–

1 Heat some oil in either a frying pan or on a griddle.
2 Crack the egg into the hot oil.
3 Allow the egg to cook to set the egg white.
4 Flick hot oil onto the egg with a fish slice to cook the yolk. If using a griddle, you may need to turn the egg over to set the yolk. How firm the yolk should be will depend on the customer's requirements.
5 Remove the egg from the pan, drain off the excess oil and serve.

Omelettes – these are shallow fried using butter in an omelette pan. They can either be served flat or filled and folded into a cigar shape depending on the type of omelette. For example, a Spanish omelette – an omlette with the addition of potatoes, peppers and onions – is served flat.

Omelette

Preparation	1
Cooking skills	2
Finishing	–

Medium eggs	3 per person
Butter	25g

Method

1 Beat the eggs well and season with salt and pepper.
2 Heat the omelette pan and add the butter.
3 Allow the butter to melt and bubble, then add the beaten egg.
4 With a fork, shake and stir the egg mix to allow even cooking.
5 Just before all the egg mixture is set, reshape the omelette and allow it to finish cooking.
6 If using a filling, add this in the centre of the omelette.
7 Roll into a cigar shape and serve.

Variations

Some popular omelette fillings are:
• sliced cooked mushrooms
• tomato concasse
• grated cheese
• diced cooked ham.

Chef's tip

The completed omelette should be lightly coloured and soft inside. The omelette will continue cooking due to its residual heat.

Flour-based products

Flour-based products suitable for shallow frying include pancakes and drop scones. Pancakes are normally served on Shrove Tuesday, served with lemon and sugar. They can also be savoury and used as a main course, e.g. filled with vegetables and served with a cheese sauce, or filled with minced beef.

Preparation	1
Cooking skills	2
Finishing	–

Pancakes (Makes about 20 pancakes)

Plain flour	250g
Salt	pinch
Medium eggs	3
Milk	625ml
Melted butter	30g
Caster sugar (optional, for sweet pancakes)	125g

To make the batter:

1. Sift the flour and salt together into a bowl.
2. Make a well in the flour and add the eggs.
3. Add half the milk and whisk slowly, incorporating some of the flour.
4. Continue adding the milk until a smooth batter is achieved.
5. Add the melted butter.
6. Allow to rest for at least an hour before using.
7. Whisk again to ensure the batter is smooth.

To cook the pancakes:

1. Heat a little oil in either a frying pan or a **crêpe** pan.
2. Pour off any excess oil. This helps prevent burns when tossing the pancake.
3. Add enough batter to the pan (depending on the pan size).
4. Lift the pan from the heat and twist the pan to make spread the batter evenly across the pan. (The pancake should be very thin.)
5. Place the pan back onto the heat and allow to cook. Once the wet look has gone from the pancake, it is ready to be turned.
6. Lift the edge of the pancake from the pan and shake to make sure the pancake isn't stuck. (The first one often does stick.)
7. Gently move the pancake to the furthest side of the pan and toss it to turn – see Chef's tip.
8. Cook on the other side for a few seconds and serve.

Variations

Herbs and spices can be added to the batter to add additional flavour.

Chef's tip

When tossing a pancake, the aim is to make the pancake flip from the furthest side of the pan onto its uncooked side. Make the movement at your wrist. This takes practice. Use either a palette knife or fish slice to help.

Definition

Crêpe – the French word for pancake.

Pancakes can be pre-cooked and then reheated. Turn over a small plate and place the cooked pancakes onto the upturned pate. Pile the pancakes on top of each other, keeping them flat until required.

Drop scones – also known as Scotch pancakes, these are shallow fried on a griddle or in a heavy-based frying pan.

It is a thicker batter with a raising agent to make them lighter.

Drop scones

Self raising flour	100g
Salt	pinch
Caster sugar	50g
Medium egg	1
Milk	100ml

Preparation	1
Cooking skills	2
Finishing	1

Method

1 Make batter as for pancake batter with the addition of the caster sugar.
2 Heat either a griddle or frying pan and very lightly oil the base.
3 Pour approximately a tablespoon full of batter onto the surface and cook. Once golden brown and the batter is set, turn over and cook the other side.
4 Continue cooking; once cooked serve warm with jam or syrup and butter.

Ready–made products

Ready-made products include:
○ pre-coated fish fillets
○ poppadums
○ pre-coated chicken pieces
○ ready prepared steak pieces.

They should be cooked according to the manufacturer's instructions.

Poppadums

This traditional Indian snack is served with curries and chutneys and pickles. They are bought dried and need to be cooked in hot oil.

Preparation	–
Cooking skills	1
Finishing	–

Method

1. Heat some oil in a frying pan.
2. Add a poppadum and fry for 5–6 seconds.
3. Use two fish slices to help spread the poppadum as it cooks.
4. Once fully expanded, turn the poppadum over and cook the other side.
5. Remove from the hot oil and drain.
6. Serve cold.

Test yourself!

1. Why should old and new fats or oils not be mixed when deep frying?

2. Why do food items need to be dried before deep frying?

3. List three items of equipment that are used for deep frying and shallow frying and their uses.

4. Why are certain products coated before deep or shallow frying?

5. What type of sauce is normally served with fish in breadcrumbs?

6. Why should fruit being used for deep frying be cut into even-sized pieces?

7. Why should yeast products that are going to be deep fried not be proved in a steam prover?

8. How long should pancake batter be rested before use?

9. What shape should omelettes be after cooking?

10. How can you tell if a shallow-fried egg has been cooked in oil that was too hot?

Practice assignment task

Task 1

Write a report on the process of frying. You should include the following points:

- State the difference between deep and shallow frying.
- List the quality points.
- List the types of coatings that can be used and explain why foods are coated prior to frying.
- List foods that are suitable for frying.
- Describe the term "blanching".
- List the mediums that can be used for shallow and deep frying.
- List the rules to follow when shallow and deep frying.

Regeneration of pre-prepared foods

11

This chapter covers the following outcomes from Diploma unit 111: Regeneration of pre-prepared food

- Outcome 111.1 Be able to identify pre-prepared food that can be regenerated
- Outcome 111.2 Be able to regenerate pre-prepared food

Working through this chapter could also provide the opportunity to practise the following Functional Skills at Level 1:

Functional English: Reading – utilise information contained in texts

In this chapter you will learn how to:

- List different types of regenerated pre-prepared foods
- Describe the difference between regenerated pre-prepared foods and other food types
- Explain the purpose of regenerated pre-prepared foods in the food industry
- State the possible limitations of using regenerated pre-prepared foods
- Use the correct methods to regenerate pre-prepared food
- List the tools and equipment needed to regenerate different foods
- State the quality points in pre-prepared foods for regeneration
- Explain the how eating excessive amounts of regenerated pre-prepared foods can affect healthy eating and nutrition

Identify pre-prepared foods that can be regenerated

The purpose of **regenerating** food is to make food edible and safe to eat. It can give food an enhanced flavour. Using pre-prepared food also ensures that you can produce a product of a consistent standard.

> **Definition**
>
> **Regenerate** – to bring food back to its original condition ready for service.

Different types of regenerated pre-prepared foods

There are six main categories of pre-prepared foods that can be regenerated – see Figure 11.1 for examples.

Fresh food	Frozen	Pre-prepared	Canned	Dried food	Ready-made food
Broccoli	Chicken curry	Steak and kidney pie	Mushroom soup	Vegetable stock	Lasagne
Poached egg	Desserts	Stews	Baked beans	Pepper sauce mix	Quiche
Soups	Cakes	Braised lamb shanks	Sauces	Dried soup	Bread
Sauces	Ready meals		Carrots	Cake mix	Buns
	Oven chips		Corned beef	Pasta	Sausage rolls
			Tomatoes	Couscous	Cakes
			Peaches		
			Strawberries		

Figure 11.1 The categories of regenerated pre-prepared foods, with examples

> **Try this!**
>
> Go to your local supermarket to research pre-prepared **dried** foods that can be regenerated. Make a list of all the different dried foods that you find.

> **Definition**
>
> **Blanching** – fruit and vegetables are immersed in boiling water for between ten seconds and two minutes depending on size and type.

Fresh food

These are food items that have been **blanched** to partially cook them, quickly chilled and then held in refrigerated storage until required. They are then rapidly regenerated as required during service – e.g. pre-blanched vegetables such as carrots or broccoli.

Figure 11.2 Vegetables are blanched in boiling water and then plunged into iced water

Frozen food

There are two types of frozen foods available to the food industry:

○ those that have to be completely defrosted before using or regenerating

○ those that can be regenerated from frozen.

Some frozen food, such as desserts or pastries, only needs to be defrosted to be ready for serving, while other foods need to be cooked. You must follow the manufacturer's instructions very carefully to ensure that the end product is regenerated by the correct method.

Freezing is a good method of preserving foods for later uses – e.g. soups and sauces which can be produced in bulk and then frozen in smaller quantities.

Marcus says:
Follow the health safety rules!

Pre–prepared foods

These are foods which are prepared in advance and then reheated as required for service. The foods best suited to being pre-prepared are pies, stews and braised dishes. These can safely be regenerated before or during service and the quality of the dish should not be affected. The foods may need **rehydrating** during regeneration, as the sauce may have thickened during the holding process.

The regeneration process is not suitable for fried or grilled foods such as fish, as during the regenerating process the item may overcook and break up.

Definition
Rehydrating – adding liquid to a sauce or dish to bring it back to the right consistency.

Canned food

Canning is a way of preserving foods for long periods. A large variety of canned foods is available to the industry. Soups and sauces are good examples of canned pre-prepared food that can be of a good quality. However, some foods can become soft during the canning process. For example, vegetables like baby carrots will lose their crispness.

Dried food

Dried foods are food items that have had the liquid removed, by one of two methods: heat drying or freeze drying. Examples of dried foods are: powdered soups and sauces and bread and cake mixes.

Fig 11.3 Canned foods and dried foods

287

Ready-made food

Ready-made foods can be placed into two categories:

1 foods that do not need any further cooking or heating – e.g. cakes, breads and cold savouries like quiche
2 foods that need regenerating to ensure that they are safe to eat – e.g. soups, sauces, ready meals (e.g. chicken curry) and part-baked breads.

The differences between regenerated pre-prepared foods and other food types

Pre-prepared foods, except those that are freshly prepared in the kitchen, usually contain additives, such as preservatives, colourings, flavourings and in most cases excess salt. These are added during the preparation process because they help to extend the shelf life of the products. The addition of these additives affects the nutritional value and also the taste and texture of the products. For example, if you compare tinned stew with a fresh stew, you will find that the meat in the canned product is soft and stringy in texture, whereas the fresh product generally has a better texture and taste.

The techniques and equipment required to regenerate and serve pre-prepared food are much simpler than those required to cook food from scratch. For more on techniques and equipment, see the next section on pages 291–294.

The advantage to a chef of using pre-prepared foods is that it saves time in preparation, but more often than not this comes at the expense of quality.

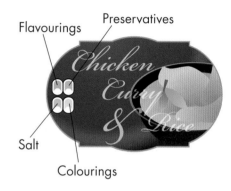

Figure 11.4 Additives are present in many pre-prepared foods

Why do we use regenerated pre-prepared foods?

The purpose of using pre-prepared food items within the catering industry and regenerating them for service is because it can help in reducing labour costs. This is because the staff required for the regeneration of food items do not have to be highly skilled. They need only a basic knowledge of cooking food, although it would be desirable for them to hold a basic food hygiene certificate.

Time is a major cost to any catering business. Regenerating pre-prepared food takes less time than cooking it from scratch. This can helps to increase the profitability of the business.

Quicker preparation time also means that establishments can meet consumer demand for variety whilst still providing a fast service. Many customers have only a short time to spend eating – e.g. if they are on a business lunch – but they will still want a choice of different styles of food and they don't expect to pay too much for it.

By using pre-prepared foods you will also be able to provide a consistent product. By following the instructions, the staff regenerating the food can reproduce the same standard of product time and time again.

Limitations of using pre–prepared food

Pre-prepared food that has been processed in any of the processes previously mentioned has many limitations in its use or the effects it can have on the diet.

Healthy eating

Pre-prepared foods generally contain more salt, flavour enhancers and preservatives. Eating any of these in excess will result in an unhealthy diet. Essential nutrients, such as vitamins and minerals present in fresh foods, are often lost during the preparation of these foods. Excessive amounts of pre-prepared foods in the diet could also be a cause of the increase in cases of obesity in the UK.

Other health issues that need to be considered are food allergies, heart disease and other related illnesses. With the use of additives and preservatives in pre-prepared foods there is the risk that consumers may have allergic reactions to the food. This could be a nut allergy as some pre-prepared foods contain oils that are derived from nuts and a customer eating one of these meals could have an analeptic fit and as a result could die. So always be careful to read the packet or manufacturer's ingredients list and inform customers of food items on the menu that may contain traces of nuts.

Another concern is that of heart disease – some pre-prepared foods contain large amounts of saturated fats which can cause cholesterol to build up and cause heart problems.

The use of excess salt in the preparation of pre-prepared foods can be harmful to people who are suffering from high blood pressure so again care must be given when finishing dishes and checking the taste so as not to increase this by adding more seasoning.

Recently high-profile chefs have been taking the lead in trying to highlight this problem, especially in relation to school meals. People in the UK generally do not eat enough fresh foods and this is one of the reasons that the government and food agencies are advertising and promoting healthier eating – e.g. the 5 a day campaign, which encourages us all to eat more fresh fruits and vegetables.

For more on healthy eating, see Chapter 4.

Quality

The quality of the food that has been pre-prepared is never as good as that of fresh produce. You only need to compare tinned or frozen fruit (especially the soft fruits) to fresh fruit. When regenerated they often do not come close to the fresh variety in terms of looks, texture or taste – e.g. defrosted frozen strawberries could never be a substitute for fresh. There are exceptions to this – some frozen vegetables (e.g. peas) compare well with fresh and are available all year round at a consistent quality.

Regenerate pre-prepared food

Equipment

An establishment that is using mainly pre-prepared food items only needs a small kitchen area and basic equipment.

The tools and equipment required for the regeneration of pre-prepared foods are shown below.

Heavy equipment	Light equipment	Small equipment
○ Microwave ovens	○ Pots	○ Ladles
○ Gas/Electric stoves	○ Ovenproof dishes	○ Spoons
○ Bratt pans	○ Baking sheets	○ Knives
○ Steamers		○ Tongs
		○ Slices

Figure 11.5 Equipment needed to regenerate pre-prepared food

Remember!

Take care when using a microwave to regenerate food. You can only use non-metallic equipment, otherwise you can damage the microwave oven and cause a possible fire or health risk.

Methods used to regenerate pre–prepared food

There are four basic methods of regenerating pre-prepared foods.

Reheating

Foods that have already been prepared and cooked are often either frozen or chilled for later use. They are then regenerated by reheating for service. The food types that should be reheated include: ready-made meals, soups and sauces which have been either produced and sold by a manufacturer or pre-prepared in the kitchen from fresh ingredients; vegetables and accompaniments.

Rehydrating

Many pre-prepared foods are dried to preserve and extend the shelf life of the product. Drying also makes the food safe as the moisture in food is one of the major factors for the growth of harmful bacteria. Rehydrating means adding liquid to foods that have been dried

Once a food item has been rehydrated it can be safely prepared and cooked ready for service. Food types include: powdered soups and sauces, dried beans and couscous.

Cooking

Many pre-prepared foods will need to be cooked before they can be served. These include foods that have been prepared in advance and stored under refrigerated conditions, which will need to be cooked before they can be served, as well as manufactured ready-meals. Some ready-meals may contain raw high risk ingredients that require cooking thoroughly to make them safe to eat.

Types of foods that need to be cooked include: frozen breaded fish fillets, pre-prepared pasta dishes such as lasagne and part-baked breads.

Defrosting

Usually defrosting is associated with products that do not require any further cooking. For example, pre-prepared gateaux, cakes, pastries and desserts only need to be defrosted and served.

To safely defrost, the product should be placed in the refrigerator to ensure that a controlled atmosphere is maintained. This ensures that no bacterial growth can occur.

Health and safety points

Health and safety points that need to be considered when preparing and cooking pre-prepared foods are:

- **Storage** – if the pre-prepared foods are stored incorrectly there is a possibility that bacteria can grow and cause food poisoning.
- **Cooking temperatures** – always follow the manufacturer's cooking instructions otherwise the finished product may not be cooked through properly or may be overcooked.
- **Packaging** – ensure that any packaging is intact and not damaged. Any damage to the packaging could cause either bacteria or foreign bodies to be present and contaminate the food.

Quality points

Quality points to consider when selecting and regenerating pre-prepared foods include the following.

Quantity – Is there enough of the food required for the purpose?

Freshness – Is the food item fresh and in good condition – i.e. not damaged, no blemishes or bruises? Fresh foods should be firm to the touch.

In date – Is the food within its use by/best before date? Out-of-date foods may not be of the required quality. They may also contain harmful amounts of bacteria and could cause food poisoning.

Appearance – Does the food look appealing? The quality of food can be checked by its appearance – e.g. its colour, shape and size.

Smell – Does the food smell right? There should be very little smell from pre-prepared foods. The only noticeable smell should be subtle and fresh. The only exception is fresh foods that have been blanched, chilled and refrigerated ready for regenerating at a later service time. These items can sometimes have a stronger smell, for example blanched broccoli has a stronger more distinct smell than when it is raw.

Temperature – Food items should be stored at the correct temperature depending on the type:

○ frozen foods should be stored at –18°C to –25°C

○ fresh foods should be stored at 1°C to 4°C

○ dried foods should be stored in a cool, dry store room in sealed containers.

During regeneration

During regeneration of pre-prepared products always follow the manufacturer's instructions and guidelines. Make sure that you:

○ use the correct amount of liquid and at the correct temperature

○ monitor the temperature throughout the cooking process to ensure that a safe product is served – core temperature should be 75°C.

○ cook for the correct length of time

○ check and adjust the consistency and appearance of the finished product before serving – e.g. should it be soft, crisp or firm?

○ taste the finished product to ensure that it has good flavour and that it is seasoned correctly.

Finishing

When finishing or serving regenerated pre-prepared food, you should consider the following points:

○ Is it the correct colour?

○ Is it at the correct temperature?

○ Does it smell and taste right for the product?

○ Does it have the correct appearance?

○ Does it have the correct consistency/texture?

○ Has it been portioned correctly?

○ Has it been correctly seasoned?

○ Has an appropriate garnish been added to enhance the appearance?

Associated products when serving regenerated foods

Regenerated foods can be enhanced at service with the addition of an appropriate garnish, sauce or suitable accompaniment. For example, serve tomato soup with a swirl of fresh cream, a sprinkle of chopped parsley and croutons.

Preparation	2
Cooking skills	2
Finishing	2

Broccoli Polonaise (Polish style)

Broccoli (fresh)	400g
Butter	50g
Breadcrumbs	25g
Sieved hard boiled egg	1
Chopped parsley	garnish

Method

1. Trim each broccoli spear to 50 mm beneath the leaf. Remove any discoloured parts.
2. Cut into equal sized florets and wash in cold salted water.
3. Plunge into boiling salted water and simmer until just tender (approximately 4 minutes).
4. Drain and plunge immediately into iced, cold water and drain again. The broccoli can then be kept covered in the refrigerator until needed.
5. When required, the broccoli can be reheated by plunging into boiling salted water for approximately 2 minutes, drained, put in the serving dish and kept in a warm place.
6. Heat the butter in a frying pan, add the breadcrumbs and fry until golden brown. Pour over the broccoli and sprinkle with sieved hard boiled egg and chopped parsley.
7. Flash the completed dish under a hot grill to heat the egg garnish. Serve immediately.

Test yourself!

1 List three quality points associated with regenerating pre-prepared foods.

2 When regenerating cooked foods for service, what should the core temperature be?

3 Give three examples of foods that are regenerated by each of the following methods.

Reheated	Rehydrated	Cooked	Defrosted

4 What is the purpose of regenerating food?

5 Where and how should dried pre-prepared foods be stored?

6 List four points that you should consider when finishing regenerated pre-prepared foods.

7 Describe how you could use an associated product when serving regenerated pre-prepared foods.

8 Name four types of ready-made meals.

9 Give two reasons why food is blanched before regenerating for service.

Practice assignment tasks

Task 1

Think of six pre-prepared foods and list an appropriate garnish and/or accompaniment for each of food. (Copy and complete the table below.)

Pre-prepared food	Garnish	Accompaniment

Task 2

List four pre-prepared products and the cooking method required. (Copy and complete the table below.)

Pre-prepared item	Cooking method
Bread mix	Baking

Task 3

Use the internet to research reasons for and what effects pre-prepared foods could have on health. (Copy and complete the table below.)

Reason	Effect on health
Excess salt	Increase blood pressure

Cold food preparation

12

This chapter covers the following outcomes from Diploma unit 112: Cold food preparation

- Outcome 112.1 Be able to prepare cold food
- Outcome 112.2 Be able to present cold food

Working through this chapter could also provide the opportunity to practise the following Functional Skills at Level 1:

Functional Maths Interpreting – use data to assess the likelihood of an outcome

In this chapter you will learn about:

- The food items used in cold food preparation
- The quality points for preparing cold foods
- The types of meals at which cold food could be served
- How to prepare and serve range of salads, hors d'oeuvres, canapés and sandwiches
- Service and service equipment

Prepare cold food

Cold food preparation involves putting together different cold food items and presenting them in an appetising way that will appeal to the customer. There is a fine line between making food look appetising and over-garnishing. Garnishing should only be used to complement the dish and not replace the main ingredients.

Marcus says:

Of course use the correct coloured boards for food preparation but also have another board for strong flavoured food. It isn't good to taste cold food that has been chopped on the same board as garlic!

Foods that can be used in cold food preparation

There are five main categories of foods that are used in cold food preparation – see Figure 12.1 below for examples.

Fruit & vegetables	Cooked & cooled foods	Pre-prepared foods	Dairy	Breads & pastries
Melons	Roast beef	Smoked fish	Cream	Rolls
Grapefruit	Roast lamb	Pâté	Creme fraiche	Loaves
Avocado pear	Roast pork	Raised pies	Yoghurt	Wholemeal
Oranges	Roast turkey	Terrines	Cheese	Granary
Apples	Roast chicken	Pies	Milk	White
Grapes	Ham	Chorizo	Sour cream	Naan
Plums	Fish/shellfish	Parma ham	Butter	Chapati
Lettuce	Poached fish	Salami	Margarine	Ciabatta
Cucumber	Prawns	Cured meats		Foccacia
Tomatoes	Crab			Wraps
Carrots	Lobster			Pastries
Onions	Mussels			Barquettes
Peppers	Cockles			Vol au vents
Radishes	Potatoes			Bouchées
Mustard cress	Beans			
Spring onions				

Figure 12.1 The main types of food used in cold food preparation with examples

Quality points of food for cold preparation

- Only use the freshest of food items – e.g. ripe fruit and vegetables and freshly caught fish. The smell should be fresh.
- Appearance of the ingredients is very important as the colour or shape of the ingredient is vital to the presentation of the dish.
- Cut the food carefully to specification, with pieces of even sizes. Trim carefully to minimise waste. Fruit such as oranges should be segmented neatly, leaving no pith, pips or membrane.
- Complex dishes such as salads should be carefully mixed in line with dish specifications.
- Portions should be correct and even.
- Storage of the food at the correct temperature is very important to maintain the freshness of the product. It also ensures that the dish is safe to eat.

Chef's tip

Using only foods items of the best quality will allow you to produce a high-quality finished product.

Cold foods to serve at different meals

Examples of cold foods to serve at different meals are shown in Figure 12.2.

Meal	Image	Examples of foods
Breakfast		Croissants, jams, marmalades, yoghurts, fruits and speciality breads Cold meats and cheeses
Lunch		Sandwiches Salads Cold meats Starters Desserts Cheese board
Afternoon tea		Sandwiches: open or closed Pastries, e.g. Danish Scones with jam and cream Cakes

Functions Receptions Cocktail parties Promotional events Snacks	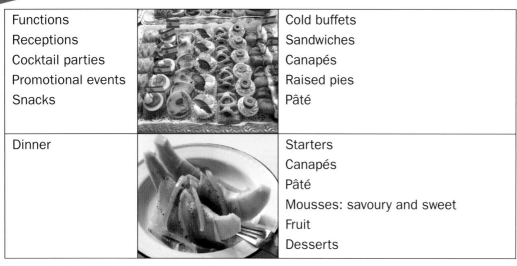	Cold buffets Sandwiches Canapés Raised pies Pâté
Dinner		Starters Canapés Pâté Mousses: savoury and sweet Fruit Desserts

Figure 12.2 Cold foods to serve at different meals

Salads

Salads are classified as either **simple salads** or **compound salads**.

> **Definitions**
> **Simple salad** – a salad with one main ingredient.
> **Compound salad** – a salad made with more than one ingredient, usually bound together with a dressing.

Investigate!

1 **Copy and complete the table below with six more simple salads and four more compound salads.**

Simple salads	Compound salads
Tomato	Coleslaw
Cucumber	Russian salad
Beetroot	Waldorf salad
	Potato salad
	Florida cocktail

2 **Find out what the ingredients of all the compound salads are. There are recipes for some of them in this chapter.**

Different types of salads are only limited by your imagination and the ingredients available. Salads can be served as a complement to dishes, as the main part of the dish or as a selection of starters.

Florida cocktail

Orange	1
Grapefruit	1
Pineapple	¼
Mint leaves	2–3
Serves	4

Preparation	2
Cooking skills	–
Finishing	1

Method

1. Peel the oranges and grapefruit using a sharp knife in order to remove all the white pith and skin.
2. Cut into segments and remove all pips.
3. Place the segments and juice into a bowl.
4. Cut the pineapple into slices and add to the bowl.
5. Arrange the segments and slices neatly in a **coupe**, small bowl or plate, dressed with the juice.
6. Decorate with the mint leaves and serve very cold.

Definition

Coupe – a stainless steel, glass or silver bowl on a stand.

How to peel an orange

1. Cut the top and bottom off the orange to show the flesh beneath.
2. Remove the pith and skin to show the orange flesh.
3. The whole orange should now have no pith or skin.

How to segment an orange

1

Hold the peeled fruit in one hand and run a paring knife down towards the centre of the fruit just inside the segment membrane.

2

Once the centre is reached, push the segment away from the centre.

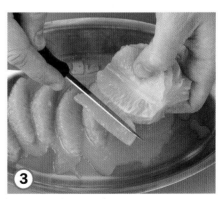

3

The segment should come away from the membrane on the other side. Continue until all the segments have been removed.

Tomato salad

Tomatoes	200g
Lettuce	¼
Vinaigrette	1 tbsp
Chopped onion or chives	10g
Fresh basil	to garnish
Serves	4

Method

1 Remove the skin from the tomatoes by plunging into boiling water for 12 seconds, and then refreshing in cold water.
2 Slice thinly and arrange neatly on a bed of lettuce.
3 Sprinkle with vinaigrette, onion, chives and basil.
4 Serve cold.

Variation

Arrange alternate slices of tomato and mozzarella on a plate. Serve with the same dressing.

Preparation | 1
Cooking skills | –
Finishing | 1

Vegetable salad

This salad is also called Russian salad.

Preparation | 1
Cooking skills | 1
Finishing | 1

Carrots	100g
Turnips	50g
French beans	50g
Peas	50g
Vinaigrette	1 tbsp
Mayonnaise or natural yoghurt	125ml
Salt and pepper	To taste
Serves	4

Method

1 Peel and wash the carrots and turnips. Cut into 4mm dice or batons.
2 Cook separately in salted water, refresh and drain.
3 Top and tail the beans and cut into 4mm dice. Cook, refresh and drain.
4 Cook the peas, refresh and drain.
5 Mix all the vegetables together with vinaigrette and then the mayonnaise.
6 Correct the seasoning and serve neatly dressed.

Salad dressings

Preparation	1
Cooking skills	–
Finishing	–

Vinaigrette

Mix 3 parts oil (olive or suitable flavoured oil) with 1 part vinegar. Then add a little mustard to bind. Add salt and pepper.

Variations

Blue cheese dressing – crumble in some Danish blue, Roquefort or other blue cheese to the strength desired.

Thousand island dressing – mix 300ml vinaigrette with 2 drops Tabasco, ¼ red pepper and ¼ green pepper finely diced, 1 grated boiled egg, a little chopped parsley and 1 tablespoon of tomato ketchup.

Mayonnaise

Preparation	2
Cooking skills	–
Finishing	–

Salt	pinch
Pepper	pinch
Mustard	1 tsp
Vinegar	1 tbsp
Egg yolks	3
Vegetable oil	300ml

Method

1. Place the salt, pepper, mustard, vinegar and egg yolks into either a glass or stainless steel bowl.
2. Whisk together until light and the egg yolks are slightly thickened.
3. Very slowly add the oil, whisking well as you do so. (Be careful not to add the oil too quickly, as the mixture will easily curdle – this means that the ingredients separate). The protein in the egg acts as an **emulsifier**, absorbing the oil and keeping the sauce bound together.
4. Once made, cover and store in the fridge.

Variations

Green sauce – add chopped tarragon, chervil, chives, spinach and watercress and blend.

Tartare sauce – add chopped gherkins, capers and parsley.

Tyrolienne sauce – add chopped parsley, chervil and tarragon.

Cocktail sauce – add 1 part tomato ketchup to 3 parts mayonnaise.

Andalusian sauce – Add julienne red peppers.

Definition

Emulsifier – an ingredient that binds oil and other liquids together.

Did you know?

Cocktail sauce is also known as "marie rose" sauce.

Investigate!

Research using the internet, recipe books or magazines and find out all the many sauces that can be made using mayonnaise as the base.

Hors d'oeuvres

Hors d'oeuvres can be served cold or hot. They can be served in two styles:

○ hors-d'oeuvres variés – contain more than one main ingredient

○ hors-d'oeuvres single – with one main ingredient.

Definition

Hors d'oeuvres – a French term meaning a dish served as an appetiser before a main meal.

Preparation 1
Cooking skills –
Finishing 1

Egg mayonnaise

To hard boil eggs, place the eggs in boiling water. Re-boil and simmer for 8–10 minutes. Refresh under cold running water until cold.

As part of a selection of hors-d'oeuvres – Cut the hard-boiled eggs in quarters or slices, dress neatly and coat with mayonnaise.

As an individual hors-d'oeuvre – Allow one hard-boiled egg per portion. Cut in half and dress on a lettuce leaf. Coat with mayonnaise and garnish with tomato quarters and slices of cucumber.

As a main dish – Allow two hard-boiled eggs per portion. Cut in halves and dress on a plate. Coat with mayonnaise sauce. Surround with a portion of lettuce, tomato, cucumber, potato salad, beetroot salad or coleslaw.

Investigate!

Find a selection of hors d'oeuvres on the internet or in recipe books. Copy and complete the table.

Hors-d'oeuvres variés	Hors-d'oeuvres single

Chef's tip

If the eggs are overcooked, iron in the yolk and sulphur compounds in the white are released. They form a blackish ring (ferrous sulphide) around the yolk. This will also occur if the eggs are not refreshed immediately after they are cooked.

Canapés

Canapés are small bite-size items that can be served as a pre-dinner appetiser, at cocktail parties or promotional events. They can be made using a variety of different bases, for example:

○ shaped pieces of fried bread

○ shaped pastry cases

○ fresh breads

○ blinis.

Figure 12.3 A selection of canapés

Some canapés do not need a base – e.g. stuffed cherry tomatoes, chicken goujons, etc. There are limitless possibilities of food items that can be used to produce canapés. You must use your ingredients to provide a good selection of well-presented canapés containing a variety of textures, colours and flavours.

Quail eggs, tomato and mayonnaise	Tuna mayonnaise
Smoked salmon and cream cheese	Prawns
Parma ham	Crab meat
Asparagus spears	Lobster

Figure 12.4 Some suggested toppings for canapés

Curried shrimp tartlet

Curry powder	good pinch
Butter	5g
Mayonnaise	20g
Finely chopped onions	10g
Roughly chopped prawns	100g
Lemon juice	squeeze
Precooked savoury canapé tartlet cases	10
Chives, chervil and cayenne pepper	garnish
Serves	10

Preparation	1
Cooking skills	2
Finishing	2

Method

1 Fry the curry powder in the butter for a few minutes.
2 When cool, add to the mayonnaise.
3 Mix in the chopped onions and prawns.
4 Add lemon juice and correct seasoning.
5 Fill each tartlet with the mixture.
6 Garnish with chives or chervil and a sprinkle of cayenne pepper.

Smoked salmon tartare

Chopped smoked salmon trimmings	100g
Chopped red onion	20g
Chopped capers	20g
Cayenne pepper	pinch
Seasoning	to taste
Chopped chives	15 g
Lemon juice	squeeze
Toasted bread croute (bite sized)	10
Chive/chervil leaves	garnish
Serves	10

Preparation	1
Cooking skills	–
Finishing	1

Method

1 Mix the smoked salmon, red onion, capers, cayenne pepper, chives and lemon juice together.
2 Season to taste.
3 Place a spoonful of the mixture onto each bite sized bread croute.
4 Garnish with a small piece of chive or chervil.

Mushroom bouchées

Butter	10g
Coarsely chopped mushrooms	100g
Chopped shallots	20g
Chopped garlic	1 clove
Chopped parsley	garnish
Double cream	50ml
Madeira sauce	20ml
Precooked bouchées	10
Serves	10

Preparation	1
Cooking skills	1
Finishing	1

Method

1 Sweat the onions and garlic in a pan with butter for a few minutes.
2 Add the coarsely chopped mushrooms and cook for 3-4 minutes.
3 Add the Madeira sauce and reduce by half.
4 Add the double cream and bring to the boil.
5 Once boiled, add parsley and fill the bouchées.

Toasted brioche with chicken liver paté

Preparation	1
Cooking skills	1
Finishing	1

Chicken liver paté	100g
Double cream	15ml
Seasoning	
Brioche	sufficient for 10 portions
Gherkins or olives, sliced	garnish
Serves	10

Method

1 Toast the brioche and cut into required shape (round, triangle etc.).
2 Mix the chicken liver paté with the cream.
3 Pipe, using a star nozzle, onto each brioche.
4 Decorate with sliced gherkin or olive.

Sandwiches

Sandwiches are a very popular and nutritious cold food. They are enjoyed by lots of people every day, either as a snack or as part of a lunchtime meal. There are hot and cold varieties of sandwiches, but in this chapter we only need to concentrate on the cold variety.

The types of cold sandwiches include:

○ closed sandwiches
○ open sandwiches
○ wraps and pittas.

Closed sandwiches

A closed sandwich is two slices of bread with a filling between – e.g. meat, vegetables, cheese or jam, together with condiments, sauces or other accompaniments to enhance the flavour and texture. The bread can be used plain, but it is usually spread with butter, oil or mustard.

Did you know?

In the 18th century, John Montague, the 4th Earl of Sandwich, liked to gamble at cards for hours at a time and sometimes refused to stop playing, even for meals. It is said that he ordered his valet to bring him meat tucked between two pieces of bread. Other people began to ask for "the same as Sandwich!" – and this is apparently how the sandwich got its name.

What were sandwiches called before they were sandwiches? They were probably simply known as "bread and meat" or "bread and cheese".

Open sandwiches

Open sandwiches use a single piece of bread, usually rye bread, with a hot or cold topping. They are then usually garnished with various items to enhance their appearance. As with closed sandwiches, the choice of toppings is virtually endless. It is up to the chef to use his or her creative flair to make them appetising and appealing to customers.

Figure 12.5 A selection of sandwiches

Wraps and pittas

Wraps are becoming very popular these days and can provide a good alternative to filled rolls or sandwiches. The filling is placed inside a wrap such as a tortilla, which is then rolled up.

Pitta bread is a flat bread, usually oval in shape. Pittas are cut lengthways down the side and then filled. Fillings can be as numerous and diverse as for sandwiches.

Presenting sandwiches

If sandwiches are being presented as part of a finger buffet or an afternoon tea menu, they may have the crusts cut off the bread and be cut into small shaped portions such as triangles and circles. This makes them more appealing to the eye and also easier to eat.

Did you know?

Open sandwiches are popular in Scandinavian countries such as Denmark, Norway and Sweden, where they are a big feature of the traditional buffets – called "smorgasbord".

Egg mayonnaise	Cream cheese
Ham and tomato	Cucumber
Beef and horseradish	Roast beef and tomato
Smoked salmon	Scrambled egg and bacon
Cheese and pickle	Bacon, tomato and lettuce (BLT)
Tuna and sweetcorn	Curried chicken mayonnaise (coronation chicken)

Figure 12.6 Some suggested sandwich fillings or toppings for canapés

Present cold food

Food safety

Pre-prepared food for cold presentation is generally high risk food. It must be stored and held for service at the correct temperature, otherwise the risk of causing food poisoning is extremely high.

The storage temperature should be below 8°C (ideally 5°C) and throughout service should be 5°C or below. The foods should not be displayed for longer than four hours. Any high risk food items kept on display for longer than four hours should be disposed of.

Equipment for serving cold prepared food

The equipment required to serve cold prepared food depends on the type of service, meal or event.

Starters or lunch

Cold food that is being served as a starter or main meal at lunch can be plated by the kitchen staff and then served by the restaurant directly to the customer at the table.

Alternatively, it could be served from a self-service, refrigerated cold display counter. This will require:

○ service tongs
○ spoons
○ dishes
○ plates
○ containers to hold the food items.

The cold counter could also be used in the service of cold breakfast items.

Figure 12.7 A fully equipped cold service counter

Dinner menus

Cold, prepared foods are mainly used as starters. They are plated by the chefs in the kitchen as soon as the order comes in from the restaurant.

Cold buffets

Service for cold buffets is either help yourself or assisted service. Assisted service is when a chef serves the main food items – e.g. sliced meats or cold prepared fish –and the customers help themselves to the salad items. Often labels are used to tell customers what each of the dishes is, and to indicate any ingredients such as nuts which may cause an allergic reaction.

Figure 12.8 Assisted buffet service

Canapés

Canapés being served at an event should be arranged and presented on a salver. Waiters or waitresses then offer these to the customers.

Sandwiches

Sandwiches can be served either:

o presented on salvers or trays with various garnishes and then arranged on the buffet tables

o or individually packaged in purpose-made packages.

Any cold food prepared for selling individually to customers should be packaged in the purpose-made containers and then labelled with details of the contents, ingredients and the sell-by or use-by date.

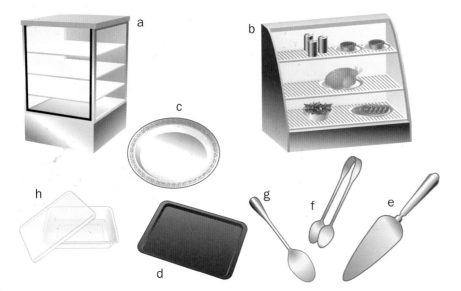

Figure 12.9 Equipment for the service of cold prepared foods: a) display cabinet, b) refrigerated open counter, c) salver, d) tray, e) slice, f) tongs, g) spoons, h) takeaway containers

Cold foods for a buffet

Pies

Cold pies are a common food used for buffets. They are high risk foods and must be stored in the fridge before service.

Pies are available in many different flavours and shapes, ranging from chilled home-made game or chicken and ham pies to bought-in pork pies.

To serve: portion the pie as per the establishment's requirements. Only place enough portions on the service dish to meet the immediate service period. Garnish with vegetables, fruits or herbs as required. The garnish should complement the product inside.

Cooked meats

Cold cooked meats such as beef, lamb, chicken or pork are often served on cold buffets. The meat can be sliced either by hand or by machine. If slicing by machine, you must be 18 or over and trained to use the equipment.

When slicing meats, the slices should be kept in the order they are removed from the whole piece. This way, the meat slices can be fanned out and the shape of the meats will be uniform and will look more appetising.

Display the meat on trays, keeping the slices as equally distanced as possible, but allowing enough space for the customer or serving staff to lift up the edge of one slice of meat for service.

The meat can then be garnished, but only sparingly to complement the display. A selection of cold sauces can also be served as an accompaniment. These are often brought ready-made. Some examples of garnishes and sauces are shown in Figure 12.10. These are just a few suggestions. Each establishment will have its own preferences. Some of the sauces are the classical sauces normally served with hot, cooked meats. With modern trends and international influences, the number of possible accompaniments is vast.

Remember!
Slicing machines must not be used by anyone under the age of 18. These machines are extremely dangerous, because they have the ability to remove fingers! (See the section on Gravity feed slicer in Chapter 5, page 160.)

Figure 12.10 Garnishes and sauces to serve with cold meats

Garnishes	Sauces
○ parsley – chopped, picked ○ tomatoes – rose, whole, wedges, slices, swans ○ cucumber – slices, wedges, fans ○ lettuce – leaves, chifonnade – very finely shredded ○ fruits – carved, wedges, fans	○ beef – horseradish sauce, English mustard ○ pork – apple sauce ○ chicken – satay sauce, lemon sauce, black bean sauce, barbecue sauce ○ lamb – mint sauce, redcurrant jelly, Cumberland sauce ○ turkey – cranberry sauce ○ duck – plum sauce, orange sauce

Fish

Fish can be smoked, poached or even fried before being served cold. Fish portions or even whole fish can be poached and decorated for display.

Smoked trout and herrings are served with horseradish sauce and lemon wedges. All other cold fish can be served with other dressing as determined by the establishment.

The skin can be removed to expose the flesh, making the fish look more attractive to the customer.

Fish that can be served cold include:
- salmon – poached whole or sliced, or smoked (normally sliced)
- trout – smoked or poached
- tuna – cooked or tinned
- mackerel – smoked
- herrings – smoked or pickled
- sardines – tinned.

Investigate!

Search the internet for cold sauces. List three sauces that can be served as an accompaniment to meat and fish listed – do not include the ones already mentioned.

Chef's tip

Pâtés and terrines will discolour and dry out very quickly, so must be kept covered until ready for service.

Pre-prepared terrines and pâtés

A terrine is a mixture of different meats, fish or vegetables of different textures. These are layered inside a mould, then poached, chilled and turned out. Once chilled the terrine should be set and can be sliced and served as a starter or as part of a cold buffet.

The terrine can be served alone, with a sauce to enhance the dish or with salad items to enhance the presentation.

Pâtés are prepared and cooked in the same way as terrines but are normally smoother than a terrine.

To slice a terrine or pâté, it is best to have a large container of water to dip the knife into. This keeps the blade clean during slicing and ensures each slice is neatly cut.

They should both be sliced and then covered and stored in the fridge until ready for service.

Figure 12.11 You will need to dip the knife in water when cutting terrines and pâtés

Cured meats

These are meats that have been either salted to preserve the meat or processed in another way (e.g. smoking) to extend the life and introduce different flavours into the meat.

The two most common ways of curing ham are salting and smoking. The ham can be salted either in **brine** or in a dry salt mixture. The mixture of ingredients and processes vary depending upon the type of ham being produced – each process adds a characteristic flavour to the meat.

Parma ham is the best-known type of cured meat. It is supplied either whole and requires slicing very thinly or, more usually, pre-sliced in packets. Each slice is separated by a piece of plastic, which allows the slices to be picked up without tearing the meat.

Other types of cured hams include:
○ Bayonne – France
○ Bradenham – England
○ Seager – England
○ Westphalia – Germany
○ Serrano – Spain.

These are only a small selection of the hams available. All of these cured hams should be sliced extremely thinly. Because of this they will dry out very quickly, so they must be kept covered until service.

Other regions produce cured meats. A popular one at the moment is chorizo, which is a spicy Spanish sausage made with pork and hot pepper. Some cured meats are fresh, but mostly they are dried and smoked. They are used cold and sliced or may be added to cooked dishes.

Another popular type of cured meat is salami, which is prepared from pork. Many countries have their own variety of salami and they are often spicy. Salami is usually thinly sliced and can be served individually or with a variety of different types.

Shellfish

Shellfish includes prawns, crabs, mussels, cockles and lobsters. Some will be supplied pre-cooked and frozen and must be defrosted thoroughly under controlled conditions to prevent food poisoning. Ideally they should be defrosted in a defrosting cabinet or a fridge.

Definition

Brine – A mixture of salt and water.

Did you know?

Parma ham is cured at Langhirano, near Parma in Italy. Only meat that has been processed in this region can be called Parma ham.

Shellfish are categorised into two main groups:

o **Crustaceans** have an external skeleton – e.g. crabs and lobster. They must be as fresh as possible when cooked to prevent food poisoning.

o **Molluscs** have shells – e.g. cockles, mussels and whelks.

Prawns in their shells should be shelled by removing the outer casing from the tail and then served with the head either still on or removed.

The digestive tract should also be removed. Use the tip of a small knife to remove the dark line that runs down the back of the tail. This is called diving.

Ideally shellfish should be served on crushed ice to keep them cool. Some will be coated in a sauce. All shellfish must be kept at less than 8°C until ready for service.

Cheese

Cheeses provide the chef with a wide variety of different flavours and textures. Cheeses can be presented as they are – either sliced or cubed and arranged, with suitable garnish on flats for the buffet table. Grated or sliced cheese can also be used in sandwiches or filled rolls. Cheese is used in other cold dishes such as quiche.

Some varieties of cheese include: Cheddar, cottage cheese, Stilton, Roquefort, Edam, Gorgonzola and Danish blue.

Eggs

Hen's eggs are the most popular type used in cold preparation although quail's eggs are also used. Shelled hard-boiled eggs can be used and presented in many ways.

o cut lengthways, arranged on a plate and covered with mayonnaise

o quartered and used in salads or as a garnish

o grated, sliced or chopped and used in sandwiches

o as Scotch eggs – covered in sausage meat, then flour, egg and breadcrumbs and deep fried.

Eggs are also used in cold cooked dishes such as quiche.

Bread

Bread of all types is used for cold buffets and special events – for example:

○ white and wholemeal rolls

○ loaves – sliced

○ French sticks or ciabatta, sliced and toasted to use as a base for various canapés.

Filled rolls give the chef another alternative to sandwiches to present a variety of fillings.

Sliced breads of different types make for good presentation on a buffet table and also gives the customer choice.

The different breads available to choose from include: white, wholemeal, granary, soda bread, pitta bread, naan bread, ciabatta and French sticks.

Test yourself!

1 Name four toppings that can be used for an open sandwiches.

2 List six hors d'oeuvres variés.

3 List four bases that can be used when making canapés.

4 Explain the difference between a simple and a compound salad.

5 List five sauces that have mayonnaise as their base.

6 How should you prepare tomatoes for a tomato salad?

7 What safety points should you consider when preparing food items for cold preparation?

8 Why must cold products be kept in the fridge until service?

9 List five cold preparations that contain eggs.

10 List five things to consider when choosing a garnish.

Practice assignment tasks

Task 1

List six hors d'oeuvres single and six hors d'oeuvres variés. Copy and complete the following table giving the ingredient(s) for your selection.

Hors d'oeuvre single	Main Ingredient	Hors d'oeuvre variés	Ingredients

Task 2

Use the internet or textbooks to research the varieties of cured meats that can be used in cold food preparation and their country of origin. Copy and complete the table below.

Cured meat	Country of origin

Task 3

Use the internet to find out about the history of the sandwich from its origins to the present day. Using this research produce a short document showing a time line and explaining how the sandwich has become so popular on the high street today.

Glossary

Bacteria: micro-organisms which cause disease.

Baking parchment: paper that has been coated with silicone and which is used to prevent food from sticking during cooking.

Barista: a term used for a trained individual who is capable of producing, presenting and serving a full range of non-alcoholic hot and cold beverages.

Baste: to moisten during cooking by spooning a liquid over the food.

Bed of root: chopped root vegetables which act as a base to put the bird on to prevent sticking and burning on the tray.

Beurre noisette: butter that has been melted until it turns golden brown.

Blanching: fruit and vegetables are immersed in boiling water for between ten seconds and two minutes depending on size and type.

Blast chilling: reducing food temperature from +70° C to +3°C or below within 90 minutes.

Blast freezing: reducing food temperature from +70°C to −18°C in no more than 240 minutes.

Blind baking: cooking a flan case without the filling in it. The flan is lined with greaseproof paper (cartouche) and filled with baking beans. The beans help to keep the shape during cooking.

Blown can: a can which has not been properly sealed during the canning process and has bulging ends. The contents are dangerous and should not be eaten.

Brine: a mixture of salt and water.

Cartouche: a greased greaseproof paper that is placed over food while it is cooking to prevent the food drying out.

Catering service: a catering operation run by the company or organisation itself.

Catering: the business of providing food, drink and entertainment.

Caustic: a substance that will stick to a surface and burn chemically. It is used for heavy duty cleaning.

Collagen: a very strong protein found in meat that breaks down if enough heat is applied to it.

Compound salad: a salad made with more than one ingredient, usually bound together with a dressing.

Concasse: coarsely chopped tomatoes.

Condensation: a coating of tiny drops formed on a surface by steam or vapour.

Contract catering: where an outside company provides the catering service.

Cooling wire: a wire rack which allows air to circulate around the product to prevent the creation of steam.

Court bouillon: a flavoured liquor for cooking fish, made by adding vinegar, parsley, thyme and peppercorns to water.

Crêpe: the French word for pancake.

Dariole moulds: cylindrical moulds which are available in a variety of sizes.

Dilute: to add extra liquid (usually water) to make the solution weaker.

Disability: a physical or mental impairment which affects a person's ability to carry out normal day-to-day activities.

Dock: make holes in the surface with a tool called a docker or a fork. This allows steam to escape during cooking and prevents the item rising.

Documented: making a detailed record of information.

Dormant: not active or growing.

Due diligence: that every possible precaution has been taken by the business to avoid a food safety problem.

Dysentery: a food-borne disease causing mild to severe diarrhoea and fever. It can be fatal.

Escalope: a thin slice of meat or fish.

Excrement: solid waste matter passed out through the bowel.

Faeces: solid waste substance from the body.

Fat: is solid, whereas oil is liquid. Both are classed as "fats" when talking about nutrition.

Flambé: to flame food that has a spirit added – e.g. brandy. This burns off the alcohol content but the flavour remains.

Flammable: describes a substance or material that can catch fire easily.

Flashpoint: the temperature at which oil ignites.

Franchise: an agreement to sell a company's goods or services in a particular place.

Game chips: thin slices of potato deep fried, very similar to crisps.

Glazed: browned in the oven or under a grill.

Gluten: the protein found in flour which gives it its strength. The strength of the gluten depends on the type of wheat and when and where it was grown.

Hazard: anything that can cause harm – e.g. a knife, a slicing machine or a slippery floor.

Health: good condition of the body and mind, with no illness or disease.

Hors d'oeuvres: a French term meaning dish served as an appetiser before a main meal.

Hospitality: the business of providing services such as catering, accommodation and entertainment.

Hyperactivity: more activity than is normally expected of the child. Hyperactivity can cause concentration difficulties and affect the child's learning.

Impervious: does not allow water to pass through it.

Inedible: cannot be eaten

Inert: has no reaction with any other substance.

Infuse: to extract flavour into a liquid by warming gently.

Infused liquids: liquids used in the cooking process that have herbs and spices added to provide a particular flavour – e.g. saffron in Spanish paella or a studded onion in a white sauce.

Kneading: pressing and stretching the dough with the heel of the hand. This assists the development of the gluten and helps to make sure that the yeast is distributed throughout the dough.

Knocking back: removing the air produced during proving. It is done by kneading the dough again.

Leaven: to raise dough with an added ingredient – usually yeast.

Liable: legally responsible.

Lyonnaise: the addition of sauté onions to a dish.

Marbling: the thin fine lines of fat running through the lean part of the meat.

Marinate: to immerse meat or fish in a flavoured liquid allowing the flavours to be absorbed by the meat or fish.

Meunière: to shallow fry.

Micro-organism: a very small life form which cannot be seen without a microscope.

Mise en place: basic preparation of ingredients before service.

Monitoring: regularly checking condition and progress.

Navarin: a French lamb stew, usually cooked with root vegetables. If possible use new season spring lamb which has the very best flavour.

Non-toxic: not poisonous or harmful.

Nutritious: containing nutrients required for a healthy diet.

NVQ: a qualification gained while working. NVQ stands for National Vocational Qualification.

Obesity: being very overweight.

Organism: any living animal or plant.

Osteoporosis: the loss of bone mass. It can be treated with hormone replacement treatment and is helped by a calcium-rich diet.

Pané anglaise: a mixture of flour, egg and breadcrumbs.

Pané française: a milk and flour coating.

Pasteurised: has been heat treated.

Pathogen: an organism that causes disease.

Pin out: roll out using a rolling pin.

Plankton: a layer of tiny plants and animals living just below the surface of the sea.

Prosecute: to bring a criminal case against someone who has broken the law.

Prove: to allow dough products made with yeast to ferment in a warm place and double in size before cooking.

Proving cabinet: a steam heated cabinet used to ensure even proving.

Refined: describes food that has been processed to make it look or taste more appealing.

Refreshing: cooling food after blanching or boiling by plunging into cold water or running under cold water.

Regenerate: to bring food back to its original condition ready for service.

Rehydrating: adding liquid to a sauce or dish to bring it back to the right consistency.

Render: to use medium heat to turn animal fat into liquid.

Rennet: a product produced from a calf's stomach used to harden cheese. A vegetarian may well refuse cheese made with rennet.

Risk: the chance of harm being done. A risk usually involves a hazard – e.g. the risk of slipping when walking across a wet floor.

Safety: freedom from danger or risk of injury.

Sauté: to cook quickly in a shallow pan with a minimum of fat.

Scaling: cutting and weighing the dough to the required size pieces.

Simmer: to gently heat food just below boiling point.

Simple salad: a salad with one main ingredient.

Sinew: tough cord joining muscle to bone.

Skinning: this is when dough is left uncovered and the surface of the dough starts to dry out. If this skin is mixed back into the dough, it will create dry pieces in the finished product.

Sleeve: a type of mould used for making steamed sponges, consisting of two halves that fit together to make a seal.

Smoulder: to burn slowly with a red glow and not much smoke.

Sous vide: food is vacuum sealed in a pouch and later cooked at comparatively low temperatures for relatively long periods of time.

Spores: cells produced by bacteria and fungi.

Stock: a broth used as a braising liquid (see Chapter 8), a sauce base or liquid for soup. It can be made from chicken, beef, veal, game, fish or vegetables. Ready-made stocks are used in some establishments for speed and convenience.

Subsidiary company: a company is a subsidiary if another company holds more than 50% of the shares.

Swab: a sterile piece of cotton used to take a sample for chemical analysis.

Sweetbreads: a dish made of the pancreas glands of a young animal, usually a lamb or calf.

Synoptic tests: these tests cover different parts of the qualification at the same time. They are important because they demonstrate that you can manage your time and resources as well as cook.

Tempura batter: a light batter made of very cold water and flour. Beaten egg white is then folded in to give a light crisp texture when deep fried.

Toxin: a poison produced by bacteria.

Trivet: a bed of vegetables that lifts meat off the roasting tray. Also, a roasting tray which holds the meat still during carving.

Unpasteurised: has not been heat treated.

Vegan: a strict vegetarian who will not eat anything that comes either directly (such as meat) or indirectly (eggs or dairy products) from an animal.

VRQ: stands for Vocationally Related Qualifications.

Recipes Index

Index